Judi James is a leading television expert in social behaviour, image, workplace culture, communication skills and body language. She appears regularly on *Newsnight*, *Sky News* and *The Paul O'Grady Show*, and was a regular expert on *Big Brother on the Couch*.

Judi started her career as a leading catwalk model and trained many big names at her modelling school in Chelsea, including Naomi Campbell. She has had six novels published, including the bestseller *Supermodel*, and has written 13 non-fiction books. Judi also writes regularly for newspapers and magazines. She is *Heat* magazine's body-language analyst, has a weekly celebrity body-language column in *You* (*Mail on Sunday*) and writes as an agony aunt expert for *More!*

BEING CONFIDENT

Tips and Techniques to
Help You Unlock Your Potential

Judi James

Vermilion
LONDON

3 5 7 9 10 8 6 4

Published in 2011 by Vermilion, an imprint of Ebury Publishing

Ebury Publishing is a Random House Group company

Copyright © Judi James 2011

Judi James has asserted her right to be identified as the author of this work in accordance
with the Copyright, Designs and Patents Act 1988.

The Random House Group Limited Reg. No. 954009

Addresses for companies within the Random House Group can be found at
www.rbooks.co.uk

A CIP catalogue record for this book is available from the British Library

The Random House Group Limited supports The Forest Stewardship Council (FSC®), the
leading international forest certification organisation. Our books carrying the FSC label are
printed on FSC® certified paper. FSC is the only forest certification scheme endorsed by the
leading environmental organisations, including Greenpeace. Our paper procurement policy can
be found at www.randomhouse.co.uk/environment

MIX
Paper from
responsible sources
FSC® C016897

Printed and bound by CPI Group
(UK) Ltd, Croydon, CR0 4YY

ISBN 9780091929558

Copies are available at special rates for bulk orders. Contact the sales development team
on 020 7840 8487 for more information.

To buy books by your favourite authors and register for offers, visit www.rbooks.co.uk

The information in this book has been compiled by way of general guidance in relation
to the specific subjects addressed, but is not a substitute and not to be relied on for
professional advice on specific circumstances and in specific locations. So far as the
author is aware the information given is correct and up to date as at January 2011.
Practice, laws and regulations all change, and the reader should obtain up-to-date
professional advice on any such issues. The author and publishers disclaim, as far as
the law allows, any liability arising directly or indirectly from the use, or misuse, of the
information contained in this book.

CONTENTS

INTRODUCTION

There are three key things you need to know about confidence: firstly, like money and sex, everyone claims to want more; secondly, for most people the display of confidence is a big fat lie. The world is divided between those people who show their anxieties and those who manage to mask them. Looking confident and feeling confident are two separate things. Sometimes they occur together but mostly they don't. The third fact is that there are several different types of confidence. Diagnosing the *type* of anxiety you suffer from is every bit as important as working out your cure and learning how to be as confident as you always dreamed you'd be.

HOW DO YOU LEARN CONFIDENCE?

I believe that genuine confidence doesn't come from being kind to yourself, writing your own sick notes providing excuses for your own fear-fuelled behaviours, or marinating in a nice warm bubble bath of self-pity. It's not about others' sympathy and support, either. Sympathy from other people might feel like a hug, but it's a hug that makes you dependent and submissive, so shun it and never seek it out.

Being confident is all about personal drive, determination and resilience. You already have all three. All you need to do is to recognise them and then develop them by learning how to become your own coach. You need to take control of yourself and be boot-camp tough.

Being confident is also about daring to be a little bit different too, because it's our differences that give us our strength and our edge.

Here's the good news:
IF YOU WANT TO BE CONFIDENT YOU CAN BE

It's up to you.

Completely your call.

Saying 'yes' is the only decision you'll have to make. After that it will be down to working through some tips and techniques, many of which are so simple and easy to do you'll be surprised to find out how instantly effective they can be. (Yes, some are tougher and more challenging and *of course* some will squeeze you so far out of your comfort zone that your pips will squeak, but I'm building your motivation and keenness here, not crushing your resolve in my opening paragraphs.)

I am confident that you can become more confident. I can't be fairer than that. The only thing stopping you is that thing you see in the mirror every morning, i.e. YOU. Because when it comes to confidence you are the only thing holding yourself back, either by clutching on to historical hurts, slights and failures like a toddler trails its comfort blanket, or by dripping poisonously negative messages into your own subconscious, turning untrue self-beliefs into irrefutable facts.

The phrase 'I think therefore I am' has never sounded as true as when it's applied to your levels of confidence and self-esteem. We are in many ways like our own advertising hoarding, creating slogans about ourselves that we then pin up there for others to read and believe. Your slogans could be telling other people that you're worthless, dull, low status and insignificant. Or they could be telling people you meet, date and work with that you warrant their interest, love and respect. This is your interpersonal signalling. But it's not just how others see you that counts. These self-created slogans have a crucial intrapersonal impact as well. By displaying yourself as unimportant you tell *yourself* you're insignificant, too. Every time you wring your hands, bite your nails, sit silent when you should speak up, say 'It's only me' when you introduce yourself on the phone, say 'Yes' when you want to say 'No', or apologise before you talk, you tell yourself that you are a low-value human being.

Now's the time to start fighting back.

The *only* sad thing about learning how to be confident is realising you could have done it years ago. How do I know? Because that's exactly what happened to me.

I know these techniques work because not only have I been training people in all walks of life in them for the past 15 years (including and often most frequently people at the highest levels of their careers), I have also had to learn them and use them myself.

I have been painfully, witheringly shy for most of my life and by allowing myself to be shy for so long I have annoyed myself with my own wussy behaviour more times than I can remember. It was only when I realised that shyness is a lifestyle choice rather than an affliction, and it was only when my annoyance at the card life had dealt me turned instead to anger at my own stupidity that I began to take control of my own behaviours and change the way I thought and acted. Like everyone else I still have a mix of confident moments and moments that cause anxiety, plus those odd, extra-daunting moments that I find I have to urge myself through by placing an invisible boot to my backside and kicking myself up my own bum, but at least I know it's my own foot kicking my own bum rather than someone else's size sevens either booting me on or stamping on my self-belief.

I know (as will you when you've read it) that I can call on all the mechanisms in this book to get me through the important challenges in my life, even though I might let some of the less important ones slip, and for me that's good enough to ensure I enjoy life and feel in control of my fate but without getting so arrogant that I have an unrealistic estimation of any risks.

Stars get nervous too

However you're feeling right now at this stage of your life in terms of confidence levels you should know that *everyone* battles their own demons. One of the things that prompted me to write this book is to share the astonishing secret that I discovered both when I worked with leading businesspeople and when I work with top performers on live TV. Do you believe there is a 'have' and 'have not' system when it comes to confidence, as though some people were touched with the confidence stick at birth, just like the lucky stick or the beauty stick, and some were not? If you do you're wrong because that's not how it is.

I can honestly say I have never worked with anyone who is naturally confident and who finds it all easy. I have worked with top conference speakers who pace like tigers before they go onstage (I watched one leading academic on the circuit rip his notes into thin shreds, roll them into balls and begin to eat them just prior to stepping onstage at one conference), and TV presenters who are whey-faced and silent before they step out in front of the cameras. I have watched leading politicians indulge in a whole ritual of those anxiety touches and tics before they appear in public, and I have worked with more than one performer who admits to being physically sick each and every time before they step out onstage.

How does sharing this help you?

The key point here, the point you need to remember above all else, is that they were all good. Regardless. They all learnt to conquer their feelings so that instead of allowing themselves to become overwhelmed by their fears they learnt to control and harness those nerves and recycle them into a stunning performance.

And so can you. Learning how to be confident is no harder than learning any other skill, which is why this book will be taking you through the process in much the same style that you'd use for more practical or technical competencies, like tips and step-by-step work that is easy and enjoyable to follow, plus some more specific techniques for more specific problems, moments or occasions when you find yourself struggling.

I see most confidence as 40 per cent ability and 60 per cent performance.

There are more people out there bluffing their way through life on 99 per cent performance than you'd think. These are the people who achieve the knack of taking a very small amount of ability or talent and puffing it up to look bigger or better than it is. The principle is simple: by looking as though they think they are good they market the same opinion to everyone around them. They're the ones who sit, stand and speak well enough to let us know they have a lot to offer.

So, hike your trousers, gird your loins and otherwise brace yourself for the ride because here's how your new confidence game plan is going to work:

YOUR FIVE STAGES TO CONFIDENCE

To boost your own confidence you will be working through the following five key steps:

1. **Diagnosing**
   Did you know there were different kinds of confidence problems? You could be suffering from shyness, low self-esteem, stress or performer anxiety. Each one of these problems is different from the next, and your way of dealing with them should be equally variable. For instance a shy person might have no problem standing up onstage acting a lead role in a play, while someone with low self-esteem wouldn't even think of applying for the role in the first place.

2. **Understanding**
   Knowledge is power, and understanding why you suffer from anxieties or shyness while other people seem to be able to be at ease in all sorts of challenging situations will be of huge benefit, but only if you use that knowledge wisely. Self-pity and victim thinking are not on the menu. Marinating in the misery of self-awareness is indulgent and pointless at best but at its worst it's destructive as it uses time that could be spent on recovery. When you learn why these feelings happen you will only be learning them to use as part of the cure, not as an excuse. We'll be using the term sick notes to describe the excuse-based thinking we do to allow ourselves to duck out from doing anything we find too challenging or scary. Knowing why you behave in a certain way is only valid if it does not then get used as a sick note.

3. **Boosting your inner confidence**
   The clue to boosting your own confidence lies in the phrase

itself: this is DIY time with a vengeance, meaning you will need to become your own coach and support system. I'm a great fan of task delegation, but delegating your ego-boosting is admitting defeat before you've even started. All the time other people prop you up by providing encouragement and compliments you are vulnerable to outside influences. If you place others in charge of your confidence-boosting it leaves you vulnerable because it means that they can also be responsible for bursting your ego, too. If your ego were a very precious Ming vase where would you keep it? Out on the street so that everyone could touch it and admire it so you could be sure it was a beautiful object? No, you'd keep it indoors under lock and key because you could see for yourself how beautiful it was and those people in the street might drop it, chip it or break it. Get the point?

4. Creating your own override button
This is where you recognise the fact that some genuine fear responses are kicking in, but ones that are either redundant in modern life, or which you wish to choose to ignore to enable you to function in a calm and professional way. This means using techniques that you will have pre-learnt to deal with your historical fears.

5. Acting confident
Remember that by acting the part you will end up feeling it, too. Those outward signals like your vocal tone and your body language will con you as well as others around you, allowing your inner confidence to grow along with the outward display. Changing your non-verbal state is easy, quick and painless. Really, what's not to like?

THE ROUTE

So now you've started on your path towards confidence you might like to know what kind of form your training and work is going to take. Do you think you will be:

Take your pick. If you like
then you can stop reading
approach appeals to you we
booster that will start to for
strength and courage. You h
to do is to get back in touch
bravery and ability to cope
this as your Confidence Cor
personal Core later in the bc

So now you have begun
confidence is about; now
started to take control of you
dribbly old cardigan and p
your shoulders; now is the t
and confident stages of your

And do remember:

Confidence is an ongoing p
you learn from this book
something you buy and ke
improving. The work is wc
without it you will never fu

CONFIDENCE RULE
Kick ass on a regular basis, espec

---

1. Spending a lot of time looking at all those problems in your life that have made you the weakling you currently feel yourself to be?
2. Throwing blame at all and sundry, i.e. everyone from your parents to the school bully?
3. Building up your confidence slowly and carefully by learning how to love yourself and realising you deserve to be loved and respected by everyone you meet and work with, too?
4. Taking a realistic, good-humoured but boot-camp approach to confidence, cutting corners where possible and telling yourself to 'get over it' on a regular basis under the understanding that this lack of confidence is probably pretty self-indulgent in the first place and that, because you've already missed out on a lot because of it, there is no time to waste playing at coaxing it out, so just go for it and then get on with your life?

I hope you chose '4' because that's where we're going. Tough love. Action-focused effort.

I'll guess '3' looked tempting but we do need to get real. Many books on confidence and self-esteem focus on telling you that you are wonderful/lovable/a beautiful person who deserves to be full of self-admiration. In fact this is not absolutely true. We're all full of flaws. Not everyone is talented, witty and exquisitely beautiful. To assume we're some kind of walking perfection would be reckless or arrogant. It's vital you know your product objectively before you begin to market it. The ability to evaluate your weaknesses as well as your strengths is important, because honest evaluation (devoid of paranoia but also devoid of delusional thinking) will help drive you towards genuine confidence rather than fake bravado.

We have to earn things in life and earning them will often mean change and growth. You're not perfect, none of us are. Accept that and then move towards confidence.

Or maybe you liked the sound of suggestions '2' best: blaming other people? While this sounds great, blaming other people can be very dangerous. It places control of yourself in other people's laps. If others hold all the power, you might as well roll over and suffer whatever has happened as a consequence because you have

no power and therefore
allow that school bully to
blame for our own respor
the power to find the cure

If the fear I experience is
the power to make it sto
victim, powerless in my s
be suing my school for sit
like iron girders who sat b
me?).

Blame yourself. Please.
stop because you can.

Th

1. **Stop blaming**. We kr
   mother/father, teach
   blaming them for yo
   control over you and
2. **Start taking control**.
   to achieve your goals
   be you need to take
   They provided the sti
3. **Get over your old ca**
   with personality.

Your first lesson is that sl
not fixed. You choose th
choose clothes out of y
or lack of confidence is
dribble-stains that you w
bed each morning. You c
your arms into the ropey
just because the garment
Or you can choose to shu
that's in your wardrobe.
ACTUALLY' embroidere

1

SO WHAT IS CONFIDENCE, EXACTLY?

Confidence looks good to everyone but it looks different to each of us, too. You know when you feel confident and you'll know when you don't, but describing that feeling is more difficult than just being aware when you have it. However, defining the behaviours those feelings produce is much easier. Here's a list of some of the behaviours that will be occurring in your life at those moments when you lack confidence.

Lacking confidence means:
- Not speaking up
- Not speaking up at first but letting rip after bottling it all up
- Sitting at the back during meetings
- Trying to look invisible
- Dropping hints rather than speaking straight
- Lying to get out of things you don't like
- Taking on too much work
- Moaning to others rather than discussing your problem with the right person
- Reminding yourself of all your mistakes and failures in your life rather than focusing on your achievements
- Being unable to make decisions
- Turning up at social events with a ready-made excuse for leaving early
- Hating confident people
- Blaming other people for your own lack of confidence

- Being emotionally impotent: 'It's how I am, I can't do anything about it'
- Over-analysing things you said. 'Did that sound wrong?' 'Did I upset that person?'
- Apologising, even before you have done or said anything
- Trying to please everyone
- Not pleasing yourself
- Does any of this sound familiar to you? I hope it wasn't too hard to read, but it's important to recognise what are and are not confident behaviours as accuracy is important when it comes to tackling your fears. So what is the alternative?

Being confident means:
- Getting noticed (and being confident with any attention)
- Speaking up
- Listening to others
- Imagining how things feel for them
- Taking responsibility for your feelings and actions
- Watching confident people to see what you can learn
- Negotiating things like workloads
- Speaking straight (being assertive)
- Performing to your full ability
- Enjoying meeting new people
- Being able to sell yourself at meetings, business presentations and sales pitches
- Talking and behaving normally on dates

However,

Confidence is not:
- Starting every sentence with the word 'I'
- Hogging the limelight
- Boasting
- Self-obsession
- Narcissism
- Telling everyone you're wonderful
- Claiming you're good at things you're not
- Being pushy

- Having no talent to back up your claims
- Boring people with long monologues
- Talking loudly
- Throwing your weight around
- Being aggressive
- Industrial-strength flirting
- Putting other people down
- Getting your own way all the time
- Sulking
- Being manipulative
- Arguing
- Yelling

A BRIEF INTRODUCTION TO THE PSYCHOLOGY OF FEAR

Think 'fear' is too strong a word to describe a lack of confidence? It's not. A lack of confidence is a fear response, even though that fear arousal might be mild, and even though you might think you have it under control. Suffering from a lack of confidence doesn't make you unsuccessful or pathetic, far from it. Some of the bravest people alive have nightmares about public speaking, or social events where they have to make small talk. There are people all around you who are busy masking their own subliminal fears. The problem is we're often so busy tackling our own that we're just too tied up to notice.

Here's one quick example.

Watch high-ranking people like royalty as they walk into or across a room. Despite the fact that they have status and power and an aura of supreme confidence, how many of them still look at a loss as to what to do with their hands? How many times do you see them fiddling with their cuffs or clothing or clutching or touching their handbag? Gestures like this are part of the fear response. They provide temporary barriers between them and the people they're meeting, and those barriers provide a small surge of comfort or safety.

You probably feel the same when you fold your arms or stick

your hands into your pockets. We all experience a desire to hide from other people, and that desire is based on subliminal or even instinctive feelings of fear. Nature has you hard-wired to produce a prickle of fear as a throwback from a response that would have once saved the life of your less-cosseted ancestors.

Fear arousal, the geek version: what your fear does to your body

- Your brain perceives a threat
- Your autonomic nervous system kicks into overdrive
- Which produces a huge surge of adrenalin
- Your hypothalamus in your brain pumps out a corticotrophin-releasing hormone
- Your pituitary gland releases adrenocorticotrophin
- Your adrenal glands release cortisol
- Making you super-prepared for fight or flight

The moral? (For geeks and non-geeks)

- **Don't knock it.** Accept it. Your fear response that you call lack of confidence is nature's way of trying to save your life.
- **Do learn to control it.** You don't want to suffer the kind of response that would have had your ancestors springing off across the savannah like a rabid wildebeest at the sight of a lion just because your boss has called you into her office for a chat.

THE MOST COMMON CONFIDENCE FEARS

The following fears are some of the most common confidence-busters I encounter when I'm training. Look at the analysis of these fears and you can understand how much of it is your animal programming kicking in, despite the fact it is largely redundant in modern life. Once you get the hang of this analysis, apply it to any situation you find daunting.

Fear of networking

One very common fear is the fear of walking into a room and meeting strangers. In animal terms this fear would be hugely appropriate, even if it bordered on terror, because an animal trying to ingratiate with another pack or herd will be very likely to be attacked and possibly killed. So your fear response at the thought of networking or 'doing a room' is entirely natural in evolutionary terms.

But networking and mingling are a normal part of business and social life. The risk of getting attacked and killed at a friend's wedding or an annual accountants' conference is so low as to be virtually impossible, so you should feel well within your comfort zone. But why then do so many of us experience high levels of fear and the desire to bottle out when confronted with this situation?

The problem is that our old, historic, animal survival fears are overpowering our logical assessments of the event. We know we're unlikely to die as we walk over to introduce ourselves to the boss's husband but we're also overwhelmed with subliminal thoughts that she might start snarling and snapping. In the battle between logic and instinct it's instinct that tends to win out. So learn to override these residual fears founded on survival instinct.

Fear of speaking in public

Nobody ever died doing this and yet it still rates as one of our greatest fears. Part of this is what I will be referring to later in the book as The Alice Syndrome, which is named after the eponymous character in *Alice in Wonderland* who grew in size after drinking from the 'Drink me' bottle. It refers to the way shy people feel when the attention of a large group of people is focused on them – as if their tics, habits and foibles are magnified. Fear of public speaking also stems from deep inside our animal psyche that tells us that when a room full of other animals are all staring at us it must mean they are about to attack. It's another prime example of a situation where you need to override your fear that is based on ancient survival instincts.

Fear of dating

This can be an ego-crushing experience but it's rarely body-crushing as well. The bruises that occur from laying out your stall in the hope of luring a buyer, only to find they have walked away and rejected you, are largely emotional rather than physical. It hurts, but it's mainly hurt pride. But you should remember that the date you have just been on was one of the early steps in the mating process (Yeah, as though it never crossed your mind!) and that it's mating and breeding that prevents us from becoming extinct. Nature has made the urge pretty strong. Humans have created a complex ritual around mating and your date is just a part of it. This is why your fear kicks in. However, it's the fear of bruised pride that needs to be dealt with. No other animals consider extreme cosmetic surgery, dieting and/or a vat of cookie dough ice cream as a way of dealing with the sting of rejection.

Despite feeling that you have a lot riding on your date, fear of survival is not a useful response (unless you're dating a weirdo, of course!). Use override techniques to enable you to blossom during the date, showing yourself as your relaxed, charming and witty self.

CONFIDENCE TRICKS: FEELING LUCKY

Lucky charms can work! Taking that favourite teddy bear to an exam or wearing your lucky pants to a client pitch can help make you feel more positive. Don't take the charm effect too literally though, and don't become obsessive with them – the trouble starts when you believe it's down to cosmic influences and freak when you discover those 'lucky' pants are in the wash on the day of a big interview!

Fear of looking stupid

This is an underpinning fear, i.e. one that lurks behind many of your other, more specific fears. We all have our own levels of pride, pomposity, cool or egotism. Some people's levels are pitched quite low, meaning they don't care too much if they make other people laugh. These are people who are comfortable being teased and even more comfortable acting the fool. Many comedians employ humour to deflect and control their tendency to make people laugh so their audience laughs with them rather than at them. People who lack confidence often have a dread of looking stupid, meaning they either opt out of the limelight altogether or act the fool on a regular basis.

The very best therapy is to look very stupid deliberately. Dress up in fancy dress for a party. Make a show of yourself now and again. Anything less will be a walk in the park. I had several major disasters when I was a catwalk model, including opening a coat to display the matching dress underneath but finding I'd forgotten to put the dress on. It's moments like that that make you what you are later on in life. I have very little fear in front of the TV camera because of that moment of uber-embarrassment.

Fear of being looked at

Again, this goes back to feelings of animal threat because attracting attention could mean getting singled out for attack. However, because humans have the power of speech, many of our attacks are verbal rather than physical. In a safe environment like the workplace, keeping a low profile will often mean you're more likely to be singled out behind your back for critical comment or even bitching!

CONFIDENCE TRICK: TAKING FEAR OUT OF THE FRAME
There is one very easy way of finding out whether you should boot up your confidence to go for a goal or whether you should trust your fear instinct and take a detour, and that is to imagine that you have no fear in the first place. Close your eyes and sit quietly for a moment. Clear your mind. Then imagine doing the thing you are contemplating, only with confidence. Ask yourself: if I felt more confident and less fearful of doing this thing would I do it? If you come up with the thought that it's only your lack of confidence that is holding you back then you have your answer. Do it. Only learn to manage your confidence first.

MOTIVATING YOURSELF THROUGH FEAR – YOUR FIRST STEPS

Although appropriate fear can save your life, your inappropriate fears will blight it because they can make you guilty of the only real failures, which are:

- NOT TRYING or
- GIVING UP

How many times have you passed on an opportunity because your fears have resulted in a lack of confidence? How often do you duck out of that social event, get someone else to do the business presentation, fail to make your point at a business meeting or dream about your ideal job or lifestyle rather than taking steps to make it happen?

The choice you make under those circumstances is one of comfort. Why swap comfort for possible pain? Isn't it better to imagine you could have written that great novel than to have written your book and seen it turned down?

My book *The Tall Poppy** is about the way the public love to idolise someone before pulling them off their pedestal and pecking them to death. It's also about the way we tend to do the same to ourselves, allowing levels of success into our lives before self-destructing with a vengeance. Not all of us do this, of course. There are thousands of examples of people who became deeply successful in their lives. But there are also those world-class footballers who drink themselves to oblivion, singing stars who choose a life spent in and out of rehab or politicians who allow their wallets to rule over their hearts and heads. 'They had it all,' we say, 'why did they choose to go into meltdown?'

HOW THE TALL POPPY SYNDROME CAN AFFECT YOUR CONFIDENCE

There are two aspects to this and you should consider both important points before taking the steps towards personal confidence that I will provide in this book.

We are often destined to self-destruct when:

We find we have chased the wrong dream or the wrong goals.
Either they were someone else's goals, and we were pushed into working towards them because it was what we were expected to do, or we failed to spot the fact that the goal wasn't one that would lead to personal happiness. Success is not generic but we treat it as though it is. You get promoted to boss and you're seen

---

*The 'Tall Poppy Syndrome' refers to cutting down the tallest and the best flowers, so that the smaller ones don't look worse by comparison.

as successful even though you were genuinely happier doing the job you were originally employed to do. You're a singer who adores a simple life of writing and singing songs, but your songs are so good you land a multi-million pound deal and you're pushed to produce more commercial songs and live one big haze of meetings, promotions and nightclubs. You're a home-loving footballer who enjoys the game when it involves dedication and teamwork, but your skills take you into a league that involves constant travel and press attention.

Or we self-destruct when we realise success is an ongoing expectation. The phrase 'resting on your laurels' rarely applies, especially in our instant-gratification-seeking, fast-moving, short-attention-span society. The greater the success, the bigger the capacity for failure. Miss a kick down the local park and you'll groan about it but it will soon be forgotten. Miss a penalty in the World Cup final and you'll know you have let down the hopes and dreams of your entire country. When you're self-employed and business dips you look at your household bills and work out how to make cuts, but when you own a business empire and business dips you're responsible for the livelihood of thousands of employees.

Dealing with success

Why do I mention this now? Because these are genuine considerations you need to take into account before embarking on a transaction where you will be calling on confidence. Low self-esteem and shyness can make the discomfort of a situation appear to be terminal, i.e. 'It's not worth it'. But it is vital you dig deep into your honesty reserves to decide whether your 'not worth it' genuinely refers to your goal or whether it is just prompted by laziness or fear, i.e. 'My goal *is* worth it but I will delude myself into pretending it's not so I can bottle out of attempting something that will make me feel uncomfortable or anxious.' When you think like this you need to evaluate your few moments of miserable discomfort against the kind of lifetime of discomfort that occurs when we know we have never bothered to pursue our goals or dreams.

Doing so involves dragging out your crystal ball and seeing what your 'successful' future looks like before you commit. I recently spoke to a woman who had just been chatted up by a famous actor who was known for his drop-dead looks. Had she agreed to a date? No. Why not? Because she knew she'd be unhappy and terminally anxious in a relationship with a guy every other woman fancied. She preferred a man who would be beating other men off *her* with a stick to one where she'd need to be taking that same stick to other women. It wasn't low self-esteem talking; it was accurate evaluation of the future. She preferred people to think it was her partner who had got lucky, rather than her.

A vital rule before you go further:

CONFIDENCE RULE

Understand the difference in your fear. Is it **goal-related** fear or **process-related** fear?

One is valid and one is not. Here's the difference:

- **Goal-related fear:** If the goals and dreams you are pursuing are not your own, compromise your values or are opposed to your basic motivations. This is where you are employing considerable effort and energy to achieve something that you do not want.
- **Process-related fear:** This is when you want a certain goal but you lack the confidence and courage to achieve your dreams. This is where you allow the risk of short-term discomfort to scupper your long-term happiness.

It's very important to understand your goals and see what it is that is holding you back. If it's the case that you actually don't want the goal that's been set, then good for you; it's important to work out what you do and don't want to do. But if it's the case that you desperately want to achieve your goal but it's fear that's holding you back, then read on. I'll provide you with the confidence tools you need in order to realise your dreams.

IN A NUTSHELL

- Address your fears. What are the fears that are prompting your own lack of confidence?

- Discover your underlying fears. The Tall Poppy Syndrome shows how your assumed successes might not be motivating you in the way you expect. Are you aiming at the wrong goals in life?

- Be honest with yourself. Admitting your genuine goals to yourself is the first stage of countering your fears and building your confidence.

2

THE CONFIDENT APE

Although we think of ourselves as modern beings, much of what we do has been programmed into us in a biological and evolutionary sense. We fear things not because they are inherently scary, but because our fears were developed when meeting strangers or putting ourselves on display could have put us in danger.

Status also has changed. In the ape world the hierarchies are well defined but in the world of the human animal we have blurred the boundaries to the point where confidence has become a bit of a chimera. Physical clout has little relevance in the world of computers, and hierarchy these days tends to be dependent on job title rather than bicep-girth, although interestingly the young bucks who rule by PC will often still feel the need to spend hours in the gym to get six-packs and triceps, even though their jobs do not need physical strength.

With our hierarchies gone wrong in animal terms it's little wonder we lack confidence. They're skewed, meaning we need to straighten them out in our heads before we can face the world with the kind of jauntiness we all desire.

This chapter will help lay out your goals by explaining the evolutionary uses of confidence and why you struggle to apply confidence to apparently non-threatening situations in modern life.

By studying an explanation of your lack of confidence you will also find the key to your cures. One basic point to remember:

Your lack of confidence is a **fear response**.

In modern life that fear is **perceptual**, meaning it's often stimulated by tosh. I am rarely asked how to be confident in a house fire or car crash. I am frequently asked how to be confident at social events or business presentations.

What this tells us is that the key to daily confidence lies in our ability to change our perception of certain events that are currently scaring us and to see them for what they are. In order to do this we must understand how circumstances that would have meant life or death to our ancestors are no longer a threat, and to learn to master and manage that historical fear response accordingly.

It will explain how to recognise Right Fear from Wrong Fear before you move on to take control of your responses.

THE WRONG TYPE OF FEAR

First, a health warning: Confidence kills.

In animal terms what we perceive as modern forms of confidence are entirely unnatural.

Why?

Well, begin by looking at your capacity to survive. Your presence here on earth today is largely thanks to the ability of your ancestors to stay alive, at least until they were old enough to mate and breed. To do that would have required enough confidence to either hunt or negotiate for food and sex, but not so much confidence that they took daft risks, meaning that a degree of timidity, fear, anxiety and awareness of danger is very likely to be part of your DNA.

So if you're looking for universal confidence, i.e. a feeling of confidence that is with you at all times, or the kind of confidence that enables you to tackle tasks and situations that you have neither the skills nor the experience to deal with, you are going against your survival instincts. It's right to feel fear under the right circumstances.

However, times change and so do threat levels. What would

once have been Right Fear might need downgrading in modern society. For instance, your ancient ancestors would have been fearful of:

• Other animals that could attack or cause harm, from large beasts (including strange humans) to smaller things like snakes and poisonous insects
• Injury or illness
• Environmental dangers like cliff faces, cold or the dark
• Being trapped or unable to escape

Any of these things would have been stimulus that would cause the fear response that in turn would help to save your ancestor's life, because all that adrenalin and cortisol would have made them stronger and faster. And we know they survived, otherwise you wouldn't be here today.

Your parents and their input in your fear response

As a child *you* were born in a state of spontaneity and relative fearlessness, but your survival depended on your ability to learn from both experience and your parents that there are many things that can harm or kill you. This makes sense, because the animal that is alert to danger usually lives longer than the animal that is oblivious to threat, brave beyond its abilities and takes risks without calculating the odds first. The animal that lives to fight another day is usually the one that avoids or runs from attack rather than the one that meets it square-on, constantly trying to punch above its weight by taking on enemies and situations that it has neither the muscle, skills nor experience to deal with.

Unfortunately parents can allow their role as protector to usurp their role in teaching you how to be self-sufficient as soon as possible. When this happens they'll often plant extra worries and cautions in your mind that can make you uber-fearful as an adult. They just hope cowardice will keep you out of danger.

So cowardice is good?

On the whole cowardice is about as good or as bad as confidence, meaning that at some levels it can be helpful to the point of being vital, but that there is also a point where it becomes downright dangerous, exactly like confidence. This isn't as confusing as it sounds.

An animal needs sufficient amounts of fear to avoid danger, but then it also needs sufficient amounts of confidence to get food, mingle with other animals and not get seen as the runt of the litter.

Apes are our nearest animal relatives and in many respects we still think and behave in similar ways to simians, with ape behaviours giving us clues about our own, often-puzzling, behaviour patterns. Like our workplaces, ape colonies tend to be hierarchical, but whereas humans have mutated to allow even puny people to rule the roost, ape hierarchies tend to be based around strength and muscle-power first and foremost, with intelligence and delegation coming second. Like us, apes need to be able to evaluate risk. Pick on a bigger ape and you could end up dead. But make no approaches at all, or show you're too much of a weakling, and the same could easily be true.

The fear response and the confidence or lack of it that it triggers will advise an ape whether to fight or run. And if running is not an option, i.e. the bigger ape is a grade 'A' sprint champion, then that ape will know tricks of ingratiation and submission-signalling that should mean it doesn't get picked on.

This is an important point. If an ape is overconfident it could end up taking on other apes that will kill it in combat. Or it will stray too far from the other apes in its group and get picked off by a predator. Or it will try to steal its food rather than waiting its turn and get into food-fights that might turn nasty.

PRESENT DANGER: HOW THIS IMPACTS ON YOUR CURRENT CONFIDENCE

Can you see how all these ancient, animal instincts affect your ability to be confident or not today? Many of the fear factors are the same, although our relatively suppressed and civilised society has created rules so that safety and status are no longer dependent on size and strength. So there is no need to fear that tribe of strange animals that sit in front of us during a business presentation, or the group we need to approach at that networking event.

Humans have evolved, of course. But even when it comes to our 'low-threat' scenarios the same rules of confidence vs overconfidence need to apply. Even when your life is not in danger your lower-grade risks need to be assessed according to skill and ability. Otherwise your confidence could cause you more problems than it solves. Overconfidence that is not backed up by skill and talent might not be lethal but it will be destructive to your career and relationships. The key to your confidence lies in your ability to understand and master the science of fear, telling good fear from bad fear and controlling responses that – despite being instinctive – have no real use in the current life of the animal known as man.

How this works in your life

As I am a life-long fan of simplicity, here is an example of the theory.

You travel to work on the underground.

How much should you fear that journey?

In pure animal terms you should fear it a lot. You go under the ground and climb into a small metal capsule (remember that ancestral fear of being trapped?) with hundreds of other humans that are all strangers to you (remember that instinctive fear of strange animals?) and then you are sealed together in that capsule, pressed tight together with no means of escape until the doors are opened again. You have no idea who is piloting that capsule and you have little understanding how it gets from A to B. You are aware that several of your fellow passengers are potentially dangerous or harmful to you.

Do you:

    A. Avoid the journey altogether?

    B. Travel on the tube but in a state of gibbering panic?

    C. Travel on the tube but avoid carriages that are too full or too empty and keep an eye out for trouble?

    D. Push into the crush and then read your newspaper until it's time to get off?

    E. Travel and play dare, winding up other passengers and yelling 'bring it on if you think you're hard enough' to anyone who looks at you twice?

Everyday scenarios like this show us all about the science of fear and confidence, because they illustrate how we need to evaluate ideal levels of both, creating order out of the confusion of mixed messages.

Ask anyone if they want to be more confident and they're likely to say yes, but confidence is a bit of a myth that rarely exists in reality, at least not in the form that we think. Would you really want to be the guy provoking trouble on the tube? Or would you prefer to go with all your intrinsic animal instincts and either walk to work every day or sit quivering in the corner of a carriage?

Your ideal tube-travel behaviour probably lies somewhere between behaviours C and D. This means suppressing normal fear, because no other animal would feel anything but threatened being placed in similar circumstances, but not pressing the 'override' button to the point that you're placing yourself in unnecessary danger. Without realising it, commuters have created a middle-ground survival state for their daily journey, which involves crushing up with animals that are strangers to them while dog-facing, which means sitting with a blank, expressionless face, using no eye contact, using little body movement and not speaking at all until the journey is over. This body language is the closest thing we can get to making ourselves invisible. By sitting still and staring into space we avoid engaging with our fellow passengers and therefore (hopefully) lower our risk of trouble or attack.

Ape actors

• How about people who mask their fear? How useful is that? For an ape, as for most humans, part of staying alive means acting your little socks off. For every ape that goes around being himself there is the ape version of Dame Judi Dench and Sir Ian McKellen. Here are a few occasions when apes use their acting skills to either save their lives or sustain their lives:

• **Using ingratiation techniques** to get food. Most baby apes rely on the generosity of adult apes to get food. This means they are forced to beg or ingratiate themselves with those bigger apes. **How does this relate to you?** In the workplace we need effective teamwork and cooperation to achieve most of our tasks, meaning we tend to be nice to people we find objectionable, especially if they are clients. Most customer-care techniques are based on the negotiation and ingratiation techniques a small ape uses to charm a bigger one into food-sharing.

- **Using submission signals.** The smaller or less-powerful ape needs to send out signals of submission, no matter how angry he is with the bigger ape. Simple submissions include lowering the head and/or the body.
  How does this relate to you? When you meet people socially or in business it's usual to dip your head slightly to show rapport rather than conflict.

- **Using re-motivational techniques.** Apes use a couple of techniques when they feel under threat from a bigger ape. One is pseudo-infantile, the other pseudo-sexual:
  * By using body language that resembles that of a baby ape – i.e. squawking and rolling on the ground on its back – the threatened ape hopes to get the bigger ape to walk on by rather than fight because fighting a baby ape just doesn't feel right (i.e. Pick on someone your own size).
    How does this relate to you? See how many of us use infantile behaviours to avoid attack, both socially and at work. How many women resort to talking in a baby voice when they want to ask a colleague to do something? How many people begin to look winsome or cute in a bid to avoid conflict under pressure?
  * The ape alternative is to indulge in some industrial-strength **'flirt' signals** in a bid to move the bigger ape's mind from 'fight' to 'fornicate' (not necessarily with the smaller ape, by the way – the flirting can often be same-sex).
    How does this relate to you? How many people use workplace flirting as a manipulative tool to persuade and influence?

- **Not showing pain.** Badly injured apes rarely show their pain, sitting quietly rather than acting out their agony. The reason for this is obvious: showing weakness can lead to attack from other apes.

How does this relate to you? It's common to mask a lack of confidence in the workplace as it can exacerbate what is already a difficult situation. Business leaders especially are expected to mask fear or anxiety as not only does it look bad for them, it also makes that fear spread to the troops that they are responsible for motivating. Would an army fight if its general was seen crying into his comfort blanket? Would shareholders hold on to their shares if an MD was seen sitting rocking and sucking his thumb? You mask your fears as a survival technique. You did it during your recruitment interview because you were trying to provoke their confidence in your abilities and you do it now to look professional, even when you're not feeling in control of a situation.

• **Not showing any emotion.** Alpha apes are known to register their status via their lack of movement. For most of them much of the day involves sitting still a distance away from the rest of the colony. Unlike the apes that are lower in the hierarchy, who tend to spend a lot of time fighting and socialising, the alphas are often sitting doing what to all intents and purposes looks like thinking.

How does this relate to you? Status techniques in the workplace involve little in the way of muscle competition but quite a lot in the way of masking movement to look cool and in charge. The higher the status the less you want to be seen dashing about, waving your arms or gesticulating or even being emotional. One slight abnormality to all this studied calm comes in the case of that alpha known as the political leader. Prime ministers and presidents put a lot of work into their alpha performances, walking tall, moving little and gazing out at a far horizon in a bid to register calm omnipotence. But the electorate has developed new demands. We don't just want a leader; we want a human being as well, with the correct emotional responses in place. And we want a leader who can fight off other alphas, either abroad or in the leadership debates. This has resulted in some odd body-language displays with the likes of Tony Blair using exaggerated hand gestures, Gordon Brown getting tearful on TV and David Cameron and Nick Clegg acting like best buds straight after an election they had fought as rivals. These days confidence is seen as having its less alpha side, causing problems for leaders with less in the way of acting abilities.

- **Aggressive arousal displays.** To ward off an attack an ape will often perform rituals of strength and power that it might not be able to prove if a real battle kicked off. This is preventative aggression, like the classic chest-banging.
  How does this relate to you? This fake form of confidence in your ability to win a fight in a bid to prevent one occurs all the time in the average workplace, only more often via email than actual chest-thumping. Even low-ranking employees can be guilty of sending snippy messages to higher-ranking staff or customers, just to show who's actually the boss in terms of real power. When spats turn into conflict you often do begin to see body-language signals that resemble those used in the jungle, though. Watch union leaders and strikers versus the bosses. When sides have been taken and strikes are being threatened it's common to see group leaders shouting, fist-waving and using a raft of pseudo-aggressive display rituals to prove they shouldn't be messed with.

Defining your fears in animal terms helps create an understanding of emotions that might otherwise feel chaotic, random and confusing.

But it is also vital you have an equally in-depth understanding of your confidence. This might not appear to be relevant for a quick-fix cure, but it is vital for the kind of prolonged confidence that will stabilise your positive and negative emotions and create success and happiness in your life.

UNDERSTANDING YOURSELF: THE PSYCHOLOGY OF CONFIDENCE

Understanding yourself is the first step towards a cure. You don't have to read this section but I hope you will. Unlike other parts of the book that are more action- and tip-packed and directly problem-solving, this chapter is less about bullet points and slightly more about theory, but it will throw some light on the complex mix of emotions you call a lack of confidence, plus it will give you some fascinating angles about dealing with it.

It will also help you ensure your goals are achievable. We often yearn to be totally confident and totally stress-free. We say things like 'I just want to be happy' but psychologists and zoologists would question those goals and suggest they're far from natural. No animal spends its time in a state of permanent happiness, confidence and calm, without the aid of drugs or alcohol that is. If your life gets so completely rid of challenge you will probably be bored and depressed. For years I wondered why my cats were so keen to get out of the cat flap every morning, especially when it was raining or cold and even more especially as they seemed to enter a zone of peril and danger, fighting with other cats and frequently coming off worse. But I suppose it made the experience of coming back into the house and snoozing in front of the fire even nicer. If they never moved from the fire then they'd be bored and fat. Humans need stimulus and challenge, just like other animals. We also need to feel fear and worry, otherwise we'd be an extinct species. Wariness is a natural and desirable state, which is why I have said that confidence is an unnatural condition in most of the circumstances in which you're seeking to achieve it.

OUR HORROR OF REJECTION

Trying to date or do well in life at the same time as protecting yourself from rejection is like wanting to learn to swim but not wanting to get wet.

Rejection is a fact of life unless you're not trying. Every time you see an actor in a starring role or a comedian doing stand-up to a huge audience or a business person with a successful company you're looking at a tip of a success sitting atop a whole iceberg of rejection and failure.

Coping with the knock-backs: how you protect your ego

Your ways of handling your confidence might be instinctive and spontaneous or they could be remedies you have thought out beforehand. When we lack confidence as a child we cry, fight or run away. As adults we prefer to be less obvious though, masking our fears to other people and often to ourselves, too.

Fear-masking is okay but denial is not. Neither is being in denial about the truth behind your behaviours. Denying or lying about your motives means you're accessing your self-protection system. This is a great system because it helps prevent the ego taking a lethal pounding. It's being usefully self-delusional. But like any tool you use to fight off attacks of low self-esteem, it's a tool that needs to be used wisely. At its best it can be like emotional armour. At its worst it will make you confused in terms of your confidence goals and the work you need to do to achieve them. This is where it courts our old enemy, arrogance, i.e. it tells you that you are good when you're not.

There are good ways and bad ways of building a protective barrier around your self-esteem. The good ways create the kind of confidence that allows you to grow and improve. The bad ways lead to the kind of arrogance that leads to delusion. I know delusion might sound tempting. How nice to live in some sort of an ideal world of You, where you genuinely believe you are more beautiful/ handsome, desirable, talented and wonderful than you are.

Why you need to know about your self-protection system

Once you learn how to spot your self-defence thinking you can decide whether it is useful to you or not. 'Useful' means rejecting any unsolicited or unhelpful criticism and taking any practical lessons from any knock-backs or rejections but at the same time shrugging off anything that could be ego crushing. It's coming away from that tenth interview rejection thinking about updating your CV but not coming away believing you'll never get a job because nobody likes you. However, it's not useful to continue to clutch your really bad CV to your chest believing the only reason nobody will offer you a job is that you're just too damn marvellous and they feel too threatened by your brilliance to offer you employment.

Your self-protection syndrome

Nobody likes rejection, do they? It hurts the pride and it bruises the ego. So your ego likes to protect itself.

So far so good.

What you need to assess is how far your ego is going to keep itself intact. Imagine you think it's going to rain. What do you do?

A. Take an umbrella in your bag, just in case?
B. Forget the umbrella so when it does rain you get wet and can say 'Just my luck'?
C. Leave home with the umbrella up even though it's not raining yet?
D. Not leave home at all?

Let's apply those options to a job interview. Do you:

A. Assess your chances of getting the job, shoring up any areas you might be less proficient in or knowledgeable about before you go?
B. Go to the interview but without making any effort to improve first and then say you were unlucky when you don't get the job?
C. Go to the interview but you are so worried and nervous beforehand that you barely say a word?
D. Realise you don't stand a chance and so decide not to bother?

Of course, the best answer in both cases is A. Understanding the situation you are about to face and preparing for it will help your confidence. B, C and D are all self-defeating.

Defensive thinking at its most tragic can also make someone focus on the wrong problem. This is where you'd be in denial about the fact that you are self-obsessed and a heavy drinker but focus instead on the fact that you're a couple of pounds overweight as the reason why you can't get or keep a date. How many celebs do you see who struggle to get a loving partner despite Botox, lipo, boob jobs, diets, designer clothes, etc.? Very likely the answer to this mystery lies in the fact that they have the personality of a demanding, narcissistic newt.

When the ego-protection goes feral

It makes absolute sense to protect your ego and self-esteem. But it also makes sense to set parameters for your protecting behaviours.

Airbags in cars might save lives but driving around with yours fully inflated 'just in case' is likely to cause a crash.

So you need to create your own healthy risk assessments, based on positive optimism that isn't reckless arrogance.

It also needs to be based on your own perceptions, views and decisions.

Why? Well here's how it works otherwise:

You ask someone else if you should do something, like apply for a promotion at work or asking someone you like for a date. They give their opinion. You act on that advice, but with no feeling of control in the situation as it has not come from within yourself. This means you're in a state known as 'puppet', i.e. the other person is quietly – and possibly in the nicest way – pulling the strings. You don't get the promotion, or the object of your desire turns you down (and here comes the truly delicious part) but you are able to blame their decision for your failure. Yay!

The feeling of comfort that comes from being able to blame other people might be seductive but it can never compensate for the lack of success. Taking control of your own decisions will always give you a better chance of goal-achievement so go for the longer-term strategic behaviour of taking your own advice and making your own decisions above opting for the short-term comfort of being able to cry: 'It's not my fault!'

Buck-passing

The same is true of passing the buck. This is a slightly different form of blaming but it is almost as corrosive to our inner confidence. If you try to lead a blameless life it means you're either under-achieving by attempting to be perfect or you're screwing up but accusing others of the mistakes. Buck-passing sounds something like this:

DAD: 'You missed your mother's birthday.'
YOU: 'You know you should have reminded me!'

WIFE: 'You're putting on weight.'
YOU: 'It's the takeaway food; they shouldn't pack it with fat and calories.'

Other statements that show you are passing the buck include:

'I keep trying to give up smoking but the kids give me such grief I can't stop.'

'I can never be good at singing. I had a very critical teacher at school.'

'My parents always praised my brother but never me. That's why I have low self-esteem.'

'I wouldn't be overweight if the government gave out free gym passes.'

'I could have been a novelist if I hadn't got married and had kids.'

'I know I sent out the wrong quote for that job but it was because my manager kept going on at me to do something else.'

'My presentation would have been okay if I hadn't spoken after that other woman. She was so good I felt nervous.'

THE FREUDS' DEFENCE MECHANISMS

The Freuds (Sigmund and daughter Anna) proposed the idea of some significant defence mechanisms that we use to protect us from the thought of our own weaknesses or failures. You might use one or two of these, you might use all of them, or you might use none. They're the opposite to a reality check, allowing us to live in our own perfect little world, but prevent us from taking steps to ensure we can grow, learn and improve. They're the singer on *X Factor* pitching up in front of the judges to claim they're the next pop sensation and then blaming timing, a cold or the look on Simon's face for the fact they can't hit a note with a slingshot filled with paint bombs.

The Freuds pinpointed seven key techniques that we use to air-bag our egos:

Projection: You suffer from an unlikeable trait or urge and because you find it hard to admit you accuse someone else of having it. How many cheating lovers start attacking their partners jealously, accusing them of playing away?

Denial: You claim that failure or defeat didn't happen to you. You ask that dream from accounts out on a date and she turns you down. You then claim she is a lesbian or that you didn't want to date her anyway.

Intellectualisation: You stare into the face of disaster and use logic to pretend it's all for the good, like those reality-show contestants who act pleased to be evicted, claiming they're delighted to be able to get back to see their families again.

Rationalisation: Creating your own spin around your negative behaviour, i.e. justifying insulting and upsetting someone by saying 'I was only speaking the truth'.

Reaction Formation: Doing the opposite to what you really want to do or are urged to do, i.e. being uber-nice to someone you can't stand.

Regression: Lovely jubbly! You've just been knocked back on a date or turned down for a promotion and you find all your adult assertive techniques get up off the sofa and bid you good-bye as they walk out of the room, leaving you with an array of behavioural options that come firmly from the box marked 'childhood'. You sulk, you whine, you throw a tantrum. It was their fault, not yours.

Repression: You bury the negative thought or idea about you deep down at a level where it no longer troubles you.

EXERCISE

Look through the seven defence techniques and see how many you currently use in your life. Imagine someone has criticised you or that you have failed in a work project or college test or exam. What do you think? How do you behave? What do you tend to say?

These techniques can be useful to mitigate lasting damage to the ego.

Self-defence mechanisms can help us cope and avoid being overwhelmed by negative thoughts and behaviours, they're not always a bad thing.

However, you also need to decide how much you are using these denials to help and how much they will be causing long-term risk and damage. Are you becoming stubborn? Do you refuse to change in a way that could be positive or improve performance?

One of the most harmful consequences of denial is to put blame for your mistakes or failings on others. This scuppers your ability to improve as well as giving control over your life and your success to other people.

BLAMING AND STALLING:
THE MISS HAVISHAM SYNDROME

Miss Havisham, from *Great Expectations*, was one of Charles Dickens's greatest and most memorable creations, possibly because she touches a chord in all of us. She was the elderly woman who lived alone with her ward in a huge crumbling mansion, still wearing her wedding dress because life had stopped for her the day she was jilted at the altar. Nothing had been touched or dusted from that day so she sat in rooms full of mouldering furniture and cobwebs. She was bitter and planned revenge against all men.

Forget the jilting and the man-hating. Just focus on how many times your life has stalled like this, just because something bad happened. Miss Havisham's 'strength' came from her determination to shut her life down at that one low point, rather than having the kind of resilience that allows you to heal and move on. The Miss Havisham syndrome affects anyone who is still shy because as a kid someone laughed when they were reading out loud in class. It's the person who thinks women are not to be trusted because his ex was unfaithful, or the people who struggle to make new friends because they were never very popular at nursery school.

Miss Havisham syndrome is all those excuses and sick notes we write for ourselves to allow us to duck out, avoid, and simply not try. It's that catalogue of the kind of griefs, tragedies and bad bits of our lives that we allow to make us stall, sometimes for ever.

How to avoid the Miss Havisham syndrome

- Identify the moments when your brain starts feeding you sick notes, i.e. you start using your past experiences to validate the cop-outs you make in your current day-to-day life.
- Write down your sick notes. Having those excuses on paper in front of you will allow you to evaluate their worth far better than allowing them to exist as an unchallenged half-thought.
- Look at your sick notes. Now imagine the excuse has been told to you by a friend you are trying to coach and encourage and write a reply to each of them. What would you say to your friend? How would you advise them to deal with it? Would you really shrug and tell them it's a pity but that there's nothing they can do to help themselves cope/get over it/power onwards and upwards despite it?
- Question every negative self-belief, even (and especially) your long-held ones. The longer you tell yourself you're shy or a worrier or lacking self-esteem or confidence the more the myth becomes a form of reality.
- Remember urban legends? These were brilliant little horror stories that were told in a way that implied they had happened to someone not so far removed from you. The point is none of them were true. When you investigated the source it was always just 'A friend of a friend' but we persisted in believing the stories even though we had no evidence apart from word of mouth. Many of your negative self-beliefs are just that: urban legends. You have it in your head that they are unquestionable personality traits that you have no power to change. You believe you have evidence to back these claims up. But your 'evidence' is based on a load of half-held, half-remembered or wrongly remembered pieces of evidence that – even if it were true – should be questioned.
- You can change if you want to. Psychologists have conducted endless studies into the subject of personality and while I agree that there are factors in our lives that make us the person we are – whether our parents divorced or died or stayed together happily, whether we were praised as children or criticised, etc. – but for each person who became crushed by negative childhood experiences you will always find another who used tragedy or

a tough upbringing as the fuel they needed to power towards success later in life.

- It's not what happens to us, it's how we deal with it and process it that matters. You have choices. Stop believing that and you donate your entire life to external factors. Taking control of your own life is an intrinsic step in building your own levels of confidence.
- Write down at least four clear steps you could take to move your life on.
- Do not allow yourself to create or listen to your NID – your negative inner dialogue – that will be pitching in with the 'Yes, but ...' or 'That's all very well ...' comments.
- At least one of those steps needs to be long term and at least one should be something you can do straight away, e.g. 'I will work on my networking skills' is a step that you can work on long term; 'I will accept that invite to the event at work that I thought about turning down because I am shy' is a step towards your long-term goal that you can do straight away.

YOUR CONFIDENCE AND CELEBRITY OMNIPOTENCE

Grandiose thinking is something most people do now and again; in fact, it is claimed we all tend to suffer from it at some stage in our lives. Steering our minds away from the reality of our own circumstances, primarily to ward off thoughts of our own mortality, can be necessary, but it can also be dangerous. Look at all the egocentric people you see in the gossip magazines who really do seem deluded enough to imagine that they can avoid ageing, hammer their bodies with booze, drugs and cigarettes without any risk of health problems and then continue to reinvent themselves with marriages, exercise routines, plastic surgery and adoptions to ensure their later years are led in a way that mimics and reconstructs their youth.

Some of this denial can be useful. A little bit. A wood-shaving-sized piece, at best. It would be good if we could take a cheese-grater and pare off just enough of that celebrity ego to transplant on to ourselves to ensure we lead a happy life that doesn't involve some form of cloud cuckoo land existence, because although these deluded people might look as though they have it all we secretly know they don't. Their quest for immortality often leads to rubbish romances, weird plastic surgeries, alcoholism, drug abuse and the kind of life that – if they didn't also have money – would often be led on the streets rather than on the screens.

WHEN YOUR EGO IS LEFT TOO VULNERABLE

Thanks to the Freuds, we know when we're being too over-protective of our egos. Using defence mechanisms, we fail to learn or improve because our minds are in denial about any flaws in our behaviour. But perhaps you have the opposite problem. When we lack confidence we tend to lay our ego as bare as a builder's bum, sharing each and every limitation, anxiety and weakness to the world in a way that is borderline humiliating.

Why would you refuse to protect your ego? Surprisingly your lack of protection can have the same goals as the person who overprotects. When you indulge in denial you avoid criticism. When you overexpose your flaws it can be in the hope that other people will boost you up via their sympathy. If you tell everyone how crap you are it's odds-on that someone is going to try to disagree with you, even if it's just with the aim of shutting you up because you're becoming boring.

The big problem with expecting failure rather than success is that it's the perfect way to avoid effort. If you know it won't work, why try? Easy! Enthusiastic apathy. Pain-avoidance makes sense but only if you don't count the kind of long-drawn-out pain that can come from not bothering to try. This can lead to regret, and do you really want to end your days with the words 'I wish I'd ...' or 'I should have ...' or 'I always wanted to ...'? Do you really want your fear of failure to override your need to try to achieve what you really want?

When your animal wants get in conflict – and the effect on your confidence

It may not seem obvious to you at this point, but the desire to be self-effacing to the extent that we're too paralysed by fear to do the things that we want is something connected to our animal selves. Not convinced? Read on.

Think for a moment about two key desires:

1. THE DESIRE FOR FREEDOM AND INDEPENDENCE
2. THE DESIRE TO INTEGRATE

You probably have a healthy need to stand on your own two feet, make your own decisions and plan your own destiny.

You probably also have a burning need to be liked and accepted by other humans.

How does this affect your confidence?

The two desires cause conflict in terms of your behaviours and responses. If you agree to do what other people want and behave in a way that you hope they will find pleasing, you compromise your independence. But if you blaze your own trail in life, behaving in a way that suits you and to hell with the consequences, the odds are you'll be a very lonely person.

Now, imagine a young animal. To survive it needs to learn to look after itself. This side of the animal's confidence stems mainly from its physical strength, health and ability to sustain its own life. By the rules of the jungle, the bigger the beast the more powerful and confident it will be. Which takes care of the George Foremans and Vinnie Joneses of this world.

But for the less physically able, the ones who would be less than useful in a fight, the ability to integrate is vital for survival. Young apes have to learn to charm their way into getting food from adult apes and older apes need a degree of group cooperation for survival. Their submission rituals, including grooming, body-lowering, pseudo-infantile (behaving like a baby animal), are ingratiation techniques that gain acceptance and prevent them being attacked. Even the alpha apes will need group cooperation to hunt successfully or repel attacks from rival groups.

Your need to be liked

It's only human to want other human animals to find us agreeable. In many ways your life has been defined by your capacity to gain approval from others. As an infant, your survival depended on parental approval and if your mum or dad showed an active and open dislike of you then it's likely you're still suffering the fall-out in your mental well-being and personality. Then came your acceptance or lack of it with friends and school chums. Did your ingratiation techniques work? Were you part of the in-crowd? Or did you hang around the peripheries of school society? After you left school, were you approved of during recruitment interviews?

And when you finally got that job did your colleagues embrace you to their collective bosom? And the ten million dollar question: have you been lucky enough to enjoy a sustained sexual/romantic relationship? Did someone approve of you enough to want to meet, date and mate with you?

It's easy to believe that the acceptance and liking and approval of others somehow confers upon us the status of successful individuals. Likeability is an important factor in our lives but in terms of creating confidence and happiness it can be a bit of a damp squib.

Ideally we should obtain liking and approval from others while we are being totally true to ourselves. What we would then learn is that the authentic version of 'me' is a neat form of currency for a successful life. People will take me on my own terms and I have to put in the minimum amount of effort to be liked and loved.

But in reality we do all have to try. Social acceptance is a rare commodity when we're in our spontaneous, egocentric state of 'being myself'. We may come across as arrogant or even aggressive and selfish. As a lone individual it's natural to put your own needs first but as an animal moving in a pack we have to learn to suppress those needs and think of other people. This act of suppression is what being a nice human being is all about. It creates cooperation, empathy and altruism. But it ain't natural.

HOW TO BE PATHETIC 1

Every year I get invited to a 'woman of the year' awards, but only to the after-awards party. This year my invite told me I was invited to the prestigious awards ceremony as well, including a sit-down dinner.

'You've been promoted because your profile has risen,' my agent told me.

'Perhaps you're nominated for an award,' said my best friend.

I barely heard. I was too busy checking the invite, assuming it had been sent to me in error and imagining the scene when they either rang to apologise or turned me away at the door.

Pushing the boundaries of likeability

Often people use marriage to return to their natural state of being 'themselves'. They place themselves on the singles market wearing a polite smile, dress to impress, groom themselves to within an inch of their lives and display the facet of their personality described as 'nice', i.e. generous, reliable, honest, loving and loyal. Then once they're in a long-term commitment they no longer need to mask who they really are or pretend. All the social pretence is stripped away to reveal what lies beneath, warts and all.

When we do this, we hope that the multi-faceted view of our personality that we're now presenting to our partner will somehow prove lovable so that we can return to the same state of unconditional love that we first achieved with our parents. Why? Because that is the road that leads to confidence and a sense of security. We are hiding nothing and yet we are still loved and still have our partner's approval.

For me this explains some of the quasi-irrational behaviours that you see from celebrities and sporting stars who, despite claiming to desire a happy and loving marriage, do everything in their power to destroy that relationship. There seems to be no logic in screwing a 'Page 3 Girl' when the press are tracking your every step and your wife has sworn to leave you if you so much as breathe in the direction of a topless model. So why do it? It's easy to blame the moment and claim that men wear their brains in their underpants but I believe it's something far more devious and clever than it appears. By playing away, but then receiving the eventual forgiveness of their wife, the celebrity feels he has achieved that state of ultimate comfort, approval, security and therefore confidence that he enjoyed as a child.

Why do you need to know this? Because it's the wrong goal. It's unrealistic at best and at worst impossible. Because if you did achieve it you'd probably be obnoxious rather than lucky. You need to set your goals lower to achieve higher. For you the ideal goal is to get to the point where you are able to obtain the approval and liking of others without compromising your personality and without putting in so much effort that you feel like a phoney. By over-presenting yourself (otherwise known as sucking up on an industrial-strength scale), you will begin to lack confidence because you will feel that the real you is un-saleable.

FAKE BRAVADO: 'I COULDN'T CARE LESS'

This is a phrase you hear a lot from people who act in a way that appears confident, but is more usually arrogant. It's fighting talk, but does it work? As a mantra the over-exaggeration of the statement can be useful and I use it a lot in a bid to encourage my subconscious to care less. But as a real, everyday tool it's got to be delusional. Of course you care what people think. Your confidence problems only tend to arise when you care too much, leading to worry and over-thinking. This is when you begin to assume that they must be judgemental and that their judgements on you will be negative. Often this seems the only option. When you lack confidence it seems unbelievable that anyone would hold you in high esteem or have a good opinion of you.

Techniques we use to overcome a lack of natural social status/power

- **Humour**
  Verbal put-downs that make other people laugh can be lethal and therefore as threatening to others as a punch in the eye. Hence comics like Alex Zane can say 'I'm a little nerdy and geeky' and yet still retain (if not enhance) their status and sexual appeal.

- **Money**
  The most classic leveller. I might not have physical strength but I am considerably richer than you (and able to pull well above my weight in terms of women).

- **Fashion**
  An elite club that only the hard-core can join. Didn't know that scuffed shoes were this season's 'must-have'? Shame on you.

- **Intellectualism**
  Having a brain the size of a kitchen unit can have social benefits, but only if you also have the ability to verbalise all that cleverness in a way that is not instantly dull, or that you have a posse of sidekicks who claim you are a genius.

• **Beauty**
Looking lovely opens some doors but not many marked 'high status'. This is a constant confusion for girls who are bred thinking that beauty is the way to go, despite the fact that the path to happiness is littered with the carcases of models, actresses and other beauties that self-destructed or imploded with grief once their 'fairytale' lives went into meltdown.

Remember a core message from the start of the book: the only animals that sustain high and constant levels of what looks like confidence are the strongest and most powerful animals. They can fight and kill most other animals on the block and can therefore live in a quasi fear-free, confident state. In apes this would be the alpha, the leader of the pack. Alphas don't get to be alphas because they're good at singing, dancing or walking down red carpets. Alphas get to be alphas because they're big enough to take on any other ape and know they have a fair chance of pulping them. The other apes are aware of this threat and therefore do what they are told. But even the lesser apes will provide a potential threat to the alpha, as will apes from other colonies. So even the alpha ape will feel intermittent dips in his confidence levels.

Let's compare this to your own life. Are you a natural alpha? Are you the biggest and toughest person in your area, able to take on all comers should the need arise?

I suspect that – like me – your answer to this question is 'no'.

YOUR LIFE PATTERNS

Ever find yourself 'locked' in situations that recur on a repeat basis and which never seem to have a positive outcome? When we are children we experiment with behaviour techniques to discover which will get the reward we want and which behaviours won't. Usually it's the way a behaviour is rewarded that determines whether we continue that form of behaviour or not.

As we grow older the 'rewards' we seek can diminish and yet we often continue the behaviour long after it no longer gets us what we want and even long after it gets us many things we don't want.

HOW TO BE PATHETIC 2

I recently saw a dress I liked in a vintage clothes shop. When I went to buy it I discovered it had a very small moth hole in the front. I put it back, but then started to wish I'd bought it, it was perfect for my woman of the year function (the one I still thought I'd only been invited to by mistake). Despite having worked in the fashion business for half my life, I rang a friend to ask if I should get the dress.

'A moth hole is bad news,' she said, 'I wouldn't get it.'

'But it won't show,' I told her.

'Then get it,' she said.

Why did I need to have that conversation? Because I didn't feel confident enough to buy the dress otherwise. So I asked someone who works in banking rather than ask myself, who had not only seen the dress but had experience in the fashion business.

It gets worse. When I got home I put the dress on and asked my boyfriend, who thinks Primark is a diffusion brand of Prada, if it looked okay.

The moral? At least I could identify my pathetic-thinking moments. Do you know yours? Or do you think they are moments of blinding truth? Know them for what they are and deal with them, which is what I do!

What do I mean by this?

Your life patterns will be affecting your confidence and your behaviours like this:

- When you were a child you wanted some chocolate.
- You threw a tantrum.
- Your parent gave you the chocolate to shut you up.
- You continue to throw tantrums as an adult.
- People dislike you and avoid you because of your tantrums.
- You continue to throw tantrums because as a child it got you the chocolate.

Or:

- When you were a child and felt fearful you would act cute and vulnerable or cry.
- You received comfort and approval as a result. Life seemed less scary.

- As an adult you continue what you once saw was rewarded behaviour.
- When you have to give a business presentation you act cute and vulnerable.
- As a result your audience get irritated and fail to see the importance of your message.
- Which makes you feel more vulnerable, meaning you increase your needy, submissive behaviours in the vain hope people will take pity on you.

Is it this kind of false reward system that is creating the 'right thing to do' in your life? False 'rightness' based on historical habit and unquestioned behaviours can scupper your ability to be confident.

I'm not talking about moral values, but the kind of essence of 'rightness' that guides everything we do in our lives, i.e. the kind of clothes is it right to wear, the sort of homes we should live in, the type of job we should do and the way we need to behave in that job. I find it fascinating that even when those long-held 'rights' have been proved to be 'wrong' we still adhere to them, especially in the workplace. For instance we all know email to be a potential form of time-wasting hell and we all know it is one of the worst ways of handling other people. And yet we still choose to use it, even in ways that we hate having used on ourselves.

If there's one thing we as humans aren't short of in modern society it is options. And although we have choice when it comes to our own behaviour we still tend to select options that are causing us grief on a regular basis, like shyness, diffidence, avoidance and anxiety.

CONFIDENCE RULE: CARE LESS, BUT DON'T PRETEND YOU DON'T CARE AT ALL

If you **really** couldn't care less what people think of you you'll happily drop your trousers in the middle of that business meeting or go tell the boss exactly what you think of her.

IN A NUTSHELL

- Your body produces a very useful, life-saving fear response.

- Being confident means managing that response.

- Your problems with confidence arise when your fear response kicks in at times when you would prefer to be calm or brave.

- The secret is to discover your override switch, allowing you to control your fear, especially in situations that are non-threatening.

- To do this you'll need to reprogramme your thinking.

- If a soldier can override his or her fear enough to run forward under fire then you can too. Tackling that business presentation or first date will be relatively easy.

- It is important not to over-manage your response to a point where you become arrogant or oblivious to genuine risk.

3

DIAGNOSING YOUR CONFIDENCE PROBLEM

It would be comforting if confidence was a one-size-fits-all thing, but it's not. Confidence is one word that defines a whole heap of issues. If I asked when you would like to be more confident you'd probably reply 'All the time' but it's vital you get a specific answer to this question. Like every other feeling or emotion, confidence needs to be aimed at a target. The dictionary defines confidence as 'A state of trust, reliance, a feeling of hope on which one relies', which may or may not fit your own definition of it.

So how you do view confidence? How would you describe the state of 'being confident'?

EXERCISE
• Write down your own definition of confidence, listing words or sentences.
• Close your eyes and imagine yourself feeling and looking confident. Search around in your mind for anything you do that you do with confidence and any key moments in your day when you feel confident.
• Now open your eyes and add to your list, keeping in mind the feelings you have just explored.
• To make your list even more useful start with the phrase 'When I am confident I ...' and add whatever endings you would put to that phrase to your list.

Your types of confidence, or lack of it, are unique to you, and maybe even puzzling to you as well. Why is it you can blush when some people look at you and yet sitting on your mate's shoulders at a music festival, blasting out the chorus of 'Who Wants to Live

Forever' in front of an audience of millions was a walk in the park?

It would be easy to say you were sober on the first occasion and as drunk as a skunk at the festival, but that would only give part of the solution. Drink strips away inhibitions like acid strips layers of paint, but it's likely much of the confidence was down to you rather than the vodka; the alcohol just brought what was there already to the surface.

THE FIRST STAGE: DIAGNOSING YOUR FEARS

Would you trust a doctor who prescribed you drugs without asking exactly what was wrong with you first? Effective cures need effective diagnosis so don't skip this section.

Your confidence levels are a bit like your DNA: unique to you, except unlike your DNA they will fluctuate and change throughout your life. I know actors who are so shy they're almost monosyllabic off-stage and I've met people who would happily indulge in extreme sports but baulk at the idea of a spot of drunken Karaoke.

But it's not just working out what prompts your fear levels to rise that is important. You also need to analyse the type of fear you're suffering from.

Shyness, anxiety, performer nerves, sociophobia, stress or worry can all seem similar but they can be more distant than you'd think in terms of diagnosed problems.

Types of low confidence

There are seven key 'types' of confidence problems, and each have their methods of cure. When you read through the categories you may find you suffer with more than one, but do avoid assuming that you suffer from all of them. Although that is perfectly possible it's also unlikely. If you insist on clinging to my ankles sobbing then I will at least insist you admit that some of the categories tend to be worse than others. Nobody is a total wuss. Confidence-denial is silly and you need to stop it if this is where you're going.

What's a confidence-denier? They're the people who say they're rubbish at some things but then their actions tell you that in fact they believe the opposite. They're the ones down the pub who insist they can't tell jokes and then bore you pantless with a whole volley of them. They're the ones who say they hate their body shape and then turn up wearing the skimpiest outfit that reveals it all. It's fake modesty, and for mere mortals who are not in the A-list league it will scupper what talent and abilities you do have. Why? Because when you keep banging on about being scared you send a negative affirmation down to your subconscious. Your conscious brain might know that you're being ironic or even cute but your subconscious tends to believe what it's told, meaning you will be creating what is known as a self-fulfilling prophesy.

So here's your menu of confidence issues. Don't make your selection without reading through the whole list first and then going back and seeing which ones most accurately reflect your confidence levels. Be honest and *don't* be modest. The more accurate your diagnosis the more effective your cure.

LOW SELF-ESTEEM

You have low self-esteem if:
- You really do believe you have little in the way of looks, skills or talent.
- You expect negative outcomes.
- You are suspicious of successes or people who seem to like you or approve of you.
- You would struggle to use any positive terms to describe yourself.
- Your dislike of yourself means you tend to dislike other people.
- You find animals easier to love than humans.
- You have a tendency to generalise: 'All men are bastards', 'Women like that are so up themselves'.
- You look to others for reassurance or approval.
- You self-scupper – i.e. make public announcements of your own failure before you even attempt a task or transaction.
- You self-compare – you constantly compare yourself negatively with others and their skills or behaviours.
- You use self-lowering terms – this is when you use negative or diminishing terms to describe yourself, like 'I'm *just* a PA' or 'I'm rubbish at that sort of thing'.

- You over-apologise – you overuse words like 'sorry' as in 'I'm really sorry to bother you ...' or start conversations with phrases like 'I know this might sound stupid but ...'
- You reverse any praise – when someone offers you compliments or praise you either knock the comment back ('Oh this is just some old thing I got in a sale', 'It wasn't my work, it was the rest of the team really') or suspect the motives of the person praising you ('What's he after?' 'Is she only being sarcastic?').
- You expect negative outcomes – when you survey a task or challenge you immediately assume you're not up to it and assume failure, to the point where you often don't try in the first place.
- You see positive options for others – you always assume someone else would succeed. ('I knew I wouldn't get that job, everyone else there looked so much more experienced.')
- You prevaricate – you use excuses to put things off, like waiting until you've lost weight or read that book or done that course. Your whole life feels like it's moving forward but in fact it's entrenched in procrastination tactics.
- You blame yourself – you always blame yourself, even problems you had little or any involvement in.
- You stockpile negative thoughts – you store away all the criticisms, insults, negative comments and slights that you've received in your life and any new failure just confirms that what other people thought about you was true.
- You assume – you only got that job because no one else was available, or that you were only asked on that date because yours was the first number in their phone book.
- Your opinions are easily swayed.
- You suffer from mood swings.
- You're suspicious of any success – 'This is too good, what's going to go wrong?'

A quick peek: what does your self-esteem currently look like?

Self-esteem underpins confidence. We'll talk more about that later. But for now I want you to perform a vital exercise.

Close your eyes.

Think of the word 'self-esteem'.

Visualise your own self-esteem but in human or animal form. What does it look like?

If you could reach inside yourself and pull out your self-esteem like a rabbit out of a hat, what would emerge?

Your visualised self-esteem is an important factor in your programme to build your own confidence, so it's important you create an honest portrait of it.

What do you see?

A runty, consumptive maiden aunt shivering in a shawl?

A dog that might be hiding in the corner or a rescue sanctuary?

A timid-looking girl's blouse who is trying but failing to stand up for himself?

Someone resembling Russell Crowe in *Gladiator*?

Or Tiny Tim from *A Christmas Carol*?

Is your self-esteem lying back waiting to be used, abused or rescued or is it ready to fight for itself? If it's waving a white flag at the thought of a fight then it's probably safe to assume your self-esteem is low and that it's this that is prompting your lack of confidence.

Low self-esteem is a lack of confidence prompted by the notion that you really don't amount to much. It's making constant comparisons with other people and finding yourself failing on every count. It's important you spot the difference between this form of lack of confidence and other ones. With most of the other varieties you have a core of self-belief but lack the confidence to project it. With low self-esteem that core is missing altogether. You have marshmallow where your stomach and spine should be.

Low self-esteem can be an occasional or a permanent problem. It is also based on flawed programming. Low self-esteem means you see yourself as being worse than the rest of the world sees you.

What caused it?

Hell, who knows?

Probably anything, because it's not so much what happens to us in our lives that counts but the way we process that stimulus. However, the smart money seems to be on three key factors:

1. Any failures we've experienced.
2. Any moments when our expectations have taken a blow and not just in a negative way. Finding you're unexpectedly successful or unexpectedly unsuccessful confuses our brains and that confusion can make us question who we are and what we can or can't do and achieve.
3. Things that make you feel you can't cope. Times when life falls out of your control, making you feel inadequate or diminished.

It's probably important to you to know that it was your parents' fault for being horribly critical, or that bully in school that poked fun at your puppy fat, or those cruel siblings whose superior beauty and intellect left you feeling like the ugly duckling, but – really – does it matter? When we spend time blaming other people we waste time that could be spent sorting ourselves out. The other problem with blaming is that it takes much of our own perception of control away. All that energy spent hating or resenting other people for what they did, said or implied is wasted energy. 'It was their fault, not mine' is a very cosy way of ducking out of the real issue which is girding your loins and getting stuck in. So the message is:

GET OVER IT. SUCK IT UP.

Those memories might not go away but you can recycle them, turning negative stimulus into positive response.

Here's a useful image to help you cope:

STIMULUS ⟶ RESPONSE

In future, refer to what has happened to you in the past, or things that are happening to you in the present as **stimulus**. Then make sure you create as big a gap as possible between that stimulus and your **response** to it. Never link the two. That gap is going to be your confidence lifesaver because it shows you how – although the stimulus might be out of your control or it might have already occurred – the way you respond to that stimulus is within your power. Think of the power of statements like: 'I choose not to get annoyed by that comment' or 'I choose to stay calm when everyone else is flapping'. Empowering thoughts create the best underpinning for your confidence.

So next time you're looking to find someone to blame for your low self-esteem, tell whoever you've been holding responsible that it was as much your fault as theirs. Yes, really. They provided the stimulus but it was you who responded in the way that you did. You had options, although maybe you didn't realise that you did at the time. One very good option would have been to have ignored the comments or behaviour. Another would have been to use it as fuel to prove them wrong.

Negative motivators, i.e. being criticised or rubbished by someone, can be perceived as positive. Many people have achieved much in their lives by being motivated by anger or a desire to prove their critics wrong. It's your choice: you can either stall at critical behaviour or you can burn it as fuel to help achieve your dreams. The funniest comedians are always the ones who describe themselves as having come up the hard way, surviving years of working the club circuit, getting heckled and even booed off the stage. These negative experiences make them funnier and more able to challenge negativity or to lack fear in the face of any audience, positive or hostile. It gives them an edge. You could have used your negative experiences to make you razor-sharp rather than jelly-soft and the good news is it's still not too late to do so. Suck it up and move on.

SELF-ESTEEM

Some psychologists think good self-esteem makes you feel immortal, positive about yourself and your life, and therefore removes the dread of the reality of death. It is also seen as a good monitor of your levels of social acceptance. We're driven by our need to belong.

Dealing with low self-esteem

Okay, I could be more helpful than telling you to 'suck it up', but if we look at people with high levels of self-esteem, that's exactly what they do.

Psychologists have identified some of the key techniques people in the upper ranges of self-esteem use to persuade themselves of their own wonderfulness. But be careful: overestimating your good points can lead to arrogance, making you unable to adapt or improve, so don't pin this list to your fridge door as your new path to behavioural excellence, but *do* read through it to indulge in a spot of compare and contrast with your own current boosting techniques.

People with high self-esteem tend to:
- Take credit for any successes but blame their failures on other people.
- Ignore, dismiss or forget any negative feedback they get but remember any points of praise.
- View any criticism of themselves with huge amounts of scepticism.
- Dismiss any criticism as being based on prejudice.
- Indulge in large amounts of navel-gazing and self-study in a bid to boost their own importance and ego ('My ancestors were titled', 'I'm psychic', 'I have several major food allergies', 'I only put men off because I am too challenging', etc.).
- Talk about their flaws in a way to make them sound great. ('I might upset people but you can't say I'm not being honest.')
- Think that any flaws they do have are part of the common human condition ('Everyone says things they regret now and again', 'Who hasn't lost it now and again?', etc) but believe any good points are virtually unique to them.

How do these behaviours compare with your own?

If you suffer from low self-esteem you should expect your own list of processing to be almost opposite to this. Which is not a bad thing if it helps you avoid the kind of arrogance that prevents improvement, but which is a bad thing if you live life in the esteem doldrums. If you remain in the neutral range of self-esteem levels or take occasional dips into the negative level you're veering close to normal. If you're firmly stuck in the middle to lower levels of the negative range though, you can clearly self-diagnose as having low self-esteem.

Your Mirrored Self

'Mirror mirror on the wall, who is the most inadequate of them all?'

If you suffer from low self-esteem you will have a habit of comparing yourself unfavourably with other people and/or judging yourself via the opinions of others. This is usually referred to by psychologists as your 'Mirrored Self'.

By and large your Mirrored Self is pathetic. Wet. A wimp. Jelly-belly, wuss, you name it and I will happily throw that name in its face. The good news *should* be that it's too much of a twerp to fight back. Although, strangely, it somehow does.

The Mirrored Self is the You that exists in the eyes of others. It's you judging You by others' opinions and perceptions or – even worse – their imagined opinions. It's thinking you're rubbish, unattractive, lacking in sex appeal or unable to perform a skill because that's what someone else thinks of you. It's as though you've collected evaluations, opinions, slights and imagined slights throughout your life, written them down on Post-it notes and stuck them to the side of that imagined mirror.

You wait to hear what others think before you act. 'Can I get that job?' 'Does this outfit look okay?' 'Am I good at dancing?' And sometimes you create their scripts for other people, imagining they are judging you negatively. 'I'm sure she thinks I'm a bad mother', 'The way he looked at me I could tell he thought I was talking tosh.'

How this Mirrored Self affects you

If you live and trade on others' opinions of You, mainly soaking up the more negative criticisms, then externally and emotionally you will become a bit of a patchwork quilt. You'll have no skills of self-evaluation and therefore no ability to either market yourself or pitch for jobs, friends or dates. You'll expect things to 'happen' and be a victim of circumstances. If you succeed at anything you'll see it as a fluke. If you fail, you'll attach that failure to someone else's evaluation and use it to confirm their opinion of you.

How this affects your behaviour

Without a personal compass to advise and guide you, you're prey to any and every opinion, real or imagined. This will make you terminally confused, as those opinions will probably be contradictory. Your mum might have told you that you were the most adorable little person in the universe, so why did your last date jilt you for someone they said was better-looking? Is the interviewer right who told you that you lacked skill or experience for that job or is it your best friend who told you they must have been jealous of you and threatened by your talent?

The point is you have no idea. When you do feel confused you'll just go and ask someone else's opinion or harvest it in a more manipulative way by whining, whingeing or crying about what was said or what happened, or even pretending it is your own dialogue ('I think I'm not attractive', 'I know I won't get that job') to provoke some form of flattery or reassurance.

Low self-esteem: worst-case scenario

You know when your low self-esteem is causing terminal problems in your life when you find you have a habit of not trying things because you can already hear the fail. You see that promotion advertised, for example, but why put yourself through the agony of rejection? Better to give it a miss. At least you won't feel any worse than you do now.

Banishing low self-esteem

Or kick-ass time as I like to call it.

First here are some basic values for you to absorb and live by in future:

- I will be happy about successes and the good things in my life.
- I will suffer from reverse paranoia – instead of expecting the worst I will expect the best, assuming people will like me and want me to do well until proved otherwise.
- I will challenge my negative assumptions and expectations.
- When I find myself making negative comparisons with other people I will instead focus on any bad qualities or events in their lives and if I don't know of any I will make them up.
- When negative thoughts start to swamp my brain I will write them all down in a little notebook, then close it and forget them.
- Once a month I will write down all the things I have done and achieved and been good at. (Your Shield Exercise, see page 63.)

- I will stop being dependent on others' support, reassurance and ego-boosting. Instead I will find someone who I can reassure and support.
- All my reassurance and support will come from me to me.

And here is your golden rule, the one that you must keep above all the others:

I WILL NEVER AGAIN, SERIOUSLY OR AS A JOKE, PUT MYSELF DOWN OUT LOUD TO OTHER PEOPLE. WHEN I AM PAID A COMPLIMENT I WILL REPLY WITH TWO WORDS: THANK YOU.

Self-effacing humour only works when it is done by people with good self-esteem, skills or abilities. A handsome man saying he's ugly is funny. An ugly man saying he's ugly is at best pointless or at worst a tragic appeal for dishonest reassurance. Every time you put yourself down you are crying for help. We're not going to be that pathetic in future are we? We're making lots of people lie to us: 'Of course your bum doesn't look big in that!' 'Of course you stand a good chance of getting promotion!' 'Of course you're a stud in bed!' Make it stop. Now.

Sources of self-esteem

Psychologist Arnold Buss listed what he felt are the six key sources of self-esteem:

- **Appearance.** We feel good if we feel attractive. Attractive people even get better treatment, or are judged to be nicer personalities!
- **Ability and performance.** You pass your exams, you do something well and your self-esteem grows as a result.
- **Power.** When you feel you are in control of your life you feel more confident.
- **Social rewards.** Affection from other people, praise from other people and respect from other people.
- **Vicarious sources.** Having nice things or knowing/being around successful people can make us feel good.
- **Morality.** Being a good person or feeling that you've got the higher moral ground.

How can you use this list of factors?

- Study it, cherishing the ones you already have in your life and making a mental note to not undervalue them.

- Look at the two that are probably the easiest to investigate and shore up, which are the last two. Do you cherish all the nice things that you own? Do you focus on that favourite outfit, piece of jewellery, pet, laptop, painting, photo album, or do you tend to focus on the things you don't have, bemoaning the fact that your neighbour has a better car or that her husband is more attractive and better house-trained than yours? And when did you last visit your moral code? This is not an invitation to be smug but establishing your set of basic values will make you a good person with standards you admire. These standards don't need to be huge or unreal. You could be, amongst other things, a vegetarian, focus on the environment, listen to others, praise and compliment others, be reliable in terms of your business, stop putting things off, help others, cheer others up.

- When you investigate issues like social rewards or praise from others you need to study steps to both gain the praise but also learn to live without it and supply your own. Just because they can raise self-esteem doesn't mean you have to have them. Realising you have become praise/flattery-dependent takes you back to the Mirrored Self. I would prefer to nudge you in the direction of self-praise. Tell yourself you've done well. Give yourself small treats or rewards to emphasise the fact.

- If your self-esteem is already at rock bottom you probably pounced on the first two factors of being attractive and being successful. If you feel like an ugly failure you'll probably blame those factors for your low confidence. But being attractive is not the same as being classically beautiful. You can work to enhance your attractiveness and we'll cover some of the visual factors in the 'Acting Confident' section of the book. Good posture, a genuine smile and a facial expression that registers warmth and good humour can all far outweigh a frozen expression and a snooty demeanour when it comes to being seen as attractive.

- Success can raise self-esteem but not always. Much of the success we strive for comes in a never-ending stream, so that the footballer celebrating his goal knows that a bad game might mean he'll be mouldering on the benches and pop stars know they're only as good as their last hit. It's the smaller successes that will provide a sturdier shoe-in for your self-esteem because they are more reliable and more constant and less likely to be eroded overnight. I don't mean you don't bother with the big successes; it's just that en route to them you should be polishing and admiring the more everyday ones because they help you see yourself as successful in a more well-rounded way. What are your smaller successes? We're about to find out by using the Shield Exercise.

THE SHIELD EXERCISE

This exercise is a simple but effective way of evaluating your strengths and successes on a regular basis and therefore boosting your ailing self-esteem. It consists of four quadrants, like a shield, and you fill each quadrant with different strengths. Spend some moments drawing and filling in your own shield and then make sure you continue to add to it on a regular basis, entering new successes as you go along. By identifying and logging all your successes you make yourself far more able to evaluate yourself in a confident way devoid of self-pity or negativity.

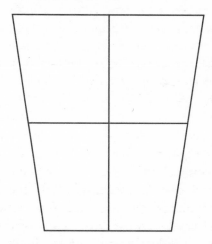

- Fill the top-left quadrant with a list of all your positive personality traits. Use no negatives or half-hearted terms.
- Fill the top-right quadrant with a list of all your skills. Make no comparisons with other people or their level of ability, just list the skills that you have.
- In the bottom-left quadrant, list all the things that you have done in your life that you are proud of. These may be things that you have achieved that you knew stretched

you, even if the achievement itself doesn't sound dramatic.
- In the bottom-right quadrant list all the values you hold dear and would be prepared to fight for.
- Your Shield does exactly what it says on the tin: it protects and strengthens you and your self-esteem. These qualities define you and your worth and they define them more accurately than the normal negatives that you probably use when you evaluate yourself.
- Compile your Shield whenever necessary and study it regularly. It is one of the most powerful ways of boosting your beleaguered self-esteem.

Banishing the self-pity that can come with low self-esteem

Self-pity is the enemy of confidence, especially if you suffer from low self-esteem. Remember that marinating in your low opinion of yourself is a waste of your life. However, you will be insulting your intelligence if you combat this via self-flattery that very clearly outweighs reality. Of course there are people better-looking than you, cleverer than you and better company than you are at the moment. If you attempt to over-elevate your ego the result will be ghastly. Realism is important, although your current version of realism is flawed as your view is way too gloomy. By realism I mean an ability to self-assess in a very positive way, making sure you allow yourself the scope to achieve your full potential. Here's a speedy way to do that.

Self-esteem repair kit
Ask yourself:
- What are my weaknesses? What am I currently poor at?
- What could I be better at?
- What would I need to do to improve?
- What are my strengths?
- How/why am I good at them?
- How could I apply those factors to some of my weaker areas?
- How important are my strengths?
- How important are each of my weaknesses?
- Which weaknesses will I work on?
- Which will I choose to avoid?
- Which will I choose to ignore?
- Which must I choose to not moan and whinge about?

By asking yourself these questions, you can realistically see what the areas are where you need to improve. And if you focus on the positive aspects of your personality, your self-esteem will start to improve dramatically.

SHYNESS

You are shy if:
• You struggle speaking to other people.
• You avoid or dread events where you will have to mix with people you don't know.
• When you want to speak to people you find little in the way of intelligent thought rattling inside your head.
• You often give a misleading representation of yourself, with people believing you are aloof or stuck-up.
• You struggle to speak during interviews and sit in silence during meetings.
• When you walk into rooms you feel everyone is looking at you.
• Your self-belief is relatively sound by comparison. You tend to be happy about your abilities or looks, but unable to communicate readily.
• You have a tendency to feel happier about performance moments, i.e. you feel more comfortable with a large, anonymous audience than you do with small groups or one-on-one with people you hardly know.

What is shyness?

Shyness is rubbish.

Shyness is not just pants, it's pants, vest and grubby grey socks. It will ruin your life if you allow it to and what it doesn't ruin it will tarnish, so that even the best of times can present you with the most miserable of responses.

I am shy, and I hate shyness. That hatred forms part of a personal vendetta, although feel free to join in if you're a fellow sufferer. Shyness can come upon you at any time, no matter what your abilities, personality or intellect. Shyness makes you look stupid and sound worse. It doesn't even create camaraderie because the last thing you want as a shy person is to be lumbered with someone else who is shy because the silence is excruciating.

EXERCISE

If you're shy try writing a list:
These are all the things I would have done if I hadn't suffered from shyness.

And then another list:
These are all the things I did but hated doing because I suffer from shyness.

The problem with shy people is that we're the world's worst cowards. Nature has given us every benefit but we refuse to exploit them because we prefer to act like children. We won't take risks, and we fear rejection or disapproval more than we fear living a life that can be terribly, awfully bland. We're also lazy gits. We give up trying because our petty fears tell us not to bother. I get shy people telling me they can't do small talk. What they mean is they can't be arsed. Nobody enjoys it, but while non-shy people get stuck in because they know it's the only way to get to know other people, shy people show you a sick note to explain why they're excused from duty.

Well any idiot can learn to do small talk. The whole point about small talk is that it's silly and easy in terms of subject matter. (We'll cover the techniques in the section on networking, see page 191.) If your life depended on it, you'd do it. (And wouldn't that be fun? 'Go talk about that woman's journey and how she knows the host or I will gouge your eyes out with this fruit kebab stick and block your breathing passage with an avocado and goat's cheese wrap.')

Shyness is like the handicap that nobody does anything about. And if it's not dealt with in the way we'll be dealing with it, it has little in the way of self-healing about it. Instead of getting better or going away it often just gets worse; in fact, I still hear people claim erroneously that you grow out of shyness. In fact you just learn how to hide it.

What tends to happen to un-checked shyness as you age is you only mix with people you know and when you don't you give the impression of being rude, cantankerous or mildly eccentric because you don't speak very much. Sort it out now or you'll be regretting it later. Once I learnt to deal with my own shyness I was angry I didn't take steps earlier.

Why am I shy?

If you're shy, congratulations! You have a very acute survival system, meaning that although you're happy to graze with the herd you don't want to stand out in case you're seen as the tasty treat de jour when the more predatory animals roam by.

There's nothing unnatural about being shy. Your problem is that it's an evolutionary survival response that is giving you grief in the modern world. While it's easy to switch irrelevant responses off because you have logic and reason on your side, disenabling the response that's telling you to keep you head down and avoid situations with other people when you have little in the way of control or self-protection can be harder. But don't give up.

Beating shyness will be like a bit of a voyage into the unknown but it's one you're going to have to make. Why? Because shyness is stupid. When we suffer from shyness we exist in a state of constant childishness, sitting in silence when we should speak up and avoiding grown-ups in case they judge us poorly.

Get over it.

The worst that will happen is that you will feel uncomfortable, but what price a little emotional discomfort if it means you can live the rest of your life like the assertive adult you know yourself to be? Stop indulging that inner brat that tells you it's far too tiny and frail to join in with the big boys. Take some risks; that's what they did.

What does shyness feel like?

Think of shyness as a behavioural verruca. It hurts a lot, it makes you limp a bit now and again and it keeps you out of the swimming pool until it's cleared up. Except shyness doesn't clear up, it just goes on staining your life **for as long as you allow it**. It stops you talking to other people or it stops you talking naturally. It makes you think of great ideas or killing one-liners that you never get to deliver out loud and when you finally pluck up courage to share that achingly funny joke you heard it makes you tell it in a way that is so exquisitely excruciating to listen to that friends will chew off their own arms in a bid to lessen their embarrassment.

It makes you start a good idea with the words 'I know this might sound stupid ...' and end jokes with 'It was funny when I heard it ...'

And to make matters worse, shyness gives you about the worst body language too. It's only the likes of Princess Diana who could make shyness look adorable with her dipped chin and doe-like upward gaze. For the rest of us it's bitch-troll miserable or monosyllabic stupid.

I have some spectacular shyness stories. Two entail moments in my life when God really did hear my prayers and offered me up exactly the men I have been asking for under what should have been ideal conditions.

The first came when I was still at school and my mother booked a member of a famous pop group of the day to open her boutique in sunny downtown Croydon. I stood inside the shop in my adorable tartan minidress with my waist-length blond ringlets cascading down my back and my hero burst through the paper doorway created for the stunt with a mob of screaming fans in his wake.

I loved Dave Davies even more than I loved my cat Sparky.

'Hi,' he said, smiling at me.

I just stared.

'Where can you go round here for a drink and meal?' he asked.

I think I shrugged. Maybe I didn't move at all. I know I didn't speak and I'm sure I looked away. It was my moment with Dave and he must have felt he'd encountered the village idiot.

My second opportunity came after years of pleading to whatever god might have been listening to set up an 'encounter' between me and Paul McCartney. I was on a train and when I walked through the carriages to get a tea I found Paul sitting by himself in an empty carriage.

As I walked past him I think he looked up (possibly to nod, who knows? Maybe he would have cut to the chase and just asked me to marry him!) and I know I looked away. I got my tea and made my way back, muttering to myself to not blow it twice in a row. But of course I did. This time I rushed past like a dervish.

I should have decided there and then that I would never allow shyness to blight my life again but of course I didn't and it's been a constant companion for five decades, leaving people thinking I'm anything, from stupid to stuck-up.

What does shyness look like?

As I mentioned above, it's the rare few that shyness looks good on – think Princess Di or Prince William. The chin is slightly dipped, the cheeks blush pale pink, the eyes move from a downward direction to faltering glances combined with the cutest of smiles and your body language resembles the very mildest form of sweet flirtation. Get it right and people will want to offer you reassurance.

At worst though, it is a nightmare. Try these for size:

- No eye contact
- Little in the way of facial expression, making the older face look dour, deadpan or disapproving
- Fake smiles
- Hair pulled over the face
- Body barriers like folded arms
- Constant self-calm rituals like fiddling, playing with hair, chewing nails, etc.

Is shyness vanity?

Oh, a big 'Yes!' in answer to this question!

One aspect of shyness is a fear of drawing attention. I hear many shy people wringing their hands over the thought that 'everyone's looking at me'. Remember that I call this the Alice Syndrome after Alice in Wonderland, who grew bigger and bigger after drinking from the bottle marked 'Drink Me'. When you're shy you feel you fill a room like the big Alice, being instantly noticeable and remarkable, so that everyone's staring and everyone's got a comment to make about you. If you see two people whispering or pulling faces it has to be about you and once you leave a room you assume that the whole conversation in that room turns to the subject of *you* and what a prize numpty you looked or sounded.

Can you hear where this is going? Most shy people consider themselves to be the complete opposite to vain but vanity is what this is all about: the assumption that other people will automatically make you their focus of attention and interest, even if it is for purposes of scorn or ridicule. Part of the shyness syndrome is the assumption of inflated self-importance, so much so that it is unimaginable that you could go anywhere without standing out or being noticed. Whereas non-shy people assume the opposite, giving themselves the freedom to behave without all that inner self-analysis or they actively seek more attention, making them seem extrovert. It's vanity that often prompts shyness; it's a low self-esteem or sense of social status that makes people outgoing and gregarious. They're not judging themselves positively: they're just afraid they won't be judged at all.

This is often the horror story for reality TV contestants. If you're shy you generally don't get put into reality shows. So those shows get all the attention-seekers. These tend to be people who have spent their entire lives vying to get attention, so much so that they never appear to have spent any time self-analysing or being self-critical. When your goal is to make people see you there's not a lot of room for evaluating the product. This often only tends to happen once they've got the attention they crave at last and are standing onstage in front of Simon Cowell or going on that blind date. It's when they're asked to prove themselves that some major meltdowns happen. They'll say 'I'm nice!' or 'I can sing!' when their actions suggest otherwise. So their voyage of self-discovery works backwards when compared to the way shy people view the world. Shy people assume they don't amount to a mess of beans and this low self-evaluation makes them avoid situations that might make this fact obvious. Extroverts have rarely assessed themselves at all; they're too busy trying to attract all that attention that the shy person assumes is theirs as a gift.

There's another aspect of shy behaviour that is equally perverse. Despite spending most of their lives avoiding attention, shy people just love going for careers in the performing arts. Show me any actor, dancer or stage performer and I'll show you someone who will claim to be shy. How weird is that?

Well, pretty weird, to be honest, although that claim bears out close examination. I find understanding this quite easy as I am a shy person who only really feels comfortable onstage or in front of a camera. I used to be a catwalk model and now I give lectures onstage and appear on live TV. But I am still shy. I've met much greater performers than me who can barely speak off set. It's as though we have a switch somewhere that we can suddenly click off to turn in a performance.

Extroverts have more of a struggle. When I sit in the green room prior to going on set I'm always amused by the split between the quiet types who sit in virtual silence and the ones who are prancing all over the place, chatting and performing already. It's the noisy ones who tend to dry up once they get on set, while the quiet ones blossom. We're the proverbial tea bags of society, we're only at our best when we're placed in hot water.

I call shy people performing tarts because we only really go for it when we've been booked or paid. Many shy performers only give themselves licence to let rip when someone else has evaluated them as being worthy of attention, or when they can perform behind a masked character. Perhaps it's because we spent so many years of childhood wishing we could sit in a sack with eyeholes, viewing the world without needing to participate that we grab at the virtual mask that is paid performance. We can 'do' somebody else; it's just doing 'me' that causes the discomfort.

Keep this 'tempted timid' theme in mind and it easily explains why most performers are bonkers. As shy people they have been tempted out of their mouse-like state into a state that would be daunting for most extroverts. There is no middle ground for the shy performer; they are either up there standing 'naked' in the spotlight or down there quivering in their little sack with eyeholes. Once they've emerged into the glare, though, they need praise and approval like a vampire needs blood. One tiny hint of criticism and their entire new world comes crashing about their ears and all those 'shy me' voices kick in to explain why they were mad to have even tried in the first place. Shy performers drag emotional baggage around like Victoria Beckham travels with designer luggage. We have airport trolley-loads of the stuff, all waiting to roll up and smack us on the back of the head. When we ask 'Was that okay?' we're not looking for half-baked feedback, we're asking for the plasma of hyperbole. We're contrary and we're often horrible and a nightmare blend of conceit and paranoia to live with, which is why so many celebrity marriages go down the Swannee without so much as a paddle.

Does this sound familiar? Do you dread standing out from the crowd yet crave (albeit secretly) fame or some other sort of professional attention where you can demand interest behind a masked personality?

If you do you're Alice from *Alice in Wonderland*, someone who can grow in the face of a real audience to the point where you dominate the room with your size but you are also a figure of mockery and ridicule, but when you're placed on a proper stage in front of a paying audience you're able to diminish to a point where you don't care who's looking because you're hiding behind your masked persona.

This complex and outwardly confusing version of shyness is magnificent in the way that it presents your cure along with your symptoms.

How to overcome your Alice Syndrome

It is a simple fact of life that other people notice you less than you think. In fact, a lot less. You think you stand out like the proverbial sore thumb but they are probably more concerned with themselves to really notice. Even if they do notice you, they probably forget you quite quickly.

The best way to ensure maximum attention is to try to vanish. Pretending to be invisible is a common habit of shy people and it is about the most attention-seeking behaviour of the lot. Animals are programmed to relax around other animals that move in the same way and at the same pace that they do. It builds rapport. If one animal is out of kilter they have to keep checking for their own safety. It could be that animal is sick or it's plotting something or it's spotted some danger no one else in the pack is aware of. Whatever the reason, it causes an animal version of a kerfuffle. The same is true when you go quiet or try to sneak into that meeting room or sit by yourself at that party or even hang around the walls at that networking event. Did you think nobody spotted you? Wrong. They not only noticed, they were subliminally freaked-out by your behaviour. One of the very best ways to obtain unwanted attention from other people is to try to avoid it. So your 'hiding' behaviour doesn't work.

At school there were three kinds of kid: the one always volunteering and trying to answer questions (the risk-takers), then there were the slightly more strategic kids who waited until they thought they knew the answer before putting their hand up (selective, still risk-taking but more strategic), and then there was the rest of us, sitting at the back, hiding under our hair, staring at the desk, wishing the ground would swallow us up (stupid but safe).

Overcoming shyness

Here's some steps that will take you through your shyness and free up that confident and competent person who lurks inside. They might not work instantly and they will stretch you but I promise you the rewards are worth it. Remember, your shyness is not the supportive friend you think it is. Using it as an excuse to hide behind – 'It's not my fault, I'm shy' – might feel comfortable but it's a dangerous comfort as it's preventing you from enjoying situations and getting your voice heard.

* **Hate it.** Hate it every bit as much as I do. Anger is good because it makes you less of a shyness victim.
* **Never forget you have a choice.** Think of your shyness as some disgusting, grubby old dressing gown that you find lying at the foot of your bed every morning and which you are currently choosing to put on. Leave it off. See shyness as optional, not compulsory.
* **Make yourself talk.** Go to places with the intention of speaking and joining in, not the intention of ducking out. Go to social events and parties with goals in mind, like chatting to at least six new people, or to business meetings with two key points to discuss.
* **Make yourself a good listener.** Good listening is often better than speaking too much anyway. Use active listening signals like eye contact, nodding and responding visually. Encourage the speaker by showing interest rather than seeing the conversation as verbal tennis (as in: You speak, I speak, you speak again, now it's my turn, etc.).
* When you're at a meeting or social gathering **make sure you speak within the first three minutes.** This three-minute rule is vital. Leave it any longer and it becomes harder and harder to break the ice and throw your voice out there into the room.
* **Never use sick notes.** In other words, never use shyness or

anything else as your excuse for not making an effort.

- **Never tell anyone you're shy**. The more you say it out loud the more it becomes concrete. You have had shy behaviours in the past. You are not a 'shy person'. Just a rather silly person.
- **Get a job where you have to meet people and speak to them**. Anything dealing with the public should do, especially if you deal with them face-to-face. Retail work is ideal, or serving in a food outlet. Dealing with the public is a bit of a shocker; you'll learn that they're worse than you thought in some ways and better than you thought in others. Whatever else, you'll have discovered the most negative side to other people and hopefully how to deal with it. Nothing life throws at you after that can possibly be as bad. Unless you work in a call centre. Remember the line that 'What doesn't kill me makes me stronger'. Work in a call centre and you'll be Herculean-strong in no time.
- **Push yourself further than your fears**. If you're dreading your own wedding because you'll be the centre of attention then get yourself off to a holiday camp before the big day and enter some hideously embarrassing competition like 'Mr Six-Pack' or 'Miss Frinton' or take the mic on stand-up night and bash out a few jokes. Whatever you choose to do it must make your toes curl tighter than the thought of your own wedding or whatever event your shyness is currently focused on. By playing bigger you diminish your fears. Walking down the aisle amongst people who like you will be easy once you've been booed off stage for telling rubbish jokes.
- **Tell yourself on a regular basis 'its fun'**. Taking yourself too seriously is a big mistake when you suffer from shyness. Tell yourself you're being a twerp because that's probably true.

PERFORMER NERVOUSNESS

You suffer from performer nerves if you:
- Know you have the talent to perform onstage but find yourself drying up or being overcome by anxiety and nerves to the point where your talents are diminished.
- Dread giving business presentations. You know your job but

prefer to speak one-to-one or via email. When you get up to present, your brain turns to mush.
• Suffer from a dry mouth, trembling, stammering, quivery voice and an ability to go completely blank.
• Have anxiety about sex that makes you under-perform or suffer from impotence.
• Know you have sound sporting skills but always blow it on the big day.
• Have a dread of public speaking that would even ruin your own wedding day.

If this is your problem you probably have talent and a desire to perform but are unable to reach your potential because you find yourself scuppered by nerves once you are in the limelight. (By talent, I mean genuine potential backed up by hard work or practice that is brought to its knees once the key moment arrives.)

Some performers 'learn' their nervousness on their first slip-up. Most actors know what it feels like to dry, for instance, but there are those who have learnt to carry on through it and beyond and those who live in such fear of repeating the experience that they make repetition a virtual dead cert, meaning that they become unable to perform altogether.

This performance problem isn't just confined to the stage. You can find it occurring in the workplace, before an important presentation or being asked to speak up during a meeting, and you can easily suffer from it in the bedroom, especially if you're a man and therefore unable to lie back and think of England.

What causes performer nerves?

I'd bet a pound to a penny that a psychoanalyst would discover the seat of all your fear, probably by hypnosis or regression. He or she would unearth the little kid who stood up to sing at the school concert and wet themselves instead, or the one surrounded by loving aunties and uncles who didn't realise the long-term trauma they were causing by laughing as you spoke your first few words.

Who knows? Who needs to know? This is just your sick note, presented to get you out of future success. Let it go. It's pure self-indulgence. You can't go back and dry those tears (or that puddle on the school hall floor) but you can conquer your fear starting from now.

We can all sing in the bath or shower. Why? Because there is no one there to hear us and we therefore have no inhibitions about warbling and yodelling away like Pavarotti. The minute you factor in an audience we begin to assess our performance through their eyes (or ears). If you have a bog-standard, tone-deaf voice this is not a tragedy, but what if you do have the voice of an angel but the nerves of a small mouse with a persecution complex?

Performer nerves can scupper the best of them and it's primarily a hybrid of shyness and stress. A performer works under pressure, often with a lot at stake. Maybe it's just themselves they'll let down if they're rubbish but maybe it's the rest of the team in a business presentation, or the rest of the cast in the case of a play.

Why you dry

'Drying' is a term actors use to describe the moment they stand out onstage and forget their next line. A small dry might lead to a pause or a swift prompt from the wings to kick-start the thought processes but a big dry can lead to career annihilation. Not because the one ruined performance is a death-knell to a career but the effect that slip might have on future performances is potentially toxic. The brain retains the problem and makes it grow in size. For the person suffering from performer nerves it's not about the 'what', it's all about the 'what if?': 'What if I dry again?' 'What if I hit the wrong notes?' 'What if that penalty doesn't go into the net?' 'What if I start stammering in front of clients?'

This thinking interrupts the free flow from your subconscious to your conscious mind. On a bad day it has it in a stranglehold. Much of what we do in the confident state needs to be subconscious, something you can do or say without thinking about it too much, if at all. There are some skills that require a low state of awareness. Can you play the piano or type? If you can you should remember that moment when you moved from that state of learning where you were focusing on every movement, and the state where you allowed your fingers to take over. Surprisingly they knew what they were doing. As I type now I look at the keys. But if I don't look and if I just focus on my words I find my fingers reach those keys anyway. Then my conscious brain wonders how it is they can do that and I start to question the technique and suddenly I can't do it any more.

Performer confidence means you stop looking at the keys and allow yourself to fly. It's that moment when you learnt to swim where you just stopped splashing and trying not to drown and pushed off into the great wet unknown to discover the less you worried the more you were able to float.

Do I need to remind you of one core point made throughout the book? Before you tackle your performer nerves you must make sure you can perform. Learn your craft. Know your script, rehearse your song, and work on your presentation. Find out how sex works. Then learn how to overcome your fears about delivering them.

Overcoming your performer nerves

- **Keep going**. Stopping or avoiding should not be an option as it can lead to your fear becoming a phobia, which is far more difficult to deal with.

- Use the phrase actors and sportspeople use: '**CANCEL AND CONTINUE.**' During your actual performance carry on without looking back. Never allow your brain to hook on that one moment. Did you ever see ice-dancers fall over during competition? One minute their bum is bouncing on the ice and next minute they're up like a little flea and off into their routine as though nothing had happened. Where you and I might give up and flounce off in a huff they carry on regardless. Why? Because they focus on going forward not back. Performances require you to live in the moment, not dwell on the minor catastrophe that just occurred. The performer brain can't function if it's aghast at the past and in dread of the future. It's too busy being brilliant in the present. Cancel and Continue. Cancel and Continue. Cancel and Continue.

- **Know what you will do if you dry**. This is not preparing to fail but it is providing yourself with a belt and a pair of braces to enable you to retain control. Create your fall-back: 'If I do dry I will listen for the prompt', 'If I fall over I will get up and carry on', 'If I happen to struggle having sex I will be open, honest and let my partner know it's not his or her fault' and focus on touching, kissing and pleasing your partner instead.

- If you dry and you have no fall-back plan, **think of nothing**. Create a gap that will allow the thought you need to pop up. It's too easy to fill that gap with panic thinking, which is busy, negative and preoccupied. Stop what you're doing if you're acting or giving a presentation, and focus on darkness. If you're presenting, take a little walk across to your notes. Or smile at your audience and create what looks like an emphatic pause.

- **Do not enact your panic**. No rushing, looking at the ceiling, fiddling, rolling your eyes, saying 'oh my God!' This doesn't just signal despair to your audience, it lets your subconscious know you're out of control too.

- **Become a reverse paranoid**. This means that you learn to thwart any thoughts that your audience are being critical of you and your performance by turning those thoughts around by 180 degrees. Tell yourself they love you. Act as though they do. If you're imagining hostility you might as well imagine admiration instead.

- **Never court sympathy from your audience** by telling them you're nervous before you start. They will think you're going to be wasting their time and they will think you haven't bothered to battle your nerves. If you are addressing them before you talk, tell them how pleased you are to have been given the opportunity to speak to them, instead. Acted nerves only work if you are an utter diva, i.e. you are fully sure you can perform in an excellent way and are therefore able to offer up a moment of false modesty to enhance the enjoyment of your audience.

FAILURE ADDICTION

You suffer from failure addiction if:

- You have a dread of doing well or succeeding to the point you bottle out or self-scupper anything you see as working to the point where it might create change and pressure in your life.

- You call bad luck what is actually self-sabotage; being late for job interviews, not leaving enough time to prepare for an exam, losing a client's phone number or delaying phoning the estate agent, meaning the dream house is gone before you can put in an offer.

- You rarely try beyond the first hit, meaning you'll go for a goal once but give up straight away if your attempt doesn't work, rather than being resilient.
- You equate failure with sympathy, cuddles and love.
- You prefer to moan about your problems rather than solve them.

Does all this sound odd? More people suffer from this problem than you'd think, living in a state of permanent bafflement over why they are always 'unlucky' or manage to lose out just as they're on the brink of doing well.

The problem with failure is that it begins to feel comfortable, even when it feels miserable. Why? Because it's a passive state, requiring little if any change or challenge, and because it can get sympathy and promote bonding rather than evoking envy and alienation.

Familiarity is a very seductive thing, even when the thing we're familiar with is unpleasant or miserable. Sometimes we structure our entire friendships or family relationships around our own capacity for failure, being with people who provide functions like emotional support or condolence, rather than people who provide fun or encouragement to succeed. I know many people who (without knowing it) enjoy relationships with their partners that involve long periods of moaning and whining about their circumstances or complaining about being taken for granted at work, just to receive sympathy and cuddles of affectionate protection. They might be people who, as children, received their most intense forms of affectionate response from their parents when they had been injured or upset by other kids, or maybe even told off or punished by the parent. Their tears would have created a positive, loving response, leaving them unsure as adults how to gain that level of affection from a position of success and achievement.

Most kids encounter a similar version of this conundrum when they start school. To begin with, a kid will measure success in terms of popularity amongst their peers. But then the school shows that success should be measured by exam results. For the clever kid this can present a conundrum because the smart-ass in class is often also the most unpopular. Other kids get jealous or feel diminished by comparison, and so – in a bid to retain his or her popularity – the clever kid will often dumb down. Until recently this pressure to dumb down to attract friendship or a sexual partner was also applied to women. Men liked women who acted less competent than them and in many ways it could be fair to say they still do. (No, I know, not all of them, although many would be surprised if they could see the sudden signals of giggling submission adopted by women when they catch sight of a potential male mate, and the word I still hear repeatedly to define a woman who is deemed admirable in the workplace is still 'bubbly'.)

How to avoid failure addiction

- Always sell the **benefits of your success** to yourself before you go for it.
- **Create visual images of your goals**. Get a photo of that house or car or holiday and stick it by your desk.
- **Visualise** living in it, driving it, living it.
- **Write two lists,** one of all the pros and one of all the cons.
- **Set yourself the task of not moaning or whingeing to anyone,** about anything. Go cold turkey. Think of uplifting, funny, optimistic subjects to talk about to friends, colleagues and loved ones.
- **Be the one who listens and helps** rather than the needy one who loves to moan.
- **Never put anything down to bad luck.** What happened? How could it have been changed? Checking your car engine over or looking to see how much petrol was in the tank? Trying again if you failed at something?
- **Lose your capacity for failure-acceptance.** Tell yourself: the only real failures are not trying or giving up. Reassess your definition of failure.
- **Avoid disparaging statements** like 'That would never happen', 'I'm never lucky', 'I'd stand no chance' and 'Knowing my luck ...' If you do use the last phrase end it with: '... I'll get exactly what I want.'

Stress

You are probably stressed if:

• You feel your negative emotions are running out of control
• You find even small knock-backs make you stall
• You get irritable or tearful for no reason
• You get feelings of dread
• Your thinking can seem muddled, i.e. you have trouble concentrating and get forgetful
• Your days are badly time-managed
• You seem to get any illness that's about and have trouble shaking them off
• You rush everything
• You can't delegate
• You worry a lot or lie awake worrying
• The pressure in your life seems relentless

How can stress masquerade as a lack of confidence? Very easily. Stress can have a profound effect on three key functions:

1. Your Intellect
2. Your Health
3. Your Emotions

When you're stressed it's very easy to view life through the opposite of rose-tinted spectacles. Stress can create feelings of doom and dread that results in a constant expectation of negative outcomes. When you are stressed everything looks and feels like a problem and every problem is too huge to tackle.

Stress makes you feel powerless, meaning you lack the ability to tackle situations with anything approaching positivity or a light touch.

Stress makes you dumb because it closes the serving hatch between your conscious and unconscious thinking, making almost everything vaguely important a conscious thought. It's your subconscious that feeds your confidence, allowing you to do things, say things and make decisions without turning into a gibbering wreck. You sit in a chair without thinking about it because you've done it countless times before, therefore your conscious brain doesn't need to get involved. You check the time on your watch and your brain assimilates the information on the dial and, without any apparent effort, translates it into commands like: 'I need to hurry or I will be late for my train'. What would happen if I stopped you just after you'd looked at your watch and asked you to tell me the time? You'd have to look again. The process would involve more effort because you'd need to translate your speedy, confident thought into actual conversation. You might even have a small problem reading the time: 'Um ... it's about a quarter to ... sorry, nine forty-five ...'

Stress can also have a devastating effect on your emotions. When we're under pressure and that pressure converts into stress we lose the ability to be calm, confident, fearless or even indifferent. Your brain and body are in fight/flight mode and your thinking has the word 'emergency' blinking away like a neon sign. What this means to you is that your negative emotions are likely to be exaggerated, making you irritable, tearful, fearful or aggressive. It is also possible for high levels of paranoia to kick in, meaning you have trouble trusting, delegating or relying on anyone, even those nearest to you. By scything off your own support system you become even more of a victim, taking on too many jobs with no one to rely on for emotional support.

And as if that's not enough, you get the physical symptoms. Stress means your brain is telling your body that you're under physical threat. This results in an amazing response as your body gets ready to fight or run. Your breathing becomes shallow and almost like a pant. Your heart rate increases, pumping blood around your body, your muscles tense, you start to sweat and your digestive system shuts down while your bowel and bladder attempt to empty.

All these responses would be useful if you were being chased by a giant squid. Your brain would be alert, your body would be faster and stronger and all that sweat would evaporate as you ran or fought, allowing you to stay cool. Sadly, though, we rarely – if ever – encounter the giant squid. Often stress happens when you have more work than there are hours in the day or a difficult meeting with the boss, neither of which will be enhanced if you're hyperventilating, shaking, dying to go to the loo and offering handshake so wet you feel like a dead haddock.

How to cope when you're suffering from stress

- Remind yourself that it's not a lion or a giant squid; it's a manageable, daily problem.
- The two key words to stress management are Control and Perception. Speak and act as though you are controlling your problems, not as though they are controlling you. And look at ways of changing your faulty perception. Look at your problem in the context of the whole world or your entire life. What would a much older version of you tell the current you to think and do about your current problems?
- Write your worries, anxieties and other thoughts down in your a little notebook. It helps empty them out of your mind. Use the three-forked way of problem solving as it helps create order out of chaos. When you have a problem there are only three possible solutions:

  1. Sort it. Solve it, take action, do something about it.
  2. Let it drop. Quit fighting. Learning to live with what you can't change is a powerful step in stress management. When you can't change the stimulus you need to learn to change your response.
  3. Moan about it. Whinge. Whine. But don't even think about choosing this option!

- Never become a stress martyr. This is where you suffer from stress, working under a period of extra pressure but instead of easing up during other parts of your life you take on more and more until you buckle. A common example would be the woman who is working flat-out in her job but who decides to invite 16 family members for Sunday lunch and insists on cooking everything from scratch.
- If your job is stressful, decontaminate when you get home. Instead of walking in blasting off about your day or rushing to the laptop to fire off a few extra emails, go and shower, change into something totally different to your work outfit and sit talking about something unrelated to work. If you are stressed at home, try to avoid chatting about your problems at work the next day. You need escapes, not more of the same.

- **Eat well and sleep well.** Look after your diet and eat healthily. Take exercise because it helps release all that pent-up desire for fight or flight, and prepare for sleep by avoiding caffeine from midday, not taking phone calls or doing any work relating to business for the two-hour period leading to bed, watch light-hearted TV and read light-hearted books during the same period.
- **Evoke the same sense of well-being and safety you felt as a child.** Children bust stress by revisiting comfort signals like thumb sucking, hair stroking, rubbing their blanket and being read to out loud. Get your partner to read to you before you go to sleep (take it in turns, of course), and acquire your own stress touch that will replicate the comforts of thumb sucking. Rub an earlobe, twiddle your own hair, rub your scalp if you're balding or short-haired, stroke your cat, play with worry beads.
- **Use music to calm you.** Find the kind of music that calms you down – different types of music work better for different people. Start with light classics but don't be surprised if you find heavy metal or jazz floats your boat. Music is hugely affecting. Keep your iPhone stocked up with the right type of sounds for the right emotions.

PHOBIAS

A phobia is a different type of fear. We all know of the claustro-phobics and agoraphobics, but sometimes the fear of things like speaking in public, meeting strangers and even networking can be upgraded to be classed as phobia. This would be called social phobia. However, I am happy to use the more generic term of 'phobias' without limiting it to social events as I know from experience that people who suffer from phobias often feel a general lack of confidence prompted by the idea that their fears make them feel they have somehow let themselves down.

Are you phobic?
- You probably are if you avoid the thing you fear. Most people fear flying, even if their fear is very slight. If you fly afraid,

you're fearful but not phobic. If you start to shun air travel you probably have a phobia.

Be aware of the difference between worrying about or fearing public speaking as opposed to avoiding it at all costs, even though it is a necessary part of your job. Or always taking a colleague to networking events because you just can't stand doing a room by yourself.

- It can lead to a situation where you begin to apply the word 'can't' to your transactions, as in 'I can't get in lifts', 'I can't do presentations', 'I can't speak to people I don't know'.
- The avoidance of fear can make you feel as though your life is less fearful than the person who is still doing all these things, even though they dread them. But phobias don't stop, they can grow like rust. Even seemingly insignificant phobias can dominate your life.

The link between phobias and confidence is interesting. I suffer from claustrophobia and have long been fascinated at the way a phobia like this can have both positive and negative effects on your overall confidence.

I'll begin by using the most useful definition I heard of a phobia, which is that it's when fear becomes avoidance.

There are many people who hate flying or using the underground but a phobic person takes steps to avoid doing what they fear. I added lifts to my own personal menu of avoidance, and there was a fantastically un-useful phase when I also wanted to avoid all small or crowded spaces, crowds in general and taxis or trains with locked doors.

Now the problem with a phobia (or should I say *one* of the problems with a phobia as they are many!) is that you tend to exist either in a state of fear or in a state of fear fear (and that's not a printer's error, you really are afraid of your fear). This either marks you out as a wuss of the highest order or as some kind of feral beast because you attempt to mask your fears, leading to a tendency to suddenly attack or turn on people who dare to question your ability to get into a lift, or to tell you to 'calm down' when you're in the midst of a crowd.

How a phobia *can* have unexpected benefits

I did say phobias can have a positive effect on your confidence, and by now you're probably wondering how.

Well, the point is your phobic fears tend to be intense but also very focused. Surf your phobia cleverly and you'll find anything that does not come under its scope is a doddle. If you're only frightened of lifts or crowds you'll do anything given the right amount of space. It's as though your fear is a see-saw: the higher it is one end the lower it is the other. When people ask how I can talk to large groups or appear on live TV, I shrug. It's not a confined space therefore it doesn't come under my scope of fear. Many phobics have the ability to be massively confident in situations that are phobia-free. My mother had a horror of spiders but no fear of humans, meaning she'd take anyone on verbally as long as they didn't have eight legs and spin webs.

I'm not saying you should embrace your phobias, but I am saying you can help yourself deal with them by putting yourself in touch with your alternative, brave side. What have your phobic fears allowed you to do without fear, as opposed to the things they have prevented you from doing?

One of the more intrinsic problems with phobias and confidence comes from the way a phobic can learn to distrust and often hate themselves. It's a baffling mental glitch that makes you feel you have no control over your responses. Fear is like a diva who appears as and when it suits her, often unannounced and always in a way that will upstage your other abilities. It respects neither intellect or courage. While the rest of the world gets on with its life, the phobic's mind feels incorrectly wired, producing illogical responses. The only thing a phobic can be confident about is what looks to others like peculiar behaviour to avoid their fear. This leads to a very intrinsic lack of self-confidence that feels far more acute than the type suffered by other people. The only advantage being that you're like an emotional piebald, a patchy mix of total confidence and total lack of it. One minute you're doing things that might scare other people and the next you're jabbering over a moth or a guy in a clown suit.

How to overcome your phobia

- **Don't stop doing**. Avoidance is the phobic state. Work through your fears instead.
- **Never duck out**. If your boss wants you to do a presentation, do it. If you're asked to speak at a friend's wedding feel flattered rather than horrified.
- **Use any opportunity to practise your skills**. Tackle your task objectives rather than marinating and being obsessed with your fear, i.e. 'I am giving this speech to show my best friend how much we all like/love him' not 'I am dreading giving this speech'.
- **Diminish your fears**. Tackle something that you dread more, it's the only way to diminish the thing itself. It will challenge you but it's better looking down on a fear than up at it. Shrink it.
- **Stop sounding fearful**. Every time you tell someone you're scared you enforce that fear in your subconscious.
- **Use positive affirmations**. They work, honest. Go for it and saturate your mind with them whether you believe them or not. 'I love speaking in public' is an example.
- **Take one small moment to overact your fear in the mirror**. Quake, knee-knock, imagine you're auditioning for *Scream IX*. Then stop, laugh out loud at yourself, call yourself a silly prat, rearrange your body language into something that looks braver and continue about your business.
- **When you approach the thing you dread do it 'The John Wayne Way'**, i.e. with the kind of bearing and facial expression that registers a complete lack of fear. Stroll, saunter, swagger, look bored by fear, like a person who would sit looking at fear across the cornflakes and laugh out loud in its face. (You might prefer other role models. I used to use Emma Peel from *The Avengers* as she was the first woman on TV who never showed fear.)

SOCIAL IMPOTENCE

How to know if you suffer from social impotence:
- Whereas the shy person is like the nervous little fawn of the social scene, the socially impotent is more like the baby elephant, blundering about in a bit of a panic.

- You are fine and dandy during in-depth conversations with anyone but you lack the skills and ability to get through those first few layers of social veneer that will crack the nut in the way you should.
- You often come across as churlish or odd, going up to total strangers at networking events and saying something inappropriate or direct.
- Your lack of social skills becomes lack of confidence as you get rejected more than you get accepted.
- This in turn can emerge as a form of hostility, as in 'They just don't get me', 'We're not on the same wavelength', 'They're not my type of person' or 'I find them too false'.
- If you're lucky (and they're unlucky) you find a partner who is more sociable, meaning you can spend the rest of your life huffing, puffing and sulking from the sidelines while they do all your socialising for you.

I use the term Social Impotence to describe the type of lack of confidence when you are over-wary of other people, meaning you bomb at social situations in a way that is not the same as shyness. There's something about other people that strikes you dumb, deaf and stupid to the point where you see them talking to you and realise you should respond but you're so keen to be showing them a clean pair of heels that the wiring in your brain that deciphers and prompts communication seems to have blown its circuits, leaving you feeling like a shell that once housed a human brain.

You cling to the thought that you're okay when you're with people you know. You bleat this excuse whenever you're asked to speak in business or make a speech, as though it will send bosses off to fill the room with all your closest friends and relatives rather than the group of clients that sit staring at you.

The fact is that we're *all* better with people we know. We can relax with people we know because the fact that they know us means they're less likely to be judgemental about that one little failure or moment of error because they either know it's out of character or because they will support us despite our slip-ups.

Like shyness this sociophobia is completely natural but it's also part fear and part laziness. Uncurling like a little leaf or petal once you're basking in the warm gaze of a friend's adoration might be fine, but you also need to hone the skills of getting those friends in the first place. Not everyone will like you. In fact, your sociophobias probably make you quite tiresome company, especially at first, and even later on in your friendships you could be high maintenance if you tend to be needy and a scaredy-cat. People around you should not always be giving you praise and encouragement just to enable you to launch yourself on the world. You're right to fear other people but that doesn't make you right to be acting on that fear and avoiding all stranger contact (at least once you've got past the 'don't accept sweets or lifts' stage in your life).

How to manage social impotence

- Now is the time to **give yourself a strict talking to**. Nobody likes small talk and 'doing a room' but we live in an era where networking is the way to get on in business as well as in the rest of your life. Do it for your career or because it will help you make friends and get a partner, even if you don't want to do it because you enjoy it.

- Networking doesn't need to be difficult or boring. Like any other business skill you need to **set yourself objectives and targets** before you set to work on the job in hand.

- **Don't get emotionally involved.** Learn how to network just as you would learn how to use a new software program. It's only when you begin to attach comparisons with real friendships and the kind of social events you do enjoy, that probably involve a ton of booze to get you to open up, that you create complications and problems for yourself. This is like comparing computer games with sending emails. Same machine, different functions.

- **Use the reverse paranoia technique.** Instead of imagining the worst about the people you are meeting, try to imagine the best, so that instead of believing them to be judgemental of you, boring or bored by you, difficult to get to know or dissimilar to you, tell yourself the exact opposite. Play a game where you go hunting for the best in people and seeking out the things you have in common rather than the opposite.

- And if you have nothing in common, **see them as a way of discovering new interests** or finding out about new subjects.

• Use the networking section in the book (see page 191) to guide you towards the techniques that anyone can easily use to tackle their social impotence.

IN A NUTSHELL

• Discover your own specific type of lack of confidence and work on managing and dealing with it based on your diagnosis.

• Use the information on other types of lack of confidence to enable you to gain a clearer understanding of the way other people view situations. That person dancing on the table could actually be shy. The one scowling or sitting quietly could suffer from social impotence or phobias, rather than dislike you. By understanding others' behaviours we help ourselves grow in confidence.

4

LOGGING YOUR IDEAL CONFIDENCE LEVELS

STEP 1: CREATING GOALS

Why goals? There are two vital reasons for creating and listing your confidence goals:

1. Behaviour is always more effective when you know what it is you're trying to achieve and why you're trying to achieve it. If you fail to identify your goals your work and effort will be aimless rather than strategic.
2. Setting a goal motivates you to achieve it, especially in the long term. Without them we become demotivated and give up faster than I can say 'Seize the day'.

Your body and your brain are capable of fantastic effort and thought, but if they're not sure what the effort or the fight is all about they'll lose interest. We can all make ourselves do things we don't want to, but only if we have first sold ourselves the benefits of doing so. You would only have gone through the hell that is the driving test because you had your future freedom, career and ability to travel in mind. You were fed up asking your parents for lifts or you had been given a car for your birthday. You visualised all the dates you could pull once you had wheels and you visualised the humiliation of being the only one still hopping on and off the bus. (Unless of course you had the environment uppermost in your mind, in which case you probably eschewed the car and learnt to ride a bicycle instead!)

EXERCISE: MAKE YOUR OWN LIST OF GOALS

If you want to fight for your confidence you need to know what you're fighting for. Write them down. This will help to focus your mind. Here are some suggestions:

- I want to be that person chatting easily at parties or speaking up at meetings without blushing or babbling their words.
- I want to have the ability to promote or pursue those skills or talents that I have that no one else knows about.
- I want to stop losing out on dates because I get tongue-tied.
- I want to be the one who can flirt with confidence, and not bottle it or break out in a sweat.
- I want my life to be more enjoyable and successful because I'm not weighed down by anxieties, self-doubts, low self-esteem or shyness.
- I want to ensure the thing I excel at, like singing, dancing or acting, isn't scuppered by performance nerves that mean I never get past the audition stage.
- I want to stop coming away from recruitment or promotion interviews knowing I have ruined my chances because of nerves.
- I want to stop quaking in my shoes at the thought of public speaking or making a business presentation.
- I want to speak up at meetings rather than allowing other people to steal all my ideas or glory.
- I want to enjoy events where I get to meet new people.

What will having more confidence enable you to do? What achievements will they help with? What parts of your life will confidence make easier or more enjoyable? Think big in terms of scope but think realistic in terms of ability. 'I want enough confidence to be famous' will rattle like a dried pea in an empty tin unless you know what talent you have that you need sufficient levels of confidence to share with the world. In any case, it's better to be specific about what you want – e.g. ask for enough confidence to book in for drama classes or voice coaching so that you can ensure you have a talent in the first place.

Once you have your goals you have the first part of your confidence game plan, like programming your satnav with your destination before listening to the directions it will tell you to take.

The tap on the shoulder syndrome

You may have already achieved your goals. In fact, your problem is that you are already successful, but suffer from the 'tap on the shoulder' syndrome. This is when you frequently wonder exactly how and why you got where you are and worry that you lack the abilities to live up to everyone's expectations of you.

If this is you, ask yourself the two following questions. They're a good place to start when you're learning how to be more confident:

1. When does your confidence desert you?
2. How are you to blame for your own lack of confidence? (Remember that the power to improve lies with you.)

By identifying when your confidence leaves you, and how you are to blame for that, you can set in motion plans to overcome the 'tap on the shoulder' syndrome.

CONFIDENCE RULES
Here's what your confidence goals should look like:
- Having the ability to act, work and perform to your full potential.
- Having the opportunity to achieve beyond your current levels of potential.
- Developing the positivity and motivation to train and learn skills that you need to reach your goals.
- Enjoying the route to those goals.
- Understanding, liking and admiring yourself.

What you should not be doing:
- Believing that confidence is either a naturally permanent state or a right.
- Believing that confidence is more important than skills, talent or attitude.
- Believing that you can achieve anything just by self-belief alone.
- Becoming self-obsessed, indulging in time-consuming navel-gazing.
- Trying the techniques in this book just to prove they don't work.

'Courage, mon brave': assessing your list of goals

Courage is the thing when you're studying your goals. Why peep at life from behind a mask of diffidence, like a giant jelly-baby? Courage will not only allow you to do things you've stalled at before, but to enjoy those things too, because I don't like to keep forcing myself to do things that I hate and neither should you.

Fun is an essential part of life and we should take active steps to seek it in everything we do. To acquire courage-confidence you must pin 'fun' up there along with your ultimate goals, especially as the steps you'll be taking towards those goals might involve the teeniest smidgeon of pain, like the emotional version of a nagging toothache. The pain is manageable unless you want to be a wuss all your life, and nothing compared to that sting of humiliation you currently suffer every time you miss out on that promotion, pay rise or even hot date just because you lacked the confidence to speak up, speak out or take a risk.

STEP 2: FINE-TUNING YOUR CONFIDENCE LEVELS

We've seen that overconfidence or arrogance can be every bit as destructive as a lack of confidence. So when you strive to achieve your goals by becoming more confident you must set yourself specific confidence goals that are relevant to your ability to survive. The technique is simple. In any scenario I want you to work on the following grid:

COWARDICE——WARINESS —— CONFIDENCE——ARROGANCE

Using your grid

This could hardly be easier. To summon up the appropriate levels of confidence for any situation you need to put two large crosses on the grid line. One according to where you are now, and the second for where you feel is appropriate. Here's what the terms stand for:

Cowardice

This will refer to a moment when you know you can do something but lack the bottle to do it. It's being over-fearful or fearful of nothing. Many phobias would come under this heading as – like agoraphobia or fear of buttons or kittens – it is based on little if anything in the way of logical thought.

Wariness

This is a different kind of fear, a much more useful fear. Wariness would be the animal busy drinking at the watering hole but keeping one eye and one ear out for predators at the same time. In human terms it would be someone who is rock-climbing being constantly aware of problems like weather or rock-falls, or a good driver being aware of potential danger from other motorists. This is dealing with calculated risk rather than imagined risk.

Confidence

This is where you either have the skills, knowledge and experience required to succeed at your task or transaction, plus the right mental attitude to be able to use those skills, or have put plans in place where you know your skills fall short and you have the correct optimistic mindset to get them. It's the Olympic sprinter who comes first but who immediately studies the footage to see if their performance can be improved. It's being in the right emotional and intellectual state to do your abilities justice.

Arrogance

We see arrogance all the time on reality TV, and for a generation it's become the new confidence. Years ago I would have spent hours in schools training school-leavers the knack of self-promotion as they were unable to say anything good about themselves at interviews. This was because – much like me – they had been brought up on a diet of modesty, gorged on self-effacing statements like a goose destined for pâté de fois gras is force-fed whatever it is they stuff down the poor bird's throat.

Now things seem to be a lot different. School leavers will tend to say they're good at anything and are capable of the highest levels of success, regardless of talent or skill. Talking yourself up is the new self-effacing modesty. I blame TV shows like *The X Factor*, *Big Brother* and *The Apprentice*, where applicants will happily claim: 'I am your next number one chart-topper' or 'I am the best salesman in the UK' or even 'I am fabulous. I want everyone to see the real me' while proving they're tone deaf, lacking in any ability to persuade and influence or in possession of the most rancid personality traits since Nasty Nick Cotton.

Blowing your own trumpet too hard is rarely, if ever, a route to success. It makes those around you feel diminished because it's competitive and crushing. It often has no concern for other people and it never ever allows others to have the ability to shine too. The only time I have seen arrogance give others the permission to shine has been in the case of some football managers whose boasting did seem to be believed by the team and therefore became catching. But going around most workplaces claiming to be 'The Chosen One' is a risky technique and more likely to lead to alienation or attack from fellow workers, so, admirable though it might have been in context, it's not a route we'll be taking towards our own goals.

Overinflated self-belief not only makes us appear vile to others, it also makes us blind to our own inadequacies and we need to have an ability to recognise those inadequacies so that we can shore them up or get rid of them.

Arrogance is the state I refer to as punching well above your weight. It's where you put in little if any effort, but expect big rewards and success. It's talking yourself up to the point where it's all puff and air, or all style and no substance, as they say in politics. It's when you're so overconfident that you're unaware of any problems and have no plans in place for dealing with them if they do occur. It's a state that many people go through at some time during their teens, but which they mostly grow out of, although not all of us do. Self-awareness and the ability to evaluate your worth and skills honestly are vital ingredients in being successful. The problem arises when we watch a successful person who is also arrogant and we mimic the only skill we can – their arrogance – without realising that their attitude is backed up by talent, while ours is all just empty bluster.

Once you have your two crosses on your confidence grid you can begin to plan how to get from your first to your ideal place. I'm guessing your first will be somewhere around the 'Cowardice' spot and that your ideal will be at 'Confidence'. Your next step is to estimate the current 'cost' of the gap. Write down what being at the wrong spot is currently costing you in terms of happiness, positivity, success or even money. What are you not doing or not doing well because you lack the appropriate levels of confidence?

Then write down the steps it will take to breach that gap. What will you need to do to move to the right place on your grid? What will it take? How will you start right now? Write down some large steps, like changing your thinking or learning new skills.

Remember, you can't expect yourself to learn confidence in great leaps. Huge strides are therapeutic and inspirational but you need regular small steps to fill up the gaps between them. What you will do, then, is to plan some regular small and mid-size steps. These smaller steps will have to be accumulative, but they must be regular and ongoing. Ideally you will rarely feel you are being pushed beyond your abilities with these smaller steps. Take a pledge now to make at least one step forward per day.

This means you will push at least one step further forward in terms of your confidence each and every day.

To make sure you feel the benefit you need to create a confidence rating that you give yourself on a weekly basis. This is simple, and I'll tell you how to do that in the next step.

STEP 3: COMPILING YOUR CONFIDENCE LOG

Once a week, I want you to sit down and give yourself an overall rating in terms of your confidence.

Your rating will be zero for absolutely no confidence at all and 20 for perfect levels of confidence.

As well as your overall rating I want you to log a score for actual events and transactions in your life. You can list any regular events that currently cause you to lose confidence and place a current rating beside each event. Then you give subsequent ratings every time you do that thing, so that you have an ongoing log of your confidence levels.

When you create your list of regular events, add some that you are currently avoiding but will be doing in future. These will be the events that stretch you and your confidence. Your list could look something like this:

	Current rating	Week 2	Week 3	Week 4	Week 5	Week 6
Going on a date						
Phoning a client						
Wedding speech						
Dealing with difficult client						
Business presentation						
Dealing with partner's untidiness						

Walking forward

You can take more steps each day and you can take bigger steps, but you must always take one step at least. Why? Because by making the steps a regular part of your daily routine you will continue to feel like a winner. When you're building and boosting confidence you must never tread water or take a backward step. Never indulge yourself. Kindness to yourself will destroy all your previous good work. Allowing a day off will be like taking a day off a diet and filling your face with cake.

Taking one small step per day is easy and fun. It also keeps the momentum going and your motivation high. You'll find lots more spontaneous ways to boost your confidence rating.

What type of steps?

You will need to plan and evaluate your daily steps because as you grow in confidence you will need to push yourself more, and because it's important you don't fail to recognise your work and achievement because the step feels mundane or not worth bothering with or celebrating.

Each morning, take one or two minutes to plan your new challenge. This means planning to do one thing that you know will stretch you in terms of your confidence. It could be doing a proper greeting to your manager or boss, making small talk with someone as you commute, asking for a discount when you buy something, speaking up at a business meeting, disagreeing and sharing your views when friends say they enjoyed a movie or walking across to chat to that eye candy you fancy in your local bar or club.

Only you will know what stretches you, so you must be honest with yourself. Picking something that is too easy will not make you feel brave, and picking something too hard or unlikely for your daily step could lead to failure.

Each evening you need to evaluate your day in terms of your confidence steps, giving yourself a proverbial pat on the back for having achieved them. If you do find you've forgotten it's never too late to add one! Ring a friend you haven't spoken to for ages and who you find daunting, go and learn a new technique on your PC or make a small speech to your family. Even reading out loud to your partner can be a way to gain verbal and performance confidence if you choose an exciting novel and really work the characters!

Eventually your daily steps will become part of your normal routine, meaning you'll be able to do them without writing your log. But you must always plot them and note them in your mind to avoid forgetting to create the right levels of stretch.

CONFIDENCE TRICK: LOSING YOUR FEARS

Stop making yourself fearful by association. The more times you tell yourself and anyone within earshot that you 'Hate' speaking in public or that you 'Can't do small talk or networking' or are 'dreadful' at understanding I.T., the more you create an untrue absolute in your mind.

STEP 4: IDENTIFYING YOUR EXISTING CONFIDENCE

When you identify, understand and analyse the moments in life when you are feeling confident and comfortable, it will help you replicate the circumstances or feelings in future and give you a hook to hang your new levels of confidence. Your existing confidence is your solid base and you might be surprised. Perhaps you're already more confident than you think!

Think you don't have any existing confidence? I don't care how bad your confidence and self-esteem levels feel to you, I will bring red-hot pliers to apply to your toenails to force you to admit that you have moments in your life when you do feel confident.

Everyone feels confident at some time or another. Often we feel so confident that we don't even register it as confidence, we just describe it as 'doing what I always do'. You probably feel confident about cleaning your teeth or ordering your lunchtime sandwich.

Let's think about the confidence your have cleaning your teeth.
Why do you feel confident about cleaning your teeth?

Don't laugh; it's a serious psychological question. What thought processes have to be in place for you to feel as confident as you'd like to feel about other transactions or actions?

Go ahead, squeeze the answer out like toothpaste and don't worry about stating the obvious.

You feel confident about cleaning your teeth because:

1. You do it a lot. Every day (hopefully). Twice a day (probably).
2. You've been doing it for so long that you hardly have to think about it.
3. You don't give a flying fig about doing it because you never do it in public.

Genuine confidence tends to occur when:
- We do something so often and with such a high success rate that we pretty much assume it's going to be okay.
- Or we feel confident because we don't have an audience. No one is watching, so who cares if we slip up?

- Or because we don't give a damn. So what if the toothbrush goes up my nose? I'll laugh it off. It won't put me off cleaning my teeth.

EXERCISE

This is the simplest exercise in the world but I want you to dig deep in order to make it effective. Just fill in the following page.

I FEEL CONFIDENT WHEN:

_____

_____

_____

_____

_____

THE REASON FOR THIS IS:

_____

_____

_____

_____

_____

IN A NUTSHELL

- Take practical steps to growing your confidence.

- Create goals and revisit and refresh those goals regularly.

- Create a confidence grid to establish how confident you need to feel in specific circumstances.

- Create a confidence log to keep track of improvements in your levels over a period of time.

5

BOOSTING YOUR INNER CONFIDENCE

STEP 1: DISCOVERING YOUR CONFIDENCE CORE

Now that you've begun to identify your own key confidence levels it's time for me to introduce you to your Confidence Core.

What is your Core?

It's your source of inner strength. We all have it but when we lack confidence we sometimes fail to recognise it or keep in touch with it. It can emerge in an emergency, or you can learn how to tap into it when you need to, but rest assured it's there whether you're tapping into it consciously or not.

- Your Core is the basis of all your confidence.
- It is vital you visualise your Confidence Core as being deep inside your body, near your spine, rather than near the outside, like your skin. Why? Because you experience the feeling of your skin all the time and the smallest of injuries can bruise it or hurt it, but your inner Core is well protected and resilient.
- It is important that you don't perceive your Confidence Core as dependent on other people. When we start to allow others to be in control of our levels of confidence we are already defeated. How many times have you blamed other people for 'making' you less self-assured, or been reliant on other people's flattery and compliments to boost your ego? Remember: when you rely on

others' support and praise to retain or restore your self-esteem you are also automatically giving them permission to destroy it.

- Praise and compliments are great confidence refreshers but they should never take the place of your Confidence Core, which you alone will guard and control.

How do I discover my confidence core?

This is relatively simple. Think.

You will have moments in your life when you feel confident and you will have moments in your life when – even though you lack confidence – your resilience and determination are greater than your lack of confidence, creating an override. This is when your behaviour and actions exceed your inner resolve, meaning you stand up to someone who you find intimidating or you pass an exam despite having been riddled with doubt, or you speak up despite having a dread of drawing attention to yourself. It might even be a moment of complete bravery.

These are the moments that put you in conscious touch with your Confidence Core. By reflecting back on these moments in your life and logging any new moments you will begin to recognise it and create connections with it.

Your next step will be controlling the use of it. Remember all those children's stories you grew up on, where a defenceless kid discovers a method of protection and bravery that it could call on whenever it needed help? The genie in the lamp? The superhero who comes when summoned? Harry Potter's magical powers? These are all fictional versions of your own inner Confidence Core and – like the genie or the magic wand – you need to find ways to tap into and use your strong Core at will.

How do I learn to control my Core?

1. First you will need to recognise it and – like Tinkerbell in *Peter Pan* – believe in it. If you don't it will become undernourished.
2. Your second step is to start accessing it during your normal day and using it when you need it. At moments when you lack confidence ask yourself how you would behave in that situation if you had confidence. What would you do? How would the outcome change? This will begin to sell the option

of confidence to you.

3. Your third step is to listen to your Core voice rather than your traditional, doom/gloom/overprotective voice, the one that tells you to sit still and keep quiet, the one that says 'anything for a quiet life' and the one that is utterly risk-averse.

4. Your fourth step is to start imagining what your Confidence Core would tell you to do. Remember it's not risk-seeking, just competent at risk assessment and risk management. It won't drive you into unnecessary danger, but it *will* help you avoid the kind of trouble you get into when you spend a lifetime choosing to do nothing when you really do need to take action.

EXERCISE: FINDING YOUR CONFIDENCE CORE

- Close your eyes.
- Bring your focus to the inside of your body.
- Do this by imagining your skin to be made of strong leather and your eyes and mouth shut firm like shop shutters.
- Imagine a thin but exceptionally strong steel pole running right through the middle of your body. This is your Confidence Core.
- Sit or stand up straighter to allow your Core to stretch to full size.
- Feel the strength emanating from this Confidence Core.
- Allow that strength to flow throughout your body like molten metal, from your spine right out through to the tips of your fingers.

From now on, when you feel yourself to be under pressure and your confidence levels dipping, fading or eroding, do this key Confidence Core exercise to sustain and strengthen your resolve.

STEP 2: GROWING RESILIENCE AND DETERMINATION

Remember that your ability to carry on and to push yourself when parts of your brain are telling you to quit because it's easier and less uncomfortable is vital to your success, as is your capacity for carrying on when something you try doesn't work well first time. To achieve this state you'll need determination, which means knowing your overall goals and sticking to your strategy for achieving them.

How can I make myself determined and resilient? I feel like quitting already

It's your goals that will motivate you. Do you want to spend your entire life standing in the corner at parties, keeping quiet at business meetings and missing out on finding the love of your life because you bottled it? Years ago a guy called Charles Atlas inspired millions of men of my dad's generation to beef up their biceps via the famous threat that if they didn't they'd be the guy on the beach who gets 'sand kicked in his face'. Now, to my knowledge my dad had never had one single holiday in his life that involved a sandy beach rather than a pebbly one, and I'm quite sure he'd never been the victim of a sand-in-face kicking incident. I'm pretty sure that even the sandier UK shores were brimming with hoards of rabid muscle-bound sand-kickers, but the idea resonated sufficiently for him and many men of his era to spend part of their hard-earned wages on chest-expanders, just in case. It was the fear of having a runty body and the risk of public humiliation in front of his girl that did the trick. So it's the thought of your runty confidence and its real and potential consequences of being a behavioural lightweight that will spur you on towards that all-essential resolve.

Resolve helps you go through discomfort

My dad used that chest expander despite the fact it trapped his chest hairs so regularly that his Tarzan-like screams of pain were famous in our neighbourhood. The pain was irrelevant compared to the benefits of a manly chest and the threat of the consequences of remaining concave. Never mind that he'd more than proved his man points by going off to fight a war, the threat of that sand-kicking seemed to scare him more than catching a sniper's bullet in Burma.

Plucking your own personal chest hairs

While there's absolutely no need for any follicle fascism when it comes to increasing your confidence, I am well aware that there will be times during the work involved when you will be yelping like an abandoned puppy, albeit silently.

I know there are confidence issues that amount to very real feelings of actual fear. I know that there will be times when your 'fight/flight' responses will kick in to the point that running away might seem like the most sensible option, even though your challenge amounts to little more than a chat with the boss or walking down the aisle at your own wedding.

We each have our own set of chest hair-plucking moments but I want to make the alternative appear unthinkable to you. Fail to face up to those moments and you've allowed yourself to have sand kicked in your face. You're a wuss, a pussy, a lightweight and a coward. Take up the challenge. It will only make your eyes water for a moment – it gets easier and better with time. Wimping out only feels better for the briefest of moments. After that it's all down to the long-term pain caused by a lack of self-respect.

But what if I don't have chest hairs to pluck? I'm a woman!

Then think Brazilian wax instead, or getting your eyebrows plucked. How painful was your first? But you probably endure it regularly because it gets you obvious benefits.

Brace yourself

So the message is 'Brace yourself' as you work to become more confident, and being confident makes us sexier, more attractive (even if you're no Keira Knightly!), nicer to be around (as Mandela once said: by allowing yourself to shine you give those around you permission to shine as well), less stressed, anxious and miserable, plus less likely to sit around with your fist in your mouth when you know you should be promoting good ideas and thoughts.

If you believe as I do that confidence is the key to unlocking your success, you'll find that with resilience, with effort, with humour and above all with an iron-clad determination you will enable yourself to change your life, making it happier, more comfortable and without doubt more profitable in both emotional and financial terms.

Resilience

Resilience is a key factor in managing your self-esteem and your confidence. It's the secret formula to bouncing back and getting on with life without brooding and pressing the self-destruct button.

For resilience to be effective it needs to either come hand-in-hand with existing skill or talent, or it needs to make you return afresh, having learnt more, achieved more or performed some kind of positive change.

CONFIDENCE TRICKS:
INSTANT BOOSTERS TO MAKE YOU LIKE YOURSELF

- Tidy your wardrobe and take all those clothes that are too small for you to the charity shop. Gazing at wannabe smaller sizes every time you open your wardrobe door is like punching yourself in the eye on a daily basis.
- Stop keeping clothes for best.
- Talk to yourself to cheer yourself up.
- Smile. Smiling makes you feel and look better. Whether you feel like smiling or not, the act of smiling lifts your mood. It makes other people respond better to you as well.
- Phone one friend every day. Make a list of the ones you like who you're gradually losing touch with and make sure you speak in person, not via email or text.
- Send brief sexy/loving text messages to your partner every day. It keeps the relationship bubbling while you're apart.
- Collect something. It gives your life an area of focus. Collectors tend to be smug, superior and happy, it's an easy hit in terms of achievement: 'Look, I found that rare 1963 bronze bottle top!'
- Stop comparing your life to other people, especially celebrities. They might be size zero, married to beautiful people, able to have babies and then be photographed in a bikini one hour later and go to A-list parties, but on the whole what you see is air-brushed living. Most of them are deeply unhappy in rotten, dysfunctional relationships, worried sick about slipping down the charts or not getting offered the best roles. You put on a few pounds or get a couple of wrinkles and it's called life. For them it's called a tragedy of such massive proportion that it's just not possible. Hence Botox, lipo, plastic surgery, hours and hours per day in the gym ... all leading to self-obsession that means they're rarely capable of holding down a happy and loving relationship.
- Don't keep looking. If you don't like the way you look or certain parts of your body, stop staring at them. Again, it's like continually poking yourself in the eye with a stick.

- Write a diary. A proper one, on paper with a pen. Imagine it's being written for the future You, to encourage and motivate him or her. Make it a good account of your life, filled with humour and positive insights. Make your tone brave and optimistic. Adopting this writing style will enable you to change your perspective of what's happening to you.
- Compliment other people. Do it well, with honesty, and they will love you more. But do it without making negative comparisons to yourself. 'You look great' is good but 'I wish I had your figure' is not. The first is a compliment and the second is an unashamed invitation for them to compliment you back. Selfish and nasty. Pay them open, honest compliments and they should do the same without feeling pressured.
- Compliment yourself. Out loud. In the mirror or during your working day.
- Eat healthy foods. It's a message to You that you like yourself.
- Do acts of kindness and appreciation to yourself by being your own servant. Sort out your clothes for the next day the night before. Valet the inside of your car. Leave little motivational notes or funny drawings around the house for yourself, especially in areas that cause you grief, like your workstation or ironing board. Put a small bunch of cut flowers in a vase next to your bed so you wake up facing something nice; change your screen-saver regularly, using funny or happy images. It's like having your own butler. If you're really busy you might even forget you've done them and surprise yourself! Lovely.
- Be a little bit daring. One small tattoo, black toenail varnish, a hat, some new cologne ... Look at those guys in the office who sport friendship bangles under their traditional business wear or the women with the little butterfly inked on their ankles. It reminds you you're more than other people think you are.
- Buy some lovely relaxing clothes. As you pull on those cashmere socks, climb into those amazingly comfortable but chic designer pyjamas (Primark counts as a designer name if you're saving the pennies) or pull on those sheepskin-lined Uggs you'll love yourself for being so thoughtful and kind to the You who comes in from work knackered.

STEP 3: BUILD A SENSE OF 'YOU'

Liking yourself is a key ingredient of resilience. Liking yourself means liking other people and expecting them to like you. If we see no good in ourselves, then how can others spot it? Your personal sense of identity is worth discovering and keeping. Knowing who you are will help to create a foundation for confidence. This 'YOU' does not have to be fixed or one-dimensional but it will help if you can look at this person as someone you like as a friend.

The media is currently full of people who lack self-awareness. Switch on any reality TV show and you will find someone wailing about the gap between their assumed self and their behavioural self. These are the people we watch being nasty, unthinking or self-obsessed and yet who then claim to be a 'nice person'. I have heard people say that 'everyone always likes me' even though they have been proved to be hugely unpopular with the other contestants.

All the time you take risks with your identity by being unable to evaluate it you take risks with your confidence because although you might be able to fool part of your mind that you are wonderful when you patently are not, there will always be a large part of your brain that can spot the discrepancy. When we bluff for long periods of time we are rarely able to feel confident inside.

When a gap between our ideal image of ourselves and the reality emerges we feel inferior

Many of us lead our lives trying to live up to our own expectations. An alternative behaviour is to learn to have low expectations about yourself so that you avoid the pain of failing to live up to them. But when we set the bar low we often lack motivation and spend our entire lives under-achieving. By creating low expectations we learn to avoid pain but by having low expectations we suffer the pain of expecting ourselves to be rubbish.

EXERCISE

Write a list of 'You' statements, i.e. comments about the way you look and how you are in terms of personality.

Then settle down and write proof for each of those statements, next to the statement itself. An example would be:

STATEMENT: I AM A PEOPLE PERSON

PROOF: I coach my local football team, dealing with players on an individual basis, using rapport and understanding to communicate with them and motivate them in a way that works.

STATEMENT: I AM THOROUGH

PROOF: When I have a work project to do I manage my time well, researching all aspects of the topic.

STATEMENT: I AM GOOD FUN

PROOF: When I am socialising with friends I find ways to make them laugh and often find myself the centre of attention when I do so.

This might sound like a very logical way to present You to yourself, but by listing and then qualifying the different aspects of You, you'll be able to evaluate and prove theories about yourself that could otherwise be flawed or just your opinion. By evaluating and then proving you'll find your confidence will increase, as long as you weigh your comments in favour of positives rather than all just negatives.

Become intimate with yourself

This is the basic skill of getting to know other people well. Without intimacy we suffer from social isolation, which sounds, and is, sad. The first step in developing intimacy with other people is developing intimacy with yourself.

We spend our growing years learning who we are, and, once we learn who we are, we are able to start learning who other people are and then seeing who we want to share our lives in an intimate way (close, not sexual, although sexual intimacy can be part of the package). The problem comes when we have no sense of 'self'. If you don't know what you're trading it can be hard to make a deal. So your sense of identity is important to your confidence. Without it you may have trouble making bonds with other people and the isolation that occurs from not making those bonds could lead to an even further dip in your self-esteem.

As I have already said quite forcibly, I'm not a fan of 'finding myself', that old hippie hobby that usually meant someone was about to embark on a voyage of self-indulgent navel-gazing that was mainly narcissistic in nature. Once we start to think we're that important we're probably going to be largely friendless anyway, due to the unmanageable size of our ego. However, as I keep emphasising, there's a huge difference between the egocentric hunt for the self and the kind of unformed, unbaked-lump-of-pastry-style sense of self that denies itself opinions, values and anything static or fully formed when it comes to personality. We need some idea of who we are and what we're like.

A personality is unlikely to be made out of granite. I prefer to think of it as a prism, showing many different facets depending on where we are, who we're with and what we're doing: you can be adult at work and childlike at home, prudish in public and a rampant stoat in the bedroom. Your personality is like a collection of skills and abilities that you use to solve problems and analyse the rest of the world. You pick a goal, you set about achieving it, and you sit back and work out whether you got there or not and if not why not. You either pat yourself on the back or beat yourself up and you either work out how to be more successful next time or you decide never to go for a goal like that again.

Integrity or stubbornness?

In the era of 'being myself' we tend to link the ability to know who we are and be true to that self, resisting change or compromise, with integrity. 'I am who I am' is seen as a statement of strength, while flexibility can be viewed with suspicion. And yet few people who claim to 'be themselves' at all times really know or understand themselves. What they've probably done is produce a scripted version and clung to it out of fear.

You could claim to be working class, with an accent, tastes and behaviours to match. So do you lose your integrity if you do well in life and begin to lose your accent and acquire more expensive tastes? Will your ancestors be frowning down on you because you're eating baguette rather than bread and dripping? If you have a temper are you compromising your integrity by suppressing it? If you are irritated by someone you work with should you let that irritation show or feign politeness? Is the masked self a dishonest creature or a survival animal? If we damn politeness and mask emotions then surely the Queen would be top of the list for criticism?

Me me me!

When you're building a sense of You to help create a strengthened self-esteem you also need to look at two sides of your personality: Your Public Identity and Your Private Identity.

Your public identity

- Your general appearance
- Your personal style, i.e. the way you move and gesticulate plus your facial expressions
- Your behaviour
- Your personality

Your private identity

- Your thoughts
- Your feelings
- Your fantasies and dreams

EXERCISE

Take a large sheet of paper. Without pausing to collect your thoughts, write a list of the roles you have in your life, again in the order that they first occur to you. This would be roles like: brother, son, father, footballer, manager, dog-owner, lover, nephew, etc., etc.

Spend some time pondering over your list. The faster you did it and the less conscious the thought involved the more revealing you should find it. Did you miss any of the big roles you play in life? Did any appear lower down the list than you would have expected? How positive or negative was your list? Does the person you've defined sound like someone you'd like to know or be? Does it sound accurate? By looking at your list does it reveal someone with a low or high self-esteem in terms of status or responsibility?

STEP 4: LEARN TO TRUST YOURSELF

The issue of trust

To exist in a pool of workable confidence you will need to develop levels of trust. When we lack trust in anybody and anything, or when we only trust the negatives, 'You can always trust him to do the wrong thing' or 'Trust me to screw that one up', it is impossible to develop any level of confidence. Sadly, the more negative forms of trust can often create feelings, speech and behaviours that sound, feel and smell like trust, although only in some bizarre, back-to-front parallel universe. When you visualise someone saying things like 'I know I could never do that' or 'You can always trust men to be unfaithful' there is potentially some degree of opinionated views put across loudly and aggressively. But this isn't genuine confidence, just anger grown over the top of miserable beliefs that everything that happens to you will be bad.

Not trusting other people is bad but not trusting yourself is a complete and utter deal-breaker in terms of confidence and self-esteem. If you can't trust yourself who can you trust? And if you don't trust yourself who else can trust you? Where is your sense of control if the You is uncontrollable, letting you down like an enemy rather than an ally?

Fear can easily create self-distrust. Phobics are afraid of their own responses to stimulus. They're not only afraid of the spider or the confined space, they're scared what their mind and body will do as a result of seeing or experiencing them. They will even warn other people: 'I will just freak if this lift breaks down.' It's as though they're hiding an alter ego, like Dr Jekyll and Mr Hyde.

The monster inside you

For those of us who get shy, stressed, anxious, or suffer from performance anxiety this monster within is a constant threat in our lives. It's the barely caged beast that threatens to escape and cause havoc at almost any moment. People who suffer from panic attacks are even more at its mercy than others. Their entire bodies are taken over by this creature in an engulfing wave of fear, leaving them helpless and frightened that they're about to die.

For other luckier souls there is just the threat of running away, saying something beyond futile, doing something stupid or going into Tussaud's style close-down, being unable to speak, move or participate in normal conversation.

The answer to this trust-deficiency is to learn to trust both yourself and the people around you. Not foolishly, blindly and unrealistically. (A friend of mine once married a man who she claimed would 'never ever lie to me'. Uh?)

Trust comes in a shade-chart of options. If you apply it wholesale to someone, you're asking to be proved wrong. It is easily possible to work with someone who you dislike intensely but who you could depend on to save your life in an emergency. I know people who would die for their wives but who wouldn't be faithful to them. You may know people you could never trust with a loan but who you would trust to babysit your first-born.

When it comes to You, it is helpful to create some parameters. Write down all the areas where you know you can trust and rely on yourself, making sure none of them are negative. 'I will always hit a deadline,' and 'I will never say yes to something I know I can't do,' are better trust pacts than 'I can trust myself to lock myself out of my car on a regular basis because I'm rubbish with keys.'

Can you be trusted with a pet when someone goes on holiday? Can you trust yourself to be brave in an emergency? Can you trust yourself to be honest with yourself? In a situation that makes you timid can you trust yourself to have a go at seeing it through rather than bottling it?

This last point of self-trust in an important one when it comes to work on your confidence. If you lack social confidence, for instance, it might be unrealistic to make a pact with yourself to 'always be good at small talk' but you could easily change that to 'always make an approach and never stand still, not joining in'. If you're claustrophobic you can self-pact to 'never stop trying to get into a lift'. That way you ensure you're always in the ball-park and never just a scaredy-cat observer in the stands.

Finding your dependable self

- Log all the things you are dependable in, like getting to work on time, having a positive attitude at work, standing up for weaker people, saving money wisely, eating healthily, bathing, cleaning your teeth, having fun on a night out. See your life from an external perspective. This is important because you're pulling the kind of traits you take for granted in yourself out of your subconscious and placing them into the conscious part of your mind.

- Is your list paltry? Why? If it's because you're having trouble working out what your 'trust' traits are, fine. If it's because you have few or none then you need to move to the next step. (If you have loads or just a case of writer's block then skip the next point.)

- If you have few or no dependable points it is vital you create some, rather than acting defeated. This is not a self-loathing exercise, it's a way of boosting your self-trust. Pick four things that you would like to be dependable in and make them your new rules in life. When you have those four mastered, add another four and so on and so on. You will find it unbelievably liberating to be able to trust yourself on some points. It places you in control of yourself, and that sense of control makes you feel more confident because it vanquishes the fear-monster.

Here are some options:

'I will always look smart for work.'

'I will keep my desk tidy.'

'I will praise or compliment someone every day.'

'If I am unhappy with someone I will tell them assertively or I will decide to let it drop.'

'If I go to my boss with a problem I will also take a solution that I have thought out.'

NB: *never use a diet as your basis for self-trust. Why not? Because diets don't work. You should never base your self-trust on a situation where only one tub of cookie dough ice cream stands between you and a whole barrel load of self-loathing.*

IN A NUTSHELL

• Get in touch with your Confidence Core. Use the Core exercise whenever you feel you are under pressure to back down or quit.

• Grow your resilience. Bad things happen and negative things happen. What matters is how you assimilate those things. Do you take them as a warning that you should never have tried in the first place or do you use them as fuel to power you forward?

• Build a sense of you. Admire yourself for what you can do rather than pitying or hating yourself for what you can't.

• Learn to trust yourself but base that trust on what you know you can do and achieve. Never get to the point where the only thing you can trust yourself to do is back out or give up.

6

CREATING CONFIDENCE OVERRIDES

FINDING YOUR OVERRIDE SWITCH

What is your override switch?

Your override switch is what you use to bypass any fears that you have around an event or performance that are not useful to you. It's creating fear control, managing the good fear and suppressing the wasteful stuff.

This chapter is about dealing with those moments when you know your fears are perceptual rather than based on real threat, when your fear response is historical rather than current and you need to find a way to override the voice telling you to avoid, panic or run away from a situation because in your current life it's scuppering your success rather than keeping you alive.

Once you have recognised these moments and understood that your fears are surplus to requirements rather than necessary, you can use any or all of the following techniques to work your way over, under or even through the discomfort they will be causing you.

Choose your own tricks

Rather than any one particular trick, your override techniques can consist of any or all the skills taught in this book, from breathing to mantras to body-language behaviours to thinking yourself up.

There is no one-size-fits-all solution, but there are many that you will be able to choose from. I will provide the steps that will work; you will learn how to assess an individual situation, recognising those points where you need to invoke confident feelings to help you succeed.

Your Key Mantra

What's that? This is a phrase you will be using as a core technique to create confidence. You should repeat this phrase whenever you are under pressure and feeling your confidence drain away. It's not magic but it will work like magic. It will make you take a pause, reflect and re boot.

Before we begin, there is something you should know about mantras and me.

I am a cynic.

As a rule I hate mantras. I hate visualisations. I hate chanting and meditation and breathing exercises and getting in touch with your inner whatever. I recently met someone who was related to someone who ran the holistic village at Glastonbury and I felt so momentarily repelled I couldn't speak. And don't even start me on 'horrorscopes'. I am terrifyingly down to earth.

But I am also open-minded enough to try things. I tried all the mantras and visualisations in this book and I have to say they work for me. Not to the point where I'm sticking flowers in my hair and celebrating the solstice, but easily enough for me to overcome my normal cynicism and pass them on to you without blushing. They work. Trust me.

So what is the mantra? Your Key Mantra is this:

I FEEL CALM, CONFIDENT AND IN CONTROL

Close your eyes and say it to yourself a couple of times. Use a soothing voice. Breathe out gently. Now use a more confident, assured voice. Do it while becoming aware of your Confidence Core. This phrase will steer you back in the direction of confidence when you've started to float, drift and cascade out of control.

Other verbal motivations

These are also supremely useful.

Verbal motivations are those mantras you call out to yourself, either inside your head or out loud, to remind yourself to keep going, even when your nerve is deserting you.

Please write your own, depending on what would sound good or useful to you. Most of them will resonate from childhood or later. They can seem silly on paper but it doesn't matter. Try phrases like:

'Go for it!'

'Seize the day!'

'Just do it!'

'Pull your finger out!'

There are other phrases to use for other occasions but as this book is all about confidence I have chosen the few I use when I can feel myself about to bottle out of a meeting or event. When you're sitting at a meeting with a good idea in your head you need a handy phrase to force yourself to speak up rather than sit in cosy but ultimately wussy silence: **GO – FOR – IT!**

Demotivational mantras

One word of warning: there are certain pseudo-motivational mantras that don't really float my boat. One is the very commonly used:

'What's the worst that can happen?'

Never say this to someone who lacks confidence, especially if the fear is extreme and especially if that person is you.

Why? When we lack confidence our brains play funny tricks on us. Say 'What's the worst that can happen?' to someone in a state of dread about giving a speech and they will immediately visualise their pants falling down, bowels emptying uncontrollably, etc. So never ask yourself this question. Instead, focus on what you gain from being confident.

I never had any problem working on live TV because the fact it was live meant no second takes and no watching it anyway because it's live. I thought this was the greatest fun until I did prerecorded TV. I found this a real challenge because more preparation seemed to go into it and because it could be refilmed people had greater expectation of the standard of your input. Then I realised everyone else was quaking at the thought of working live. So for the first time I developed a few wobblies about doing it. Like most people I started down the 'What if ...?' trail.

Until I took myself by the scruff of the neck, that is. Now I talk to myself very firmly indeed, telling myself I have to do it well. No arguments. And guess what? Messages like that work. Take away the negative alternatives. Make the positives non-negotiable. In terms of my worries it was like a good dog-training class: my mind came to heel.

Another classic demotivational mantra is:

'You can only do your best.'

This is one of the most defeatist phrases ever created and it has become horribly familiar in modern life. It puts a false lid on your achievements (you have no idea what your best is) and when parents say it to a child they're capping all kinds of effort. When you say it to yourself you're allowing yourself an opt-out. It's a lazy phrase, as though you have no real control over your achievements. If you tried your best and failed it means someone else tried better, which in turn means you could have tried better. Any professional athlete will always be looking to top their 'best'.

It's never said with a heroic, steely stare of victory: 'I DID MY BEST AND I WON!!!!' but always with the shrug of defeat: 'I did my best, what more could I do?' Think about it, when did you last hear someone successful say 'I did my best'? Winners know they should be moving onwards and upwards. For them their 'best' is something they are still striving for. 'The best is yet to come' for a winner. For a defeatist, surrendering loser it's happened already so they may as well give up.

WORKING ON YOUR CORE MOTIVATIONS

When you want to change what you do or how you feel there are the classic carrot or stick options, meaning you can use the stick, i.e. tough love and gritted teeth, to force yourself into doing something or you choose to use the carrot, and urge yourself on by reminding yourself of your goals and the benefits of your actions.

When you are taking yourself through fear it is crucial you can tap into your prime motivational factors in order to show yourself on a regular basis that any negative feelings you're experiencing are worth it. The quickest way I can lose a group on a presentation skills course is to instil fear of my criticism and possible disapproval above their own pride in getting the presentation and the performance right. Although I do give a pat on the back when things are working, the person who has sweated and suffered their way through the learning process needs to learn to pat themselves on the back. Why? Well, because I won't be around once he or she gets back to work. If my approval (or fear of my disapproval) is the sole motivator then why bother if I'm not around? People on my workshops need to be reminded they're doing it for themselves, for their career success and for their personal pride in achievement. When we lack those basic motivators we'll get away with any failures we can.

Your motivational values

To discover the basic factors behind the fears prompting your lack of confidence you need to first look at your goals and then compare them to your motivational values. You should compare the two and see if they make a compatible fit. For instance, going back to that talented footballer kicking the ball around the park. His dream is to be a world-class footballer and play for England. His motivational values look something like this:

• Having a laugh
• Acting like a big kid with other like-minded guys
• Drinking and eating a lot
• Irresponsible behaviour
• Enjoying playing football

Now the values that would be attached to his dreams might look like this:

• Unrelenting pressure to achieve
• Ability to be competitive and strategic
• Professional in terms of putting the job over socialising

- Knowing your life will be under constant scrutiny
- Acting as an ambassador for your country and a role model for the kids

Spot the difference? Of course you can, so why didn't our hypothetical footballer see it for himself? Because it's easy to take the title of your dream rather than imagining the reality of it.

So here's some points to help you steer yourself towards your ideal goals.

EXERCISE

Imagine the reality of your long-term dreams and short-term goals. Write them down and stare them in the face.

Now start to log some of your motivational values. What events/behaviours/lifestyle choices will be most likely to make you genuinely happy?

Are you:
- Task-focused, driven to do everything well and get on with the job?
- Impatient with delay and with a desire to do better than others?
- Driven by personal status and power?
- Impatient with people who waffle and take their time?
- Genuinely impressed by the trappings of status like a big car or boat?
- Comfortable working primarily by yourself, in charge of a team that respects you?
- Driven by the need to understand and trust other people?
- Made happiest by your ability to help, coach and nurture other people?
- Comfortable leading from behind rather than visible at the front?
- Motivated by empathy, enjoying chatting and face-to-face communications with colleagues?
- In need of family ties?
- Protective of your privacy?
- Driven by a need to be the centre of attention?
- Happiest going with your gut reactions, acting in a spontaneous and enthusiastic way?

Do you:
- Need the company of your team and the relationships you forge?
- Love listening to people?
- Love fun and humour, with a dread of things getting too serious?

- Suffer a real aversion to commitment or long-term ties?
- Have a horror of negativity and pessimism?
- Love the idea of fame and the trappings of it?
- Dread any jobs that involve planning and detail or a long-term attention span?
- Love talking to people more than listening to them?
- Enjoy change and seek it out?
- Enjoy drama in your life?
- Have a need for calm and quiet?
- Love long-term jobs that you can work on alone?
- Have a need to plan and be thorough?
- Enjoy thinking logically?
- Need to work at your own pace?

When you sit ticking off your motivational qualities make sure you listen to your own voice, by which I mean you need to be honest with yourself. This is not a personality quiz with right or wrong answers; it's a way of finding out what will make you happy, and through that, where to work on your confidence-boosting to help achieve that happiness.

It will allow you a first peek into your motivational traits, many of which might have been buried under piles of rubble in your job. You should avoid presenting your ideal traits as your answers and go for the ones that you know really give you the buzz of achievement.

Don't sit ticking the things you're good at; tick the ones you genuinely enjoy and get a buzz from. Don't worry if you think your ticked motivators make you sound like a nerd or an attention-seeking wannabe, but do worry if you find yourself drawn to the wrong qualities just because you want to look good.

Study your answers. If you have managed to answer honestly, tapping into your genuine values and happiness factors rather than the ones you feel you should have, you will now be getting a more accurate look at your goals and ideal achievements. What this means is that you won't end up scuppering your supposedly 'ideal' goals because they are intrinsically wrong for you. You can now start to place all your energies into building the right sort of confidence for the right sort of goals.

Logging your happiness

Knowing what *really* motivates you is the nub of the matter, then. How strange that the two key things we rarely know in our lives is what we want and what we really like doing.

EXERCISE

Spend four weeks logging your GHR (Genuine Happiness Ratings).

Keep a daily book of things you did at work or at home that gave you a genuine buzz of pleasure or achievement rather than the fake one. Did you ever find yourself thinking 'I know I should be enjoying this' or saying 'I know my life is great and that I have a lot to be thankful for ... but ...'?

Genuine happinesses will be those moments, quiet and unassuming ones as well as the leap-up-and-down-in-the-air ones that really do it for you. Evaluate your own feelings, rather than the way you think you should feel. This is not a competition.

Motivational types

I have been depressed when a new book has been published and felt churlish admitting that. With thousands of would-be authors out there it seems ridiculous not to be delighted. I use the phrase 'Of course I'm happy, of course I know how lucky I am ...' but when it comes to the real buzz of the process it's the moment I see someone I don't know sitting reading the book that I wrote and then laughing out loud at something I wrote that was funny. I get the same surge of enjoyment when I say something funny at a conference and 300 people in the audience laugh. Bliss!

I have no idea why I have this intrinsic need to make people laugh but it's in me like my DNA.

For some people it's big payments but money motivates very few people. Money is a mover rather than a motivator. We get up and go to work because we get paid for that work but it doesn't mean we also like or enjoy our jobs.

Here's a quick breakdown of some core motivational types. Can you identify yourself?

Drivers

Drivers are motivated primarily by task achievement. They like to get stuck in and tend to be competitive and into personal power/ status, meaning they like to lead a team or a task.

Actors

Actors love the limelight and being the centre of attention. They enjoy change and exciting new things. They get bored and distracted very easily. They adore humour and fun and dislike planning and detail.

Empathists

Empathists are relationship-focused, enjoying working in a team or with other people they can communicate with face-to-face. They love listening as well as speaking and value small talk and other rapport-building techniques. Trust is a big issue for them and they like to feel they know and are liked by other people.

Analysts

Analysts are into facts, figures, detail and logic. They are thorough workers who will always see a project through to the end, although they have a dislike of rushing a job to a point that they feel compromises values like research and accuracy. They love projects where they can sit down alone and work uninterrupted.

Does any of this sound familiar? Where possible peg your core motivators to your motivational values. When you're in the process of motivating yourself, base rewards on these values, too.

Motivational factors can take the form of the proverbial carrot or stick. You can threaten, cajole or bully yourself to go beyond your zone of comfort or you can bribe yourself and reward and praise yourself when you do. Most performers I work with do both. I see presenters muttering to themselves angrily, even hitting themselves, when they're struggling to memorise a script or keep fluffing their lines. But they will usually be comfortable celebrating performances or treating themselves afterwards. These most basic techniques promote excellence but non-performers rarely think to use them in the same way. Your confidence is important. Never ignore moments when you have pushed yourself further than normal or exceeded your own expectations. Like a sportsman in training you should make a point of logging your own progress, recognising the milestones and urging yourself towards success.

Modesty is not helpful when you're self-motivating.

CHALLENGING THE KNOCK-BACKS AND DEALING WITH FAILURE

Life is never peachy 24/7. If I tried to tell you otherwise I'd be a liar. One day you're doing well and your confidence levels are sky-high, then next you receive some sort of a knock-back and ...

And what? If you assumed that sentence was going to end dismally with something like '... you're back down in the gutter' you'd be wrong. Once we understand the odd knock-back will occur we can stop overreacting when it does. Only drama queens take a problem as a sign from the gods that a disaster of epic proportions is occurring. What the rest of us do is more like damage limitation to ensure we can resume our journey. By planning ahead and being strategic about any problem that might arise and taking steps to deal with those that do we're not being pessimistic, we're ensuring we have that quality I mentioned earlier in the book as being a vital ingredient of success: resilience.

Identifying the knock-backs

You should always try to identify the knock-backs because it's good to spot the brick before it hits you.

When it comes to increasing your confidence it can be very difficult to separate helpful voices from toxic voices. Sometimes toxic advice comes from people who are trying to be helpful and sometimes help can come from an enemy. Most of the worst voices will be in your own head and a lot have been planted there to aid your survival.

Any good battle plan contains a strategic assessment of the enemy. The one good thing about your own personal enemy in this particular fight is you and you know quite a lot about yourself already. Unfortunately, so does the enemy version of you. It knows exactly what to say to demoralise and demotivate you and it knows all the right ways to make you back down and quit.

Because it's you too (Aren't you loving this?) we should give it another name so you can spot the good you who is working in the right direction from the ASBO, bad-boy you who is urging you to give up.

The name you choose for your negative voice is up to you but

I'm going to suggest you try Barry because Barry is probably the least-dangerous name I can think of. If your real name is Barry you'll need to either pick another name instead or change your own name by deed poll!

Anyway, it's your inner Barry that you're going to learn to indentify and to deal with. It's his face you'll be kicking sand into and I hope you're going to enjoy it. Later we'll be creating an arch-enemy for Barry called your Leader Voice and he or she will be your uber-confident alter ego who will help kick him into touch for ever.

Getting kick-ass with Barry

Of course, the whole concept of your inner Barry sounds pretty stupid and that's exactly what it should do because it *is* stupid. Barry is the voice that tells you to beware and take care well beyond any useful remit. Life's all about pushing back the boundaries and developing. If there were a good or useful Barry it would have been the voice you hear that warns you of genuine danger. This is your survival voice and it's into genuine risk assessment, not the phoney kind. It takes over from your mum and dad when they're not about and it says that crossing the road without looking is a very bad idea and so is kissing someone with herpes.

However, Bad Barry has lost all concept of real risk versus imagined risk and he gets more confused by the minute when you're put in a situation that should lead to nothing more than mild anxiety. Where a glass of hot milk might do much to quell your mini-jitters, Barry will stoke them until you're having panic attacks and acting and feeling as though you're in the middle of a disaster movie. Barry will walk into a room full of nice strangers who mean you no harm and induce feelings of panic and fear that are so real they have you reaching for the incontinence knickers. He'll make you shake like a leaf when all you have to do is stand up and chat with some clients at work and he'll have sweat oozing from every pore when you get up to say a few words at a mate's wedding.

Barry is the ultimate drama queen because for Barry no challenge is too small to merit a severe attack of the jitters. It's all an emergency for Barry, no matter that so far nobody died asking for a pay rise or a refund or haggling the price in a PC emporium. For Barry there is no light and shade, just blinding headlights that he can get caught in like the proverbial rabbit. There's nothing Barry loves more than sparking a full-blown phobia and he does so by feeding you false information about risks, fear and the merits of running away.

Just so you can identify a good, juicy Barry-ism when it pops up in your head here's some of his favourite phrases.

Barry at a social event
- 'Everyone's looking.'
- 'You're shy. It's not your fault.'
- 'You're okay when you know people.'
- 'Nobody likes you.'

Barry during a presentation
- 'Let someone else do that presentation.'
- 'You don't have to if you don't want to.'
- 'What if you dry?'
- 'You're looking like an idiot.'
- 'You're babbling.'
- 'You're blushing and everyone is laughing.'
- 'It is actually possible to die of heart failure during a business presentation. Everyone knows that.'
- 'Hyperventilate. It will make you feel better.'
- 'Why is it everyone else looks so relaxed?'
- 'Have a drink, it will help.'
- 'If you look confident they'll think you know more than you do and start asking difficult questions.'

Barry at a business meeting
- 'Sit at the back of the room then nobody will see you.'
- 'Better to keep your mouth shut than open it and risk saying something stupid.'
- 'That really is a very stupid idea you just had.'
- 'I wish you were as confident as him or her but they're lucky.'
- 'Wait till they see you don't have any idea what you're talking about.'
- 'When you bring up that idea of yours at the next business

meeting make sure you preface it by saying "I know this might sound a bit stupid ..." It will dazzle everyone with your ability.'

Barry's version of life skills

- 'You know you're not good at technical things.'
- 'You were never good at this at school.'
- 'Keep your head down.'
- 'It's because you were an only/eldest/youngest child. It made you shy and quiet.'
- 'You can't do that.'
- 'That compliment was sarcastic.'
- 'You can't think of anything to say.'
- 'It's your parents' fault. They were always critical of you.'
- 'You can't help it, it's because you were bullied at school.'
- 'Don't volunteer.'
- 'You're rubbish at that. You know it.'
- 'DON'T PANIC!'
- 'If you tell everyone you're no good at things they'll take pity and be nicer to you.'
- 'If you tell yourself you have no chance of passing that test/ exam it will act like a lucky charm.'
- 'Saying you're good creates bad karma. Trashing yourself is the only way to go.'
- 'If you tell everyone about your big nose it will mean you got in with the insult before they did, which is good.'
- 'Worrying about a job is better than starting it.'
- 'The middle of the night is the best time to worry.'
- 'Moaning is good; it makes you feel better and gets things done.'
- 'It's other people's fault you lack confidence.'
- 'I knew they'd pick on you first.'
- 'You always get in the longest queue.'
- 'Stick with the devil you know.'
- 'You'll never get a job/new partner at your age.'
- 'You're always unlucky in love.'
- 'Out of the frying pan, into the fire.'
- 'Anything for a quiet life.'
- 'You know you can't remember names.'
- 'Wait until you've lost that weight before you try for promotion.'

- 'They're laughing at you behind your back.'
- 'He or she only asked you out for a bet.'
- 'Pride comes before a fall.'
- 'You can only do your best.'
- 'It wasn't meant to be.'
- 'Just be yourself.'
- 'There's no point trying too hard.'

SELF-HECKLING

You self-heckle when you criticise yourself, either out loud or in your own head. Self-heckling can be verbal but it can also be performed with your body language. This is where you fiddle, wring your hands, flap your hands about or fold your arms, etc., with your gestures letting both you and your audience know that your point is not worth making, or that you have little belief in it.

You might as well stand beside yourself booing and yelling out insults. Self-heckling is self-destructive. It's impossible to look or feel confident while you're doing it.

Battling Barry

There are three key routes to making the most basic changes to your confidence levels and they relate to the triangle of behaviour.

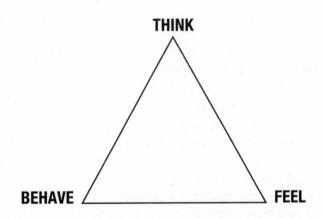

This triangle very simply and neatly illustrates the three dominant factors in your confidence levels and the impact they have on one another and on you.

At the top peak of your triangle are your **thoughts**. All the scripts and dialogues in your head are what really create your self-esteem and your confidence. If your scripts are negative you could become lacking in confidence but if they're positive, optimistic and encouraging you should begin a task or transaction with quite solid feelings of self-esteem.

These thoughts and notions of yourself and your ability will directly influence, affect and impact on the second point of the triangle which stands for your **feelings**. The thought creates the moods and the emotions, which will fluctuate according to the messages being transmitted from the brain. You know the power of the mind over the body. If you don't, try this fascinating experiment in mind over matter.

EXERCISE

In a moment (once you have read all these instructions), close your eyes and focus for a moment on nothing. Empty your mind. Then start to imagine yourself standing outside your own home. See your front door, smell the fresh air (or as fresh as possible if, like me, you live in a city) and feel the weight of your door key in your hand. Now visualise yourself turning your key in the lock and letting yourself into your own home. Smell the air inside and look round at the familiar sights.

Now walk down to your kitchen, taking care to take in all the normal sights, smells and sounds en route.

In the kitchen you can see a chopping board with a large Spanish lemon on top plus a small, serrated knife. Pick up the lemon and feel the weight of it in your hand then lift it to your nose and smell the tangy skin.

Now place it on the chopping board and take the knife and cut it in half. See all the juice ooze out and smell the sour, tangy zest.

Now raise one half to your mouth and take a large bite out of the flesh, feeling the juice run down the back of your throat. Chew, swallow and then open your eyes.

Notice anything? Your mouth will have filled with saliva, even though the lemon-eating was purely in your mind. Once your brain told your body it was sucking the lemon your body responded as though it had a mouthful of sour juice. You probably even grimaced as your took your imaginary bite of the flesh (most people I'm training do, even though they're just sitting still with their eyes closed).

This easy exercise illustrates the way your brain commands your body's responses and the experience is useful if you harness it in the way we will do in this chapter.

But before we get on to the use of this link we need to look at the last point of your triangle. This is the point that refers to your **behaviour,** and this point is in turn affected and influenced by the previous point, your feelings.

The way you feel will always have a direct impact on the way you behave. If you feel nervous and lacking in confidence, the chances are your performance during an act or transaction will be less effective than normal. Once the brain starts to question, over-assess and over-analyse the behaviour it's very hard to sustain a good performance, and that includes every performance from sex to stage-work to simple transactions like a business meeting or first date. With your mind checking and rechecking everything you do say or even wear, plus tending to evaluate them negatively, your odds of doing those things well will dramatically decrease.

So let's say you have been called on to introduce yourself at a meeting or training course. Your brain produces a 'Barry' message like: 'Oh my god. I knew I'd get picked out first. Everyone's staring. I'm never good in these situations. I know I'm going to look like a numpty.' That's the first point of your triangle taken care of.

Now let's look at the second point, your feelings. With all the compliance of a small child being led by the hand, your feelings are likely to match step with your thoughts, meaning you start to feel nervous and anxious and your confidence levels begin to dip.

Which takes us to the third point of your triangle, your behaviour. With your palms getting damp and your breathing rate increasing your body begins to respond to mental and emotional stimulus that suggests it needs to be activating the fight/flight response. In simple terms it begins planning to either stand and get stuck in or to rush off screaming like a girl. On a bad day it gets confused and plans to do both, meaning your 'run away' and your 'stay and fight' responses are both activated at once which brings about a hilarious blend of racing pulse, muscle tension, wobbly legs and shaking hands all at the same time. This can have you acting like a cross between Corporal Jones and Private

Fraser from *Dad's Army*, yelling out 'Don't panic! Don't panic!' or 'We're doomed!' in turns as the adrenalin rises or subsides.

What's happening?

This state of apparent sublime irrationality is brought to you thanks to your survival responses that have activated your fight/flight mechanisms that we discussed in the section on stress.

Now all this booting up of your body would be great if the initial stimulus was worth it. If you were being chased by a rabid grizzly or a randy alpha silverback you would need all that extra power, energy and clarity of thought. It would enable you to out-run or out-fight your opponent in a way that would have been unimaginable to you in an ordinary situation. It's the fear of pain or even death that triggers your inner super-hero, making you capable of exceptional feats.

However ...

What happens when it's not a grizzly? What happens when it's just Barry? What if your fight/flight response has been triggered by nothing more than a meeting with the boss or a small speech you need to make at a best mate's wedding?

This is where it all starts to go painfully and possibly hilariously wrong. The 'Massive Alert' button on your brain has been activated for all the wrong reasons but once the 'Panic' system has started rolling all the yelling and pleading in the world won't deactivate it. It's like a smoke alarm in your home: great when there's a proper fire but annoying when it goes off because you over-cooked the toast, leaving you standing underneath it waving a tea-towel in circles as you try in vain to get it to stop.

Like a smoke alarm that can't detect the difference between a kitchen fire and someone having a crafty drag of a Marlboro Light, your non-confident brain ceases to differentiate between a real emergency prompted by a hurtling juggernaut and a bit of discomfort caused by a job interview and spews out the same response.

This means you end up acting like a complete drama queen for no benefit whatsoever, and the more you or any well-meaning friends do the tea-towel-waving thing by telling you to 'calm down' the more your panic levels rise. Placing the words 'Don't' and 'Panic' together guarantees pandemonium, as Douglas Adams realised when he placed those two heart-stopping words on the cover of the 'Hitchhiker's Guide to the Galaxy' in his book of the same name.

Replacing Barry

Once you have learnt to identify your Barry voice, you need to challenge it while reprogramming yourself. To reprogramme you should create definitive positive inner dialogues which will saturate your subconscious making them effective, even if your conscious brain refuses to believe them. These mantras should be as upbeat as your other messages are negative. Examples would include:

- 'I enjoy meeting new people.'
- 'I'm an extrovert.'
- 'I know that queue will be a short one.'
- 'I'm a lucky person.'
- 'I can always overcome adversity.'
- 'I have some great ideas.'
- 'I know I can eat healthily.'
- 'I don't smoke.' (Rather than 'I'm trying to stop smoking'.)

Your Leader Voice

This is fabulous.

We've spoken about mantras and we've identified your negative inner voice, AKA Barry. To motivate yourself through knockbacks you need to adopt or appoint the voice you *do* want to listen to when the chips are down. All those chaotic, negative, dripping ideas of doom and disaster in your head need to be rounded up and shown the door.

The voice you'll be listening to in future will be your Leader Voice, the one responsible for making you do things you didn't think possible. The voice that will make you feel and behave in a way that is confident and assured.

How to create your Leader Voice

- Think back. Find a voice from your past or present that can get you to do things. This could be a schoolteacher, strict parent, aunt, boss, older sibling, etc.

- The voice you choose should be strong and authoritative. It should be one that could give orders that you would naturally obey.
- Once you have chosen your voice, hear it in your own ears. How did it sound? How did it bark out orders?
- Use this voice as the voice that will drive you forward in the face of setbacks, when you feel your courage is deserting you and you're thinking of backing out or quitting. It will be your bravery voice from now on. Focus on listening to it and the messages it tells you and allow it to override your negative inner dialogues.

TAKING CONTROL OF YOUR LIFE: THE POWER OF CHOICE

A sense of control is wonderful. Knowing that what happens to you is up to you will give you a feeling of command over your own destiny that creates a rush to the head every bit as good as a double espresso downed in one.

The problem is it's also frightening. Many of us spend our entire life blaming others for our own inadequacies and failures and that can feel good too. Not great exactly, not even a strong latte-size boost, but the kind of warm, safe but miserable glow you get when you take to your bed with a warm hot water bottle when you suffer a mild cold in the middle of a chilly, wet winter.

Change the script

Instead of 'I've *got* to get up, get ready for work, get to work on time, wash up after supper ...' swap the words 'got to' to 'I *choose* to'. This will sound strange and cumbersome for a while but it will teach you that everything we do in our lives has been our own choice. Sometimes that choice has been made because of lack of credible options, as in 'I chose to give that guy my wallet because he held a knife to my ribs' but even in that scenario the mugger was presenting you with options. You selected the 'give him my wallet' option because it seemed the best way to avoid getting stabbed, but that was still your choice.

This thinking is not about semantics. Choice and control recognition is one of the most powerful ways of boosting your confidence and liberating your ability to be successful. It's about being your own master rather than someone else's victim. It means you stop moaning and start planning and creating strategies. It's knowing when and how to thank and reward yourself rather than scheming to wreak revenge on other people. Control is also a vital ingredient in the skill of managing your own stress. Stress tends to occur in situations where we feel things, events and changes are happening while someone else is in the driver's seat. It was no surprise to me to learn that people who own their own businesses tend to suffer lower levels of stress than those who work in middle management who are therefore less likely to be able to make the big decisions.

Recognise your daily decisions

How many things do you choose to do every day? Make yourself identify and mentally log or acknowledge exactly how much you are the boss of your own day. Nothing should be too small to spot. What drink did you order in the coffee house? Did you email that client or phone them? Did you walk, bus or drive to work? What clothes did you choose to wear? You make hundreds of decisions every day yet we rarely recognise any but the big ones or the new ones. You might see your boss as powerful and confident because he or she strides through their day making one important call after another but so do you, you just don't realise it. And if you think some of those decisions are unimportant think how you decided to cross that busy main road. The wrong call and you could have been road kill!

Start to take genuine control over those decisions

When you start to observe the decisions you make daily you begin to understand that you have options that previously you had failed to recognise. Did you choose to accept that extra work that your manager dumped on you? Did they force you into doing it or did they ask? Did you agree? How did you agree? Did you tut? Smile? Pull a face but accept it? Puff loudly to let them know you were annoyed? Go off and moan to a colleague? Did you look pleased and say 'no problem'? Learning to say 'no' in an assertive way is a fundamental skill for confident people.

Stop being sympathy addicted

By which I mean stop being a victim. Sympathy addicts thrive on the attention they get from others when something goes wrong in their lives. They start by enjoying those hugs that their mums gave them when they fell over in the playground but they end up falling over deliberately as adults, just to get the same 'hit'. The problem with growing up is that people care far less about us when it comes to the sympathy stakes. When you get much older in life almost no one really cares in a sympathetic way because they're all struggling with their own ageing processes, bereavements and varicose veins. I believe nature created age-related hearing loss so we didn't have to sit listening to everyone else's problems. Just watch those mouths moving and nod now and again while you fantasise about sex with Robbie Williams. Of course there are people who care and people who will sympathise but it's not like when a small child falls over and an entire aisle of a supermarket feels obliged to rush to its help and offer comfort. Nobody likes to see a child cry but a grown adult whingeing is another matter entirely. It is a fact of life generally acknowledged that adult–adult sympathy is used as a tool to make people shut up, which is why we have the rise of the therapist business and pay people for what we can't get for free.

Do your own therapy

Unless you have acquired your own obsessively mad stalker I'm guessing that no one else in your life sees you as being as important as you do. You count more to yourself than you do to any other person. (If you are the proud owner of a small baby I can see you would rate yourself as a dominant and vital factor in its survival but believe me, kids tend to turn egocentric thinking into an art form!) So bite the bullet and accept the fact that you rate high only on your own self-obsessed chart in life. Which is good, because it means you don't really need other people, apart from the usual (good sex, good haircuts, back-scratching, etc.). When it comes to morale boosting, motivating and confidence coaching the fabulous news is that you can do it yourself. And the even more fabulous news is that by doing it yourself you seal yourself into a self-contained transparent bubble of strongly self-reliant independence. Which means your confidence levels will end up looking like Angelina Jolie dressed as Lara Croft or Russell Crowe in *Gladiator* (except at the end when he dies).

Wear an invisible thought hat

To take control of your thinking you need to imagine yourself in possession of a large, woolly-but-strangely-also-lead-lined pull-on hat that reaches well below your ears. When you hit any type of problem during your day wait until you feel your normal pattern of needy, dependent thinking surging up like a giant wave and then imagine yourself pulling your big hat on over your head to trap all your thinking inside it. Ask yourself what it is you need to know. Use your own brain as your confidence and motivational coach. Instead of wandering around looking for reassurance and approval, do it yourself. Does my bum look big in this? Look in the mirror. Am I good enough to get that job? Work it out for yourself. Should I get down the gym? What do you think? No part of your brain can breach the hat's parameters, not even the brain-bits that come wearing leather bomber jackets and riding motor bikes like Steve McQueen in *The Great Escape*. Steve McQueen was attempting to ride off to freedom but your brain is trying to creep off to get help. Don't let it – work it out for yourself.

What about an expert?

Okay, so there will be times when the help you need is technical or professional. For those moments you take an educated look from inside your own woolly hat to discover who you need to guide or help you. What you don't do is rush out screaming like a small child, claiming to be pathetic and wet and in need of life support. People you bring into your team of one need to be well chosen for the right reasons, just as a leading entrepreneur might bring in a good legal expert when there's a contract to draw up. That entrepreneur doesn't gasp in awe or feel life has beaten them; they just pick the right person for the job and stay in overall control. And one key tip: watch the expert as they work. Few experts are that good, it's just that we leave most of them alone to do what they do and come back to gasp in awe at the result of all the magic. Stand and watch your plumber, IT expert, decorator or nail technician. See how much of what they do you could do yourself and see how few times you feel you deserve to throw your hands up in defeat and just stand goggle-eyed in awe.

IN A NUTSHELL

- When you're faced with a situation where you lack confidence, address your fears to gauge how genuine they are.

- Where you see that your lack of confidence is out of kilter with the actual task or goal, you will need to evaluate that goal to avoid fear reactions that include not trying or giving up.

- Know your Core motivational values.

- Ask yourself if the goals you have chosen are compatible with your Core motivational values. If not, your fear response could be genuine as you'll be pursuing goals that will make you unhappy.

- Once you have targeted your motivational values you can see whether your fears are based on goal-fear or process-fear. If it's fear of the process of pursuing those goals that's the problem, you can proceed to the next steps of overcoming those fears by boosting your inner confidence.

- Get in touch with 'Barry', i.e. your inner voice that is overprotective and negative.

- Replace him with some Positive Inner Dialogues.

- Create your Leader Voice to coach you through moments when you feel you lack confidence.

- Learn how to motivate yourself through or over any dips.

7

ACTING CONFIDENT

There are two types of performed confidence, the type that sits on top of ability and inner resolve and the type that is a mask for insecurity and a lack of inner self-belief.

*CON*FIDENCE

The first three letters of the word confidence say it all. For many people the art of looking calm and brave in the face of daily pressures is little more than a con trick, a kind of behavioural smoke and mirrors that they are able to perform, and which suggests to the rest of us that they are more talented, accomplished and even attractive than the rest of us.

Sound enviable? Perhaps. Usually it looks to the naked eye as though these people have found a way of making themselves immune to self-doubt and oblivious to fear, but I do need to insert a huge, finger-wagging warning at this point, while you need to stare a couple of naked facts in the face:

1. Yes, it's good to be able to portray a confident face to the world, even at times when you are feeling less confident inside. Animals do this and humans strive to do it all the time ...

2. But it's *not* good to trade solely on a portrayal of confidence. Genuine confidence sits on top of ability, skill or experience, a bit like positive thinking. Muhammad Ali was one of the greatest exponents of positive thinking, with his famous

quote 'I am the greatest' being an example. But contrary to popular belief and the implication of some motivational coaches, he did not advocate the art of pretending to be really great when you know you're really rubbish. He did not suggest getting into a boxing ring to fight a heavyweight opponent armed only with a couple of positive affirmations. Muhammad Ali was a superb athlete who worked hard at his craft. Your confidence should be seen as a portal to allow your ability to shine, not a gleaming coat of paint covering rust on a knackered old car.

So that's genuine confidence dealt with. Now we need to go back to the other sort, the performed or acted confidence. The con. The bluff. The kind you see every day in other people but probably assume is the real deal.

When you find yourself envying people who appear to have total confidence

In psychological or even evolutionary terms total or overconfidence shouldn't exist (I explained why in Chapter 2: The Confident Ape).

Do you believe in *total* confidence? That it really exists? Do you think that there are some people out there who are able to make decisions, voice their opinions, run businesses and perform onstage without secretly keeping their fingers crossed behind their back? If so, do you find yourself gazing in awe and wonder, thinking their state of supreme calm under the kind of pressure that might leave you quaking and jibbering is like a private members' club that you feel you'll never be able to join? That they were somehow touched with the lucky stick while you are not? That they inherited the confidence gene just as they inherited the colour of their eyes and shape of their nose? People like this are projecting confidence but not always feeling it. Whereas genuine arrogance can be a killer in animal terms, your ability to project more confidence than you're feeling on specific occasions can be something of a life-saver.

How acting more confident than you feel *can* have benefits

The good news about confidence-trick confidence is that you can learn to do it too; because of course there will be times when you're feeling nervous but wanting to imply supreme confidence to those around you. You could be giving a vital business presentation to a client, knowing your product is good, but desperate to sell it because your job is on the line if your sales dip. You want to project an air of studied calm and cool, even though you're close to clutching the client around the ankles and begging them to buy. This is arguably fake or acted confidence, although the general abilities it is being stapled on to are genuine. You know your product is good and you know you have a valid argument for them buying it. You just don't want your anxieties about sales targets to scupper your delivery. Oscar Wilde wrote that happiness and pleasure are not the same thing. Neither are looking confident and feeling it. Ideally you'll learn how to do both, which is like hitting the jackpot in confidence terms. When all the good factors for confidence collide it's a bit like having a confidence orgasm, except while you always notice a sexual orgasm, a confidence orgasm can slip by unannounced if you're not careful, which is why it's important you get that shudder of pleasure that makes you want to do it again.

How and when to turn con-trick confidence to your benefit

The *really* good news about con-trick confidence is that it comes with added benefits. Acting confident tends to create the real thing: by acting, sounding and looking confident you don't just fool those other people around you; you begin to fool yourself as well. It's conning your subconscious, and it's a sublimely fabulous trick of body-over-mind rather than mind-over-body. Not so much 'I think therefore I am' as 'I am therefore I think'.

When you think small you tend to play small. All your worries and insecurities hang about your body like marsh gas and you believe your own self-created publicity. By looking and acting confident though, you can fool your mind and your emotions in a positive way, which is why part of this book is dedicated to body language and image. Changing your physical state can have a powerful effect on your emotional state.

Limited effectiveness

But you do need to decide the extent of its effectiveness. Make constant checks on yourself: am I being confident for no reason?

Would some level of fear be more appropriate? Or are my fears hampering my ability? For instance, how much does sitting and talking like a good driver make you a good driver? Can it help or does it just create dangerous levels of fake bravado?

Here's how con-trick confidence could improve your driving skills:

- First – and very importantly – you would need to separate your emotions and feelings from your basic skills. Are you a competent driver? If not, are your problems caused by a lack of knowledge, training or experience or by a lack of confidence?
- If you have been trained well and don't lack knowledge or experience, applying a more positive, confident demeanour would be a very powerful way of unlocking that potential.
- If you're quite good but lack some knowledge it would help a lot, used hand in hand with added training.
- If you've barely learnt how to adjust your seat and switch the engine on, it would be useful in unlocking the kind of confidence you need to enable yourself to learn and be taught BUT ...
- It would be very dangerous if you put confidence in place of training, like the teenage joy-rider who steals a car to race at speed despite never having driving lessons. This kind of self-belief that tells him he is capable of feats even Formula One racing drivers would know to be crazy is delusional rather than helpful.

So always consider the worth of your levels of confidence.

How not to use con-trick confidence

There is one potential downside to this ability to project confidence then, and we've all seen it in action on a regular basis. Con-artists get it wrong when they:

- Are all style and no substance, meaning they are the wrong people for the job they are doing. You can fool some of the people some of the time but not all of the people ... (you know the rest). In other words it can all end in tears.
- Imagine you're boarding a plane and about to meet the pilot. How would you prefer him or her to be, confident or skilled?

'Both!' I hear you cry. But 'skilled' would have to come first. It would be no good your pilot turning up looking like Tom Cruise in *Top Gun* if he has no idea how the controls work. If the pilot knows how to fly the plane at least you'd get off the ground but if they know how to fly the plane and have high levels of the kind of confidence that allows them to do so calmly and professionally you'd expect to complete your trip in one happy piece.

CHANGING YOUR MESSAGE: HOW TO PROJECT YOURSELF AS THE PERSON YOU REALLY WANT TO BE

Acting confident is all about looking and behaving in a way that will sell your confidence to You as well as to other people. When you look confident people behave differently to you, meaning they will seem to affirm what you display as your own opinion of yourself. When you have shyness or low self-esteem hanging about you like a shroud it's no wonder people give you a wide berth or tend to ignore you. You're telling them you are of low value, or that you are in a state of fear or self-loathing. Now, it would be true to say they should then feel and behave in a way that is protective of you and sympathetic towards you but my question is:

WHY THE HELL SHOULD THEY?

When you were a small child your signals of defencelessness and vulnerability were part of your survival system in order to make bigger, stronger adults want to protect you and nurture you. But now you are an adult (or at least old enough to read this book). Why would you think other adults would want to swaddle you? What gives us the right to expect other people to act as our own personal therapists, taking responsibility for our own shortcomings and helping us to deal with our own rubbish insecurities? This is not their job; it is our own. So stop looking like a walking cry for help.

ASSERTIVE BEHAVIOUR: ITS PLACE IN YOUR QUEST FOR CONFIDENCE

Assertive problem: your instinctive, animal responses

It's important to understand that assertive behaviour isn't natural. Your instinct for survival is strongly linked to your fight/flight responses, with the fight option being aggressive and the flight being passive. Assertive behaviour is strategic, meaning you often have to suppress your natural urges to achieve it. If someone pushes in front of you in the canteen queue you'll probably want to push back or bop them on the head with your tray. Any other animal would go on the attack or rush off, feeling threatened. But as a human animal you will have been taught to think longer term. Why get into a jostling match when the boss might be watching, meaning you lose out on that promotion? What if the pusher-in is armed with a steak knife and turns nasty? What if you hit them and get done for GBH? What if you get into a row and discover this is the new CEO?

Why do I need to be assertive?

Assertive behaviour is the epitome of confidence. It's a skill that has to be learnt, rather than one that occurs naturally but it should be seen as an important part of your quest for confidence. Assertion is easy to learn but not so easy to apply to your daily transactions, especially if you have a tendency to use passive responses.

The good news about passive behaviour is that we are usually aware that we are using it, and we normally have a desire to change and be less of a doormat. When we are by nature more aggressive though, the need for change might be less obvious. Why change what you're doing when it gets results?

Whether you are currently using passive or aggressive behaviours, assertion should be the tool in your tool kit that you pull out the most for long-term, strategic goal achievement.

What is assertiveness?

The understanding of the word 'Assertive' tends to be perceptual. I have heard people describe TV characters like Gordon Ramsay and Lord Alan Sugar as assertive and I have seen people say that they are aggressive. It is vital you understand the difference between aggressive and assertive behaviours.

Assertive behaviour is standing up for your own rights, saying 'no' when necessary and being honest with people. But all those three descriptions could also be applied to an aggressive person. There is one important factor that makes assertion very different from aggression and that is that you allow others their rights, too. You listen, you are calm, you are flexible and you are adult. In fact I prefer to describe it as levelling behaviour, meaning both people in a transaction are allowed their rights and their views. It means saying what you want to happen but being open to negotiation.

Let's define passivity, aggression and assertiveness.

I am passive if:

- I apologise all the time, even when I have done nothing wrong
- I apologise if someone else bangs into me
- I use the phrase 'no problem' all the time
- I often work late or accept too much work because I struggle saying no to people
- I tend to sit at the back in meetings
- I rarely put my point of view across
- I tend to agree with others
- I use the phrase 'anything for a quiet life' a lot
- And say 'I don't mind' when I am asked where I would like to go or what I would like to do
- I often lie to get out of doing things I don't want to do, like parties or social events
- I tend to smile a lot, even when I'm unhappy
- I tend to use status-lowering body language, like touching my neck, head or hair, fiddling or using self-comfort gestures
- I don't use a lot of eye contact, especially with people I don't know well
- I prefer to go with the flow than to cause ructions
- I use hints to get my message across

I am aggressive when:

- I work to get my own way, regardless of others
- I relish the 'win' of a transaction

- I am comfortable getting into conflict
- I use sarcasm
- I use humour to attack someone
- I use a lot of eye contact, especially when I am speaking
- I talk over other people
- I disagree by dismissing or trashing their points
- I am opinionated
- I talk loudly
- I put my wants ahead of others'
- I tell people what to do and give orders instead of asking or negotiating

I am being assertive when:
- I stand up for my own rights but am aware of the rights of others
- I am flexible
- I am honest but tactful
- I make my point clearly
- I listen as well as speak
- I think how a situation feels and looks to the other person
- I am calm
- I am logical
- I suppress my negative emotions
- I use clear, concise speech
- I act confident
- I look at the evidence rather than speculating
- I negotiate where possible

The see-saw of behaviour: raising, lowering and levelling behaviours

Often you'll be using assertion during a very quick transaction, meaning you'll need to make your behavioural call at short notice. To enable you to do this it's a good idea to pre-create a visualisation, seeing your responses as a see-saw before deciding which point of that see-saw you're going to try to achieve.

RAISING: When you do what the other person wants rather than what you want you use passive behaviour, raising them by agreeing to their needs, but lowering yourself in the process.

LOWERING: When you insist on getting your own way regardless of the other person you are using aggressive behaviour, meaning you raise yourself by lowering the other person.

LEVELLING: Assertion means you stand up for yourself in a non-aggressive way, which means you are in control, meaning your confidence in yourself and in other people will grow. See your assertive skills as creating a level, even-handed transaction.

STRATEGIC BEHAVIOUR AND WHY YOU SHOULD USE IT

When you lack confidence, as when you are overconfident or arrogant, it is easy to use behaviours that are seductive in the short term, but which might easily be counter-productive overall. In passive terms this means saying yes to more work even though you are already too busy to handle the work you have piled on to your desk, or agreeing to go out to a social event that you have neither the time nor the inclination to attend.

When we do this we are trying to be instantly pleasing. By agreeing and avoiding potential conflict we feel we have taken the easiest option. But in reality that pile of work doesn't go away and neither does the conflict. When you keep accepting work that you know you can't do you go for short-term pleasing over long-term satisfaction and trust. You end up letting other people down because it's just not feasible to get all those priorities sorted.

When we allow people to dump on us they rarely stop dumping, in fact the dumping will often increase, meaning eventually we will get into a conflict with the person who is giving us more work.

The other person we get into conflict with is ourselves. Have you ever hated yourself or been angry with yourself because you just couldn't say 'no' to something or someone? You probably tell yourself that you had no option, that they 'forced' you, but think back and reflect honestly how true that thought is.

The other obvious option is to become aggressive. Fighting your corner is a very appealing option when it makes you feel like an instant winner. When we act dominant or angry we often manage to get other people to do what we want. But the problem is we're using short-term thinking. I have spoken to many managers who feel that ruling by dominance is the only option but what they create is a team of donkeys who will only do what they're told. This means the aggressive manager is unable to delegate for fear things won't be done his or her way. Which in turn leads to over work, which in turn can lead to stress, which in turn causes paranoia and snappy, aggressive behaviour ...

So what you need are some strategies

Strategic behaviour means thinking beyond the current problem or situation and planning your communications and behaviour around long-term and possibly professional goals. It's pulling your objective out first in any situation and then seeing what strategy you will need to achieve that objective. It's realising that saying 'yes' to everything will only lead to other people thinking that you are a willing doormat. It's understanding that every time you say 'anything for a quiet life' you are probably giving other people the green light to continue doing what they were doing that lowered your status or eroded your rights.

I recently worked with a man who felt he had to argue every point I made. By the third point the rest of the audience were willing him to shut up. I was fantasising about spilling my tea down him by the first point (it's not that I mind questions or disagreements, it was the way he was arguing with me that got right up my nose!). My head was flooded with every verbal put-down in the book but, while my aggression tanks were happily filling up and my face was going red I forced myself to focus on what needed to be my professional objectives, which were to give a good talk that the rest of the audience would find entertaining and useful.

This thought led to some very different behaviours from me than the ones I was fantasising about. I was charming (so charming it hurt!) even though I kept control of the dialogue. I offered to answer some of his questions during the break and I retained the right to close him down if he became too disruptive (I noticed him being critical of other delegates too).

Pluck your overall objective out first, then plan your strategy for achieving it

This assertive strategy was only possible because I pulled out my objectives first. If you don't you could easily find yourself using lowering behaviour – acting aggressively to lower the other person just to score points – or raising behaviour, acting too passive or submissive yourself just to avoid conflict or disagreement.

Passive-Aggressive

Probably the worst option in behavioural terms is passive-aggressive. This is where you act in doormat mode for a period of time (possible a very long period of time), festering over put-downs or the inconsiderate behaviour of others, becoming filled with resentment and possible self-loathing and building up a head of steam. Every time you berate yourself for backing down or not standing up for yourself or your rights your overall confidence takes a dip. You might blame other people for taking you for granted but this victim thinking does nothing to bolster your self-esteem. Deep down you know it was you who crumbled under pressure so the blame will be like a little boomerang that keeps falling back into your own lap.

Like a pressure cooker, something's got to give and what happens is you perform the biggest about-face since Robbie sang a duet with Gary Barlow. Suddenly all the resentment blows in either a sarcastic remark, a bitchy little email, a snippy, hurtful comment, a comprehensive telling-off or an all-out conflict. Your victim will not have seen it coming because you have never complained before and are possibly only doing so now when it's too late for them to change their behaviour because as yet the Time Machine still remains a fictional device.

When we behave like this we suggest there has been something pleasurable about our suffering, as though we were saving it up to prove we were the better person all along. Last summer I watched the England football team play exceptionally badly in a World Cup match. I started the game in a state of hope and excitement but after the first 15 minutes it was obvious we were staring into the bowels of mediocre play. The thing I found phenomenal once I had realised it, though, was that after the second half had started

I no longer wanted them to score; in fact part of me was hoping they wouldn't. Why? Because by then I was marinating in self-pity and depression. We were an unlucky team as always and I was an unlucky fan. It was horrible but it felt familiar and it felt right. I almost couldn't have coped if they had suddenly booted one in the net. The emotional turn-around required would have been too great.

This experience probably goes some way to explain why we sit on our resentments for much longer than we know we should. I believe that in many ways the feeling of martyrdom has led to a feeling that we are so much the better person and that the longer we allow the negative behaviour towards us to continue the more ammunition we will be storing away so that when we finally blow it's an atomic-sized explosion rather than a small firecracker that might go unnoticed.

But of course there is no real excuse for passive-aggressive displays. By presenting ourselves as compliant and then suddenly attacking from nowhere we gain little in the way of a genuine win. Instead of pity or guilt we get the comment 'You should have said something earlier', which of course is right. 'I didn't like to!' will get the retort 'Then why bring it up now?' Always ask yourself if it's too late to do anything more than give a telling off for past misdemeanours. If it is then what is your point and where's the gain? Did you really wait that long just to hear a bewildered or grudging apology? Are you happy that your relationship with that other person will never be based on trust, just on a half-baked feeling from them that they're not sure whether you mind doing things for them or not? Or that you lie when you do have a problem?

Better to be firm with a light touch in the earliest stages of the problem than to save it all up and let rip later on.

And one more thing: when we adopt the passive-aggressive stance we often spend the passive part of the experience going round whining and complaining to other people in a bid to gain sympathy. The likelihood that those people will at some stage let drop to the person you have the problem with is enormous. Finding out that you have been badmouthed by someone else leads to friction and conflict. Either say it straight to the person causing you grief or keep it to yourself. Letting them know you've been complaining to everyone but them is an admission of passive-aggressive tendencies.

STRATEGIC ASSERTIVENESS

Up until recently it was thought that only human animals had the capacity for strategic behaviour. Then an ape in a zoo in Europe proved us wrong by calmly lining up rocks during the morning to throw at the public during the afternoon visiting hours, meaning he was planning for his anger and rage at a moment when he was calm and relaxed.

Your assertive behaviour should be primarily strategic, focused on your goals rather than responding to your knee-jerk needs. Instead of blasting out a response you will take a moment, pulling your professional or long-term goal out of the hat before planning your behaviour around working to achieve it.

Your three assertive skills

To be assertive you need to focus on each of these areas:

- **Your thinking**
- **Your words and voice**
- **Your assertive body language**

Too many people put effort into their script but forget to endorse their verbal message with the non-verbal one. This would be when you tell someone you can't do something while your fiddling gestures imply that you could back down if you were pushed harder.

Be congruent to be confident

Congruent signals are important for assertiveness. What do I mean by congruent? Congruence occurs when your words, tone and body language must all send out the same message, showing you mean what you say.

THE ASSERTIVE BLUEPRINT

This blueprint is going to be one of the core steps in your overall confidence-boosting, meaning it will return to haunt you throughout the book. It is one of the most important and fundamental stages in creating your ideal confidence levels in any situation.

Step 1: Identify and solve

• Identify your problem.
• Look at your three possible solutions. You can:

A. Sort it. Meaning you look to solve the problem. Once you make this decision you can flip to Step 2, your strategy planner.

B. Let it drop. This means recognising that you either *can* do nothing about your problem or that you *decide* to do nothing, meaning you allow it to drop away. If you make this choice you stop using all of your energies dithering or getting emotional about the stimulus and start focusing all your effort on changing your response to that stimulus. This is a very adult option. Choosing to do nothing is a million miles away from being too afraid to do anything though. Make sure which one your choice is.

C. Moan. Whingeing, moaning, whatever. What you're doing by just bellyaching about your problem is neither healing it nor allowing it to get better by itself. You're picking at it, making it like a scab that keeps bleeding. Ever ask yourself why you keep re-experiencing the pain of the problem? Because that's exactly what you're doing, no matter how many times you're telling yourself that you're 'getting it off your chest'.

Step 2: Evaluate the problem

• Take a moment.
• Evaluate what happened using the logical part of your brain. Avoid over-dramatising, exaggerating or translating.

Example: Your hairdresser has double-booked your appointment.
Over-dramatising: 'This is always happening to me! Why can't

anything ever be easy? I can't cope unless I get my hair done today!'

Exaggerating: 'He had the whole year to let me know this had happened. I had to cancel an important job to be here.'

Translating: 'I know why he did this. He doesn't want my custom any more. I'm too old for his salon.'

- Stick to the facts as they would sound in court: 'He booked another client in at the same time as me and now he's saying he can't do my hair today.'
- Identify your goal(s): 'I feel I should get a discount for the next appointment.'
- Identify your own feelings: 'I feel undervalued and demeaned.'
- Decide whether those feelings will help or hinder your transaction: 'If I get angry I could end up finding it hard to explain myself.'
- Examine their side of things. What is their view of 'right' in this transaction? 'I completely missed this other booking. I want to keep both customers happy but we're a member of staff short. I chose to do this customer first because I know the other one is a nicer person and less likely to cause a big fuss.'
- Plan your strategy based on your goals.
- Try it on yourself. 'How would that sound if someone said it to me?'
- Do it (if it sounds okay).
- Monitor the effect of your words.
- If they don't seem to be getting the right result, change your strategy.

Step 3: Boost your confidence

- Sell your idea, thought or suggestion to *You* first. Too many people try to negotiate or set their opinion or goals out without having really considered them. When you do this it has a very half-baked effect on your body language, meaning they will be able to spot a mile off that you're winging it.
- Sell *You* to you. Although assertive behaviour will create confidence, it also helps if you can embed it on a degree of existing self-esteem. What are your rights as a human being? Why do you

know you're the right person to be making this point? Again, getting into what you hope will be an assertive dialogue will be risky if you dive in without any degree of confidence in yourself at all.

- Self-coach. Hear all those negative intrapersonal messages, telling you it will be a disaster, that they'll start reading you the riot act, that it will be less hassle to shut up and put up? Well, when it comes to shutting up it's those messages you need to gag. Feed yourself some positive affirmations instead, like 'I know I can do this', 'Life's too short to be a namby'.
- Get some mood music buzzing in your head. Pick your best bravery tune or song and play it on a loop in your head to pump up your courage. It might sound like an '80s video montage but the point is that it works. It's why boxers go into the ring with the theme tune from *Rocky* pumping through the speakers and why soldiers go to war with the sound of bagpipes or marching songs. Music has a very profound effect on our moods and our courage and you should use it as a very cheap way of tapping into some bravery. I use the *Thunderbirds* theme tune but you can have it too if you want it. Corny is good. Just make sure you don't pick something by Morrissey or Leonard Cohen. Nobody won a battle with 'Bird on a Wire' ringing in their ears.

Step 4: Plan your location

- Pick your venue for your transaction. No assertive conversation should ever happen on the hoof. It's hard to make your point well when you've just happened to bump into the other person in the lift or the loo or the coffee machine. These conversations will seem like very low priority and probably end up being rushed.
- Timing is just as vital. It's pointless having a dialogue with someone who is too busy to listen or too distracted to take on board what you're saying.

Step 5: Confident speech

When you're in a transaction where you want to be assertive, keep three key stages in mind:

1. Make reference to the other person's point of view. This is a powerful technique because it shows you're being fair and

empathetic, plus it tends to open their mind to change. For instance, saying to a member of your staff 'I know the traffic can be heavy first thing in the morning ...' can lead to more chance of improvement than 'You're late'.

2. State your own view clearly and calmly.
3. Discuss and negotiate if appropriate.

Having your Assertiveness Blueprint is a great foundation for becoming more confident. Back that up with clear communication skills, and you'll soon be able to go into any situation knowing that you have the tools to deal with any problems that may come your way.

CONFIDENT COMMUNICATION: CLEAR SPEAKING, STRAIGHT TALKING

Speaking confidently involves more than just your words. Delivery is all, meaning you'll need to take care of your vocal tone, pitch and pauses. Speaking in a high-pitched breathless voice will make you sound low status and unsure of your facts. Mumbling will imply low self-esteem and using a whispery, giggly voice will imply shyness or lightweight thinking.

Trouble-shooting techniques

You talk too quickly when you feel you're under pressure
Caused by?
You are over-thinking, evaluating your words in your own head and assuming they are worthless, stupid or prompting critical thought from your listeners.

Solution:
1. Sell your message to yourself first. Evaluate its worth. Know that it needs to be aired.
2. Make your messages lively. Fresh language and a high-impact delivery will make people want to listen.
3. Breathe out before you speak. Breathing out releases tension

4. Speak in sentences not paragraphs. Launching into long patches of dialogue will leave you gasping for air and rushing to get to that breath.

5. Hold your pauses. When you get to a virtual full stop, take a moment to recover, breathe and reboot.

6. Create your own metronome. Singers and musicians use a metronome to count them in to the beat before they start. Before you start to speak, use a subtle foot-tap or beat your fingers against your leg to let your body and brain know the pace you want to use as you speak. If you find yourself speeding up mid-talk, employ the small tapping technique to reboot your timing.

You stammer
Caused by?

There are stammers that are a constant problem and there are the types of stammering that trips us all up now and again. With the occasional type of stammer it's usually down to mental rushing, i.e. thinking ahead and trying to force your speech to catch up. Once we trip once we often panic and push ourselves to speak faster to overcome the stumble.

Solution:

1. Focus on stopping rather than speeding up.
2. Pause at the first stammer, breathe. Then continue.
3. Avoid beating yourself up mentally. It happens. Move forward.
4. Don't start launching into apologies and explanations.
5. Just stop – pause – carry on.
6. Slow down using the metronome method described above.

Your voice rises in pitch under pressure
Caused by?

A shrill voice sounds juvenile, meaning you sound less confident the higher your voice rises. We equate maturity and status with a richer, deeper tone. Fear sounds like a scream and so calm sounds lower in tone.

Some people manage to grow up but their voices don't. It's

common to hear adults with high, piping voices that sound childlike and which they make no effort to mature. For women this can entail maintaining a tone that stays firmly in the back of the mouth, rather than emerging from lower in the chest. The 'girlie' voice also often entails the habit of scooping the tone up at the end of every sentence with the effect of turning statements into questions, as in: 'My name is Julie?', 'I work as an accountant?'

Talking like this not only implies a lack of self-confidence, it creates a lack of confidence in your audience, too.

Solution:

1. Breathing exercises: fill the lungs, hold the breath for a few seconds, then breathe out slowly, emptying the entire lung.
2. Pick a spot across the room and project your voice towards it, 'seeing' your voice like an arrow in your mind. How high did the arrow fly? Bring it down by bringing down your vocal tone but still projecting the same distance.
3. Relax your vocal chords. When we speak high we can feel as though we're strangling them. Feel the tension in your neck and throat and take a moment to allow each of those muscles to relax.
4. Hum. Start your hum up behind your nose, and then bring it down to the back of your throat, down to your chest then lower, if possible. Work your way around those areas slowly, holding the hum for as long as possible. The gentle vibration of humming will help relax those areas.
5. Relax your entire body. Clearly you can't do this while you're standing up onstage, but pre-talk you can lie down and relax each muscle in your body one at a time. Or gently shake your hands, feet and shoulders before you get up to speak.
6. Use your key Mantra: 'I feel calm, confident and in control.' Repeat.
7. Smile. It's hard to feel and sound so tense if you wreathe your face in smiles.
8. Take voice coaching. DIY techniques will help but if your job involves public speaking with a lot of projection, like chairing meetings or working in politics, you should consider some professional work on your voice.

You talk too quietly

Caused by?

This can be cultural, and I'm talking family culture rather than national. Some families are quiet, meaning you would naturally get heard easily, while others are riotous, meaning you learn to shout or shut up.

Some families encourage conversations that involve speaking and inspirational, encouraging listening. Others watch TV or live in their own rooms. I have no problem with the TV stuff but it's quite hard to deliver high-quality conversations when you have no real experience of them. If you're going to live in front of the TV at least make sure you're watching a few programmes that present the formula for conversation.

Low self-belief can cause quiet speaking too, as you have little or no desire to be heard.

Solution:

1. Remember that vocal projection does not mean shouting. Shouting is equated with anger, which could be why you're shying away from it, whereas projection could even involve talking in a stage whisper.
2. Projection involves using the lungs as bellows. If you speak quietly you're probably working on half-empty tanks.
3. Stand or sit with your arms uncrossed so that your lungs are completely free. Breathe in, allowing your lungs to expand, right down to the bottom of the lung. Place your hands lightly on to your ribs to feel them expand if it helps.
4. Breathe in and out a few times, expanding the lungs as you take in air and then relaxing your entire body as you empty them.
5. When you speak, imagine air moving up from the lowest part of your lungs and emerging via your throat and finally your mouth.
6. Read out loud from a book. An older child's book is ideal, full of action and adventure. Pause at the start of every sentence, breathe out then in and then project as you speak.
7. See your voice travelling like an arrow across the entire room. Launch it and see it land. Did it hit the floor midway?

Did it drop feebly at your own feet? Use the breath from your whole lung to project it across the entire length of the room.

8. Try using some listening motivators prior to speaking. These are words that announce the fact you want to speak, like 'Look ...' 'Right ...' 'You know what?' or the name of the person you're addressing, 'Carl ...' etc. Put your energy into these announcements at the very least. When you have people's attention they will often stay with you even if the rest of your speech is quieter than would be ideal.

You get verbal diarrhoea
Caused by?
Is anything sadder and funnier than your ears listening in horror as your mouth runs away with you? Verbal diarrhoea is when you find yourself babbling away when you would prefer to shut up. It's as though your mind loses its link that gives it control over your mouth. This is what low self-esteem sounds like, with your self-heckling inner dialogues prompting you to over-speak as a symptom of your own anxieties.

Solution:
1. Think concisely. Pause and create sentences in your head before you speak. This will feel like scripting yourself but becomes less painful the more you do it.
2. Think of the points you want to make in bullet-point form.
3. If you're doing a speech or talk, write your talk out in bullet-point form and keep the list where you can see it easily.
4. Get into the habit of speaking in sentences, visualising and recognising the full stops.
5. Become comfortable with pauses. It's the end of your sentences and the gaps that follow them that will be seducing you into adding more. Most of us wilt under the sound of silence, any silence, and we rush to fill it with more words. This leads to repetition and rambling. Practise speaking then stopping and allowing the silence to occur without panicking.
6. If a thought starts to form in your mind after you've spoken, allow it to become fully formed before you voice it. Making a statement, then going 'um ... ah ... or ... sorry ...', etc. shows

your brain has gone into freefall.

7. Allow other people to make judgements of your comments rather than adding them yourself, as in: '... but you might not like that idea ...' '... or we could do it your way if you prefer ...'

You keep getting a frog in your throat

Caused by?

When we get tense or nervous our mouths dry and our vocal chords tend to tense. We then try to clear the throat but this in turn leads to throat problems, meaning we end up clearing and re-clearing throughout our speech.

Solution:

1. Sip room-temperature water and keep a glass handy when you speak.

2. Avoid dairy produce prior to your talk. I'm not a medical or a dietary expert but the current wisdom seems to be that dairy products can produce more mucus. Keep milk out of your tea or coffee when you're at the venue.

3. Warm up before you speak. Actors don't just walk out onstage and speak for the first time, any more than an athlete would start running in a race without doing warm-up exercises first.

4. Warm up your voice via the humming exercise described above, and by either going through the alphabet saying each letter several times, almost as though singing them, i.e. 'A-A-A-A, B-B-B-B', etc.

5. Use throat sweets that will help lubricate your throat, but avoid brightly coloured ones. You won't want everyone dazzled by your cherry-red tongue as you deliver your words.

You keep using verbal fillers

What are these?

Verbal fillers are all those words and noises we use to fill in gaps in our speech. Here are some of the most common examples:

Um ...
Er ...
You know ...

Sort of ...
Kind of ...
Like ...
If you like ...
Basically ...
Actually ...
Per se ...
You know what I mean?

Caused by?
Filler words are like verbal comfort blankets, meaningless but familiar words that we pluck out of the air and clutch close to our chests when we feel a small loss of the plot coming on. They are the way we stall for time to think, although in confidence terms they rob our speech of emphasis and clarity and – in some cases – they bare our lack of self-belief to our entire audience.

Here's what we disclose when we use them:

Um ... er ... You've lost the plot, albeit for a split second or two. Your mind has wandered and you're desperately hunting for the next thought. These noises dilute your message.

Sort of ... kind of ... like ... You lack the ability to define your thoughts with precision. You may also be displaying your passive side as these words suggest you're too wussy to say what you mean.

If you like ... This is even more of a wimp-out as it's akin to presenting your statement out on a platter for your audience to approve or reject at will. Could anything be more of a cop-out? You choose a word you think is appropriate but then you are too terrified to use it without approval from your listeners. What if we *don't* like? Eh? Got anything better to offer us?

Basically ... Actually ... Per se ... These words that are sprinkled across your speech like confetti come from the mind that likes to consider itself a little more intellectual than most. The problem is hypocrisy. Anyone who uses the word 'basically' is never basic. It's a word that is intended to cause some verbal discipline but usually the opposite is true. When people say 'basically ...' you know you're in for a long-winded ride.

You know ... you know what I mean? When you use these phrases you instantly let the listener know that you don't know what you mean and are having to ask your listener for encouragement, despite this. Often the phrase 'you know what I mean?' is said without any other statement to hang it on, suggesting you expect your audience to be mind readers. It is a cry for help. Don't go there.

Solution:
1. You need to focus on the gaps in your speech you are trying to fill. Why are they there? Prepare your points more fully before-hand if possible.
2. Focus on what you do want to do, not what you don't. What would you prefer to fill those gaps with? Fillers lower your confidence. Small, emphatic pauses will raise it and make your speech seem far more measured.
3. But when you do pause make sure you don't display suffering or anxiety signals during those pauses. These will let both you and your audience or listener know that you've lost the plot.
4. Learn to maintain brief, confident pauses. Keep a relaxed facial expression; prevent your arms from waving or your hands from fiddling. Use eye contact as you pause.

You do the dying fall
What?
This is where your voice trails during a sentence. Sometimes it dips away completely in what would on the written page look like this:

'I thought we might go to that meeting later on but if you're not keen we ...'

This is a common problem and I see it a lot when professional people introduce themselves or come to a vital part of their pitch: 'Hi, I'm ... Denise ...' 'I'm an ... IT manager ...', 'This product costs five thousand ...'

Without doubt you let people know you have no confidence in

yourself and or your product when you do the dying fall.

I hear a very similar problem when parents talk to their kids, although the vocal trail-off can be verbal as well as vocal, as in:

PARENT: 'You'd better tidy your room right away, or ...'
CHILD: 'Or you'll what?'
PARENT: 'Just do what I tell you to for once!'

Caused by?
This is a habit that usually stems from childhood. In a busy household or noisy family, or in a grouping where one member tends to be verbally dominant, there is often no need or no possibility of ending a sentence. Some parents tend to finish sentences for a child, especially if that child is shy or a poor communicator. It's seen as helping out, although it can cause problems later in life because the odds are remote of your mum or dad suddenly appearing out of nowhere at that business meeting to finish off your thought:

(you) 'Thank you all for coming here today, I wanted to talk to you about ...'
(your dad) 'BILLING SYSTEMS!!!'

But of course we're not blaming here, as blame means we deny our ability to control our lives, our destinies and our ability to change what we don't like. (I'm sure you've got this message by now but just in case I will keep popping it in.)

Solution:
1. Read out loud, keeping the energy in your voice right to the end of each sentence.
2. Rehearse speaking as though you were speaking to someone with hearing problems.
3. Record your own voice. Hear it dipping. Imagine you're being interviewed on the radio. (This was the discipline that helped me to get over a lifetime of speaking with a dying fall.) On the radio you can't end with a dip or a mumble or a fade. People listening at home aren't there to finish your

sentences for you, they're there to listen to your points.

4. Rehearse by making yourself shout out one word at the end of every point you make, like BINGO! (This will make you anticipate and end your sentences, although clearly you will need to drop the habit when you're talking in the real world!)

Your tone scoops upwards
What?

You use the habit that was allegedly brought to the UK from Australia of ending each sentence with a rise in tone, turning your statements into questions. This robs your speech of any smattering of confidence because you appear to be asking for audience verification of every point you make. Or to put it another way, 'You appear to be asking for audience verification? Of every point you make?'

It sounds cute and we use it to encourage participation in our conversation, as in 'I saw that TV programme, did you see it too? Do you know what I'm talking about? I'm just checking.'

This might be adorable in a lightweight, social conversation but it will sound annoyingly like uncertainty during a business conversation or anything more serious and important.

Solution:

1. Remind yourself that you have a right to make points without canvassing votes as you do so. You're entitled to your thoughts and opinions.

2. Do some 'out loud' rehearsal work. Visualise the upward curve your tone is currently taking then visualise the opposite, seeing it arcing downwards instead. Begin by scooping down, and then when you have tried this several times, aim to get your tone to remain even, as though it is running in a straight line.

You have a monotonous tone
What?

You bore for Britain because your voice runs at a monotone, flat, droning and lacking energy or emphasis.

Caused by?

This is likely to be copied behaviour from someone influential in your development who spoke in a verbal flat line. It can also signal acute lack of confidence, enthusiasm for your speech or your subject, or depression.

It can also be seen as cool, as in a nasal, can't-be-bothered delivery as affected by some US comedians to suggest they are tired of life.

Solution:

1. Do try recording your voice so you can see what you're inflicting on your listeners.
2. Get your hands on a really dramatic piece of literature and read it out loud, making yourself swoop, fly, curl and dip in terms of your vocal tone. Exaggerate. Overact. And keep doing this on a daily basis; it will be like a little gym workout for your vocal chords. Build those muscles and then work them. Once you've got them pumped you'll be able to use them in real life.

THE TRICKS OF CONFIDENT SPEECH

You know words are powerful but you might not realise exactly how powerful. Although you shouldn't be overanalysing your speech while you're talking as over-thinking will lead to hesitant, under-emphatic speech patterns, you should be aware of the confidence ratings of words we commonly use.

Submissive words and terms

• **Sorry**

Although there's nothing wrong with an apology under appropriate circumstances, like treading on someone's foot or being unable to locate a product for a client, the habit of over-apologising or apologising for no apparent reason is a wussy one.

Do you start many of your sentences with the word, as in 'Sorry to bother you ...' 'Sorry, can I just have a word?' 'Sorry if this sounds stupid but ...'? Do you create a catalogue of apologies: 'I'm really really sorry ...?' 'I'm awfully, dreadfully sorry ...'? If so you need to wean yourself off the word. Only use it when it is entirely appropriate and limit yourself to one use per apology. Apart from sounding less passive it also sounds more honest if used just the once.

- **I think ... I hope ... I try**
  These are weak terms that dilute the impact of your points.
- **Just, only**
  As in 'I'm just a PA' or 'I'm only a journalist' or the dreaded 'It's only me' when you announce yourself on the phone. Weasel words that diminish you and your confident persona.
- **No problem**
  But usually it is, so why keep insisting it's not? An 'I'll roll over and you can use me as a doormat' phrase. Use it sparingly and only when you mean it.
- **I know this might sound stupid ...**
  Never put this at the front of an idea or point. It's your low self-esteem looking to be bolstered via some reassurance but you need to keep in mind that although the kindlier members of your audience might smile encouragingly the rest will be thinking you're a wet Nellie and a timewaster.

Aggressive, red rag words and terms

- '**I'm sorry you feel like that**'
- '**I'm sorry – okay?**'
- '**I've said I'm sorry, I can't do any more**'
  These are mealy-mouthed apologies of the worst kind. You're not apologising, you're just going through the motions to try to get someone off your back. Sulky, nasty double-speak.
- '**You must ...**'
- '**You'll have to ...**'
- '**You should ...**'
- '**You ought to ...**'
- '**You've got to ...**'
  These are orders, and used in the wrong way they will demean the authority of the person you're speaking to. They will also tend to elicit a rebellious child response from the other person,

meaning your order will be met with a mood of 'Says who?' leading to toe-to-toe conflict.

- **'Just this once then, but consider yourself lucky'**
And any other term that reminds your listener that you're going out of your way for them. Grudging in the extreme. What's the point in being nice or helpful if your grumbling tone makes them resent what you've done?

- **'No'**
A bald, blank 'no' with no qualification will always sound rude unless used in extreme situations. Try to offer an alternative: 'Do you have these shoes in a 9?' 'No, but we might have them in that size in another colour.' 'Is Fred around?' 'No, but he'll probably be back shortly.'

- **'Why?'**
As in 'Why do you wear red?' 'Why did you phone in the middle of that game?' 'Why do you wear your hair that colour?' Using 'why' like this will imply you're being judgemental.

- **'Whatever. Your point being?'**
There are a whole raft of words or phrases like this that seem to have been invented to annoy. Said with a stare or a shrug they are aggressive in the extreme.

- **'Stupid'**
As in 'That's a stupid idea'. There is a phrase in assertive training that says you're not rejecting the person, you're just rejecting their suggestion or idea. Putting 'stupid' into the knock-back will always be taken personally though, and rightly so.

- **'So what you're trying to say is ...'**
Implies the person speaking is not capable of making their own point clearly.

- **'I don't mean to be rude ... but ...'**
These fake apologies are horrendous. If you say this you announce you are about to be rude, so why do so if you don't want to? People think they can say what they like because this opener gives them immunity, which it doesn't. Similar phrases would be 'With respect ...' 'With all due respect' and 'I don't mean to be funny ...'

- **'Didn't you read the instructions first?'**
These words leave the words 'You idiot' hanging in the air.

- **'Obviously...'**
  Ditto. When you answer a question by plonking this word at the start of your reply you imply the questioner is a numbskull.
- **'I could have fallen over these and broken my neck!'**
  This and other drama-queen statements form a rather exaggerated attack when all that's happened is a pair of shoes have been left in the hallway.
- **'Oh really?'**
  Can sound sarcastic, implying the speaker is lying.
- **'Yes, but ...'**
  Means you're about to trash an idea.

Confident, assertive language

- **'I' rather than 'We'**
  When you use the I word you take responsibility for your ideas or comments.
- **'I know'**
  This will work, rather than 'I hope'.
- **'Thank you'**
  In reply to a compliment.
- **'Let's discuss this'**
  Rather than 'You're wrong'.
- **'I don't like toasted cheese'**
  Rather than 'It's disgusting!/ horrible/ tastes of sick'.
- **'Yes please'**
  In reply to questions like 'Would you like a cup of tea?' rather than 'If you're having one'.
- **Their name**
  Starting your speech by addressing it to the listener is a good way to ensure their attention before you speak. This technique should not be confused with the rubbish customer care technique of repeating the customer's name so many times in one sentence that they think you are a relative.
- **'Yes, and ...'**
  Means you're about to add to an idea.

YOUR CONFIDENT SPEECH PATTERNS

Headline

This means introducing your topic in the same way a newspaper headlines an article, to get your attention and arouse your interest. In normal speech this would sound like:

'Nina, about that meeting you've called to discuss the budget for the conference ...'

Rather than: 'Nina, sorry to bother you and I don't know if you've had time to think about it yet but I did send you an email to see how long you thought we might be able to talk for on Thursday ...'

With the first example your listener is immediately engaged.

With the second they will be confused, having to mentally backtrack to listen once they've worked out what it is you're talking about.

Reflect

This is a useful response after someone's spoken. Instead of churning out the line that always sounds like a big fat lie, i.e. 'Oh that sounds really interesting', you repeat back some words they have spoken, e.g. 'Sex? With a melon?'

Keep your language fresh

Clichés and jargon are the enemy of confidence because they make it sound as though you're hiding behind someone else's stale old words. There are too many to list but examples would be:

'At the end of the day ...'

'I'm on a learning curve ...'

'We're thinking outside the box.'

'At grassroots ...'

'It is what it is.'

CONFIDENCE TIP: HOW TO SPEAK UP FOR YOURSELF

Getting stuck in doesn't mean being aggressive. In fact if you deal with something quickly you'll probably find a lighter touch does the trick.

CONFIDENT COMMUNICATION: CONFIDENT BODY LANGUAGE

Your body-language signals should always endorse your words. Powerful speakers are able to create congruent messages by using their non-verbal dialogues to add emphasis to their speech, but speakers who lack confidence will often become self-absorbed, allowing their anxieties to emerge in nervous rituals like fiddling, rather than getting lost in the focus of their own message.

Communication is about more than just speaking, too. A confident speaker will be a confident listener too, sending signals of active, rather than passive listening to register interest and understanding. When you are confident enough to both speak and listen well you will be able to project charisma and status.

Here are some image goals and your ways of achieving those goals:

- **Being vivid.** Modern life requires us to stand out if we want to make a mark and achieve levels of success. The meek might inherit the earth but not in any business I have ever been involved in. Confidence means getting noticed but for all the right reasons. This is not about being an attention-seeking extrovert but it is about making high-impact entrances and sending out subtle but effective signals of self-control and power.
- **Being authentic.** This means looking as though you mean what you say. We have been through an era of the slick, the glib and the over-promising, under-delivering style of businessperson. What people want now is integrity. Even the politicians are having a stab at it. You should too.
- **Being salient.** This means tailoring your communication to make it relevant to your audience. Your style of communication is important. If a lack of confidence is making you too self-aware you will forget the techniques of rapport building.
- **Your entrances.** This should be an area of massive interest to you. You have about as long as it takes to blink to make a first impression. Never allow yourself to walk into a room and warm up once you get there or once you get to know people. Hit the ground running. You are like a strange animal about to join a

new tribe or pack and their acceptance or rejection will take
no time at all to occur. Here's your first training technique for
confident body language:

EXERCISE: MAKING A POWERFUL ENTRANCE
• Pause before you walk into a room.
• Check your hair and your clothing.
• Never be over-cluttered. Take an easy-to-carry bag that ideally leaves both hands free.
• Never walk in carrying your coat or shopping bags.
• Avoid rucksacks in the office. They were designed for hiking or mountain-climbing. Using them in business is idiotic unless you're a Sherpa.
• Before you enter the room, breathe out to release tension and anxiety.
• Pull up to full height by trying to touch the ceiling with the top of your head.
• Roll your shoulders back and down. When you get stressed your shoulder muscles contract, raising your shoulders upward.
• Pit-bare a little. Make sure your arms from the elbow upward are not pulled in against your ribs.
• Shake your hands gently to relax them.
• Draw your chin up so that it is at approximately a 45-degree angle to your neck.
• Relax your facial expression. Too many people walk into a room looking haunted and hunted or wearing their journey on their face. Imagine your face is being ironed out with a very small, warm iron. Get rid of all the facial tension, including frowns and rigid lips. Then imagine you've just been told that someone you like is on the other side of the door.
• Walk in and impress everyone.

Your Power Pose
• Confidence comes from the feet. Standing well on feet that are what I call well planted is vital. By this I mean your weight should be evenly distributed on both your feet and that you should not be standing on the outside or inside edges of your shoes.
• Your feet can be very slightly toes-out but never toes pointing inward.
• When you want to look confident, never stand with your weight on one foot, or with your legs crossed.
• Women often cross their legs at the ankles. In confidence terms this looks rank.

- Your feet should be slightly apart, shoulder-width for a man, less for a woman.
- Keep your legs straight but not so straight the knees lock.
- Stretch your spine straight and tuck your pelvis in and under very slightly.
- Head up (45-degree angle from your neck).
- Roll your shoulders back and down.
- Have your hand ready to shake hands.

When you walk, try to propel yourself across a room without looking down at your feet. Take a slightly shorter stride than normal and don't rush. Look at people, using eye contact that looks friendly and open.

STATUS AND POWER

Did you ever walk into a room and immediately have a feel for who the real leaders and power brokers were in that room, even though you had never met before? Or have you ever struggled trying to gain the appropriate levels of respect from other people, even though you have a job with a title that should imply leadership or relative status?

Words like status and power might imply a more aggressive or forceful attitude, but we all present our own role in the workplace and social hierarchies, even if you prefer to remain some way down the pecking order.

The kind of power that accompanies appropriate levels of confidence should be:

- The power to have a positive impact when you walk into a room
- The power to be taken seriously when you choose
- The power to be listened to
- The power to be treated with respect
- The power to be memorable

All of these 'powers' would be suitable goals whatever your walk in life, but you may also have a goal that involves genuine leadership power signals. Are you a manager, team leader or business leader? Or does your leadership role relate to parenthood?

All genuine power signals tend to be visual, and most of those visual signals will involve your body language. Why? Because real power will relate to your core animal signalling. An alpha animal gains and sustains his or her role via implied threat rather than the real thing. (Though note that I'm not asking you to copy silverback gorilla signals – sitting alone from your group, eating and farting like crazy, might not be the best career move!)

Study any charismatic speaker or leader and you will see they emanate a form of power. Meet them and you might find yourself automatically falling into the role of follower.

Leadership power signals will vary tremendously but they also tend to have some things in common. Think of some well-known leaders. Each leader will have their own style of leadership signals. If you take football managers, for instance, you could take the charismatic, 'wartime' leadership style of a José Mourinho, with his hands stuffed into his designer greatcoat and his boasting and sulking signals, or you could look at the more granite-faced demeanour of an Alex Ferguson or the suppressed inscrutability of a Sven-Göran Eriksson.

The one thing you rarely find with good leadership signals is a pushy promotion of status or power. Most effective leaders are subtle in their displays but ultimately more powerful for that.

Power signals

- The use of space is important as powerful and high-status people tend to have and use the most space, which is why being crushed in an underground carriage does us no favours in terms of self-esteem.
- Although over-splaying looks arrogant and aggressive, do make sure you aren't in a permanent strait-jacket, i.e. spending your whole life in a self-hug with folded arms and a tight-looking body.
- Pit-baring is an expression of overconfidence. This is an overt armpit display, when someone sits with their hands behind their head.
- Steepling is another status signal that only works if you want

to look bossy. This is where you place your fingers together, pointed upward like a church steeple.

- Placing your hands on your hips will usually be seen as overconfidence or arrogance. It relates to the way animals will fluff their fur out to look like a bigger opponent when they feel under the threat of attack.

- Splaying your legs will also look borderline aggressive. This is where you overspread your legs.

- Staring is not the same as eye contact. Eye contact will look confident, staring will look aggressive.

- Be careful where you stand or sit in relation to the other person as leaning or looming over someone or standing in their space will appear aggressive rather than confident.

- However, do stand face-to-face when you're talking as it registers undivided attention and good levels of power.

- You transmit many signals about your power and status via your handshake. Make it firm but not a bone-cruncher.

- When you touch or place your own items on furniture you create a form of territorial ownership. This means it's good to spray your own territory by moving chairs, straightening things on your desk or dinner table, and even running your hands across the surface of a table or desk after you sit down. However, be careful about doing this to other people's desks as it will be seen as an act of invasion.

- Always take control of a chair when you sit down. Never perch or occupy it timidly. Sit into the back of the chair and place your elbows on the arms. Use the space but without slumping.

- Always walk with energy and purpose. Never dawdle or dither. If you're in business walk around with documents or papers in your hand; it gives a sense of focus and importance.

- When you sit at your desk remember your status signals. Avoid slumping or leaning, no matter how long your day.

- Low-status animals register submission by using lowering rituals. Avoid hunching or head-lowering gestures.

- Nodding is a relic gesture of status lowering, although it can be used to raise status if you nod to register understanding while someone else is speaking.

- Smiling is a relic of an animal fear display so never smile too much; however, a genuine, not over-congruent smile is seen as a signal of confidence in modern society.

- Touch is a powerful way of registering status and control. By patting you signal superior status and a grooming gesture from a woman to a man will signal ownership to all other women in the area.
- Tapping is an aggressive gesture. It might be prompted by nerves but it will imply you're bored or anxious to get away.

Weaned on a pickle

It is a mistake to see leadership or power signals as being purely straight-faced and arrogant. I visit many businesses when people seem to think power comes from talking and emailing like a robot and never smiling, joking or relaxing.

Then I will see people at the other end of the leadership chain who think power and close friendship can be combined so that they can act exactly like their teams, showing flaws, weaknesses and all and vying for sympathy and acceptance as much as (if not more than) respect.

If your confidence or self-esteem is low, you will be sub-consciously sending out non-verbal messages of low self-worth via leakage signals, which other people will read subliminally as meaning you are of low importance. Although high-status people can enact signals of shyness without lowering their status this is down to their known public status, meaning they can signal low self-esteem without looking as though they mean it. The rest of us will just find that other people will believe what we tell them. You can show that you're more confident by keeping the points below in mind.

Confident displays

- Avoid barrier gestures like folded arms or self-hugging.
- Smile but without too much of a tooth display.
- Use open gestures for emphasis while you speak.
- When you use your hands, a subtle display of the palms will signal openness and confidence.
- Mirroring, i.e. subtly copying the other person's body language, will signal like-minded rapport.

- Never sit at a desk or a table with your hands invisible in your lap.
- Avoid fiddling with your hair or jewellery.
- Avoid face-touching as it looks anxious.
- Keep your hands away from your neck or upper chest as it looks nervous.
- Use active listening signals: eye contact, smiling, mirroring and nodding.
- Use a Precision Gesture to show you're in command of your facts. This involves a light pinching together of the thumb and first two fingertips.
- Avoid the fig leaf pose. This crotch-covering pose is a classic male way of signalling a feeling of being under threat.
- Avoid any pseudo-infantile displays, i.e. childish body-language rituals, like standing with toes pointed together, clutching or wringing the hands, waving your hands about above shoulder height as you talk or performing over-congruent, over-exaggerated gestures.
- Avoid self-attacks. When an animal wants to fight another animal but fears it will be too strong to beat, it will often take its state of aggressive arousal and turn it on itself. In an ape this might mean hitting itself on the head but in you it could be nail biting, lip chewing or even hair pulling or knuckle cracking.

Self-awareness

Being aware of your body language for the first time can be alarming and many people I train suffer an instant urge to go back to a state of unawareness when they're not feeling inhibited about every movement and gesture.

It's vital you push, coach and motivate yourself past this stage though. Being unaware of your body language is the same thing as being unaware of the words you are speaking, only worse, as your facial expressions, gestures and body movement account for a much higher percentage of the impact of your message than your words ever can.

You wouldn't speak without evaluating your choice of words first (well, not intentionally, I hope) so why allow your body language to do its own thing?

Working to modify or improve your body-language signals is not making you a liar. Often our signals lie for us, for instance, shyness signals can often appear arrogant. Or low self-esteem can easily be mistaken for boredom or disinterest in other people.

When you work on your body language you need to first create your goals, then to tailor your signals to help achieve those goals. You also need a pretty firm grasp of your current reality, too, i.e. the gestures you use, both when you're relaxed and when you're placed under pressure.

I'm always fascinated at the amount of business people who are unaware of their physical responses when they're placed under pressure. I've filmed them presenting and had them gape in awe and shock as they watch themselves scratching, fiddling or swaying from one foot to another as they give a business presentation. Some of them even try to argue they don't do those things, even though the evidence is there in front of their eyes!

We all have our foibles but it's important we're aware of them. Only then can we take the decision to change or modify what we do or retain it and try to turn it into an adorably quirky feature of our performances.

In order to ensure that your body language says exactly what you want it to, I strongly suggest that you create a body-language log with the following categories:

Event:_____

My image goals:_____

How I came across:_____

Why I created that impression:_____

When you're assessing your impact and image never log how you felt. Other people aren't mind readers so will only see what you choose to tell them, both with your words and your behaviour. Never say: 'I felt nervous' but do say 'I looked nervous' and limit yourself to analysing why in terms of projected signals rather than feelings. Anything else is just a sick note. Below are a couple of examples of what you might fill out.

EXAMPLE 1:

Event: Client meeting

My image goals: To look knowledgeable, professional and friendly

How I came across: Nervous but friendly

Why? I forgot to smile when I walked in and I struggled with eye contact. I did listen to the client and I gave a better handshake on the way out.

EXAMPLE 2:

Event: A date

My image goals: (Aside from the obvious!) To appear fun, friendly and trustworthy

How I came across: Shy, awkward and borderline sleazy

Why? I spoke too much after that vodka and tonic and I couldn't keep my eyes off her cleavage. My hands were really sweaty with nerves.

Your body-language themes and your signature looks

Another log to fill in:

When I am relaxed my body language is_____

When I am under pressure I_____

Please list all your regular anxiety leakage, e.g. 'I fiddle with my cuffs', 'I chew my pen', 'my leg judders', 'I fiddle with my hair', etc.

Like your verbal fillers, the best way to train yourself out of these leakage habits, all of which will tell both you and your audience that you're lacking in confidence, is to focus on what you *do* want to do, rather than what you want to stop doing. Focusing on the negative gestures will only make you do them more. Visualise some positive alternatives to help create a 'Do' rather than a 'Don't' command in your mind.

CONFIDENT CLOTHING

Your clothes have many functions as well as the most obvious of covering your body (and therefore preventing you from being arrested as you go about your working day).

Tribal function
The style of your clothing defines which tribe you belong to. We usually dress like our own social group and when we go to work we tend to dress to fit in with the company culture, showing a desire for acceptance within that culture.

Status
Clothing has always been used to define status, with the more plush and expensive the fabrics and designs the higher the class or status of the person wearing them. This has evolved over the centuries, with certain ironic status signals emerging. Years ago only rich people would have worn light colours and well-ironed fabrics but then washing machines and non-iron fabrics hit the market, meaning the wealthy moved to crumpled linens and even shabby, grungy dress in a bid to go one better. Upper classes have found shabby, worn clothing the height of good taste for a couple of centuries. The truly upper class looked down upon over-dressing and flaunting your spending power through the clothes you wear.

Personality
The clothes you choose will give obvious and subliminal clues about your personality, e.g. introvert, extrovert, boring, neurotic, chaotic, etc.

External self-esteem
We tend to use dress to reflect our own levels of self-esteem. You might dress confidently (well-chosen, well-fitting clothes), overconfidently (bright colours, flashy styles, lots of flesh exposed) or anxiously (neutral or dark colours, dull styles, body covered).

Internal self-esteem

Your clothes will also have implications as a message sent from you to You. Like your body language, your feelings of self-worth can be enhanced or diminished by the way you choose to portray yourself via your clothing, which is why shopping is such a popular form of ego-or mood-boosting therapy and why makeovers are such a regular form of entertainment.

Dressing to impress both you and your audience

- **Always look well groomed.** I once met a celebrity who was casually dressed in flip-flops, baggy shorts and a T-shirt. His grooming was impeccable, though. (I couldn't stop staring at his feet, they looked newly made!) Despite his casual dress he still exuded confidence and power via his attention to grooming detail.
- **Smell well.** Avoid too much perfume or using clashing products. Strong perfumes imply a lack of confidence but a fresh scent will reek of success.
- **Don't over-think**. Fake talons in multi-colours, hair that has been crimped to within an inch of its life, spray-tans, fake boobs, too much make-up, over-dressed outfits and over-matching accessories will all suggest the opposite of laid-back cool and confidence in your appearance.
- **Buy clothes that fit.** Please! I could weep when I see leading politicians and businesswomen wearing clothes that either never fitted or which used to fit before they ate all the pies. Weight gain is between you and You but pouring a size 16 body into a size 12 suit is not. Clothes should never pull or gape, especially formal business dress. For the women beware skirts that are so tight they show knicker lines or tops gaping and displaying any part of your bra. I'm no fan of cleavage showing in the workplace, either. Think of the male equivalent, pecs-a-go-go and you'll see why. For guys there's the horror of the trousers that are so tight the pockets gape or the shirt that barely buttons over the beer-gut or the beer-belly flopping over the top of the fall-down pants.
- **Too big is bad too.** I see many women in jackets with sleeves that are too long and cover their hands. If the body of the jacket

fits, get the sleeves shortened. Most professional dry cleaners do repairs and tailoring so there's no need to have too-long or too-short trousers or sleeves.

- **Never hide.** Whether you're smart or casual, avoid hiding in your clothes. By this I mean pulling your T-shirt or jumper sleeves over your knuckles or wearing long skirts that make you look like a Victorian mother.

- **Colour up.** When you choose the right colour for your outfit you send positive intrapersonal messages as well as looking more confident. I know there is a huge business in colour selection, mostly aimed at selecting the colours that enhance your skin tone and make you project confidence. However, do remember to take care of your inner mood, too. The colours we wear have a strong effect on our self-esteem. If you lack confidence or feel anxious you could move to remedy that by selecting a bright red outfit or tie. But also keep an eye on your psychological palette; we associate different feelings with different colours. I can look in the mirror and see that navy blue suits me and flatters my skin tone. But because that was the colour of my school uniform and because I hated school I never feel good wearing that colour. Black makes me feel good and confident in a way that bright colours like pink or bright blue never do. When I wear black I feel cool and stylish and ready for anything. When I wear some bright colours I feel ridiculous. Therefore the black option would win out over the better colour in terms of projected image.

- **Wear clothes, don't allow them to wear you.** If your items of clothing are high maintenance, i.e. they need regular checks in the mirror or re-arrangement, or if they are difficult to wear, like high-heel shoes, pick an easier option. However, I'm not advocating a life spent dressed comfy. Smart gear makes you feel higher in status. It's hard to feel powerful when you're wearing espadrilles and leggings.

- **Go for detail.** It's the smaller details that will define you in a confident way: good bags that aren't stuffed with rubbish, nice pens, a good comb or brush, a nice phone, a stylish notebook; never settle for rubbish as that's how you'll be evaluated.

PSYCHOLOGICAL IMAGE CONFIDENCE

What follows is a quick guide to the impact of different types of clothing. You might like to argue with some of the assertions but I have generalised to keep it simple. Of course David Beckham looks the bee's knees in a tweed three-piece suit, but he is a leading sportsman, captain and personality, with a body to die for. It would be hard to dress him in a way to make him look lacking in charisma or power. Even in his huge woolly hats and baggy knitwear he looks confident. Put most of us in similar gear though and we'll either look like a bashful Hobbit or a low-status historian.

Confident clothes: men
- High-contrast colours
- Navy, black or charcoal grey
- Cotton, linen, wool, or blends that resemble them
- Slight shoulder pads
- White or blue business shirts
- Plain ties in strong colours, silk
- Plain socks in black for business
- Well-polished shoes

Confident clothes: women
- High-contrast colours
- Or violet, deep pink, flesh colours, rich yellows
- Cotton, linen, wool, or blends that resemble them
- Fabrics and cuts that drape on the body
- Slight shoulder pads
- Skirts: knee-length or up to three inches above the knee
- Metal buttons on jackets
- Matching underwear

Unconfident clothes: men
- Sandals with socks
- Funny ties
- Funny socks
- Short socks
- Socks that shin-flash

- Shorts that ride up your bum
- Trouser pockets stuffed with stuff
- Trousers too short
- Tweeds
- Brown shades
- Anything too tight

Unconfident clothes: women

- Pashminas
- Shawls
- Cardigans
- Florals
- Showing a camel-toe
- Pop-sox
- Sleeves too long
- Long skirts
- Tweeds
- Brown shades
- Beige
- Brooches
- Crocs
- Satin
- Heavy jewellery
- Scarves
- Anything fluffy
- Pastels

Know what floats your boat

We all tend to have garments or accessories that we wear to make us feel confident and successful. These clothes can be useful even if their benefit is only perceptual, meaning you might look like a pile of old rags in them but if you feel like George Clooney on a good day then go ahead and wear them. The benefits will normally come under one of six key headings:

Trophy clothing

Expensive jewellery and designer clothes or bags, worn to project an aura of high status or wealth. Some people wear expensive jewellery with a new date in an attempt to seem more desirable, as though they are adornments from other admirers. Egyptian women of high rank were buried with their adornments to look classy in the after-life. Victoria Beckham just wears hers dangling over her arm. I doubt yours will be so enduring, but if flashy helps your confidence levels, it might be useful.

Armour-plating

Tailoring, shoulder pads, leather, big hair, gelled hair, high heels, these all qualify as garments or styles than induce a look that in animals would be called aggressive arousal. They make you look (and feel) bigger and more threatening. Your padded jacket could well be the equivalent of chest-banging in an ape.

Talisman clothing

You wore it once and you got lucky in terms of that promotion or date. Or people complimented you while you wore it. Now it brings you luck. As I said, if it works in your mind it works for me!

Nostalgia wear

You gain a sense of comfort or well-being from wearing familiar styles, fabrics or colours from your youth. This is a more passive form of confidence and only to be recommended in an emergency, as it is akin to lugging a comfort blanket around with you.

Safety clothing

These are clothes that hold you in, squeeze you up and out or generally act as figure-enhancing under-garments, like thick elasticated knickers that keep your tummy flat. Again, this is passive confidence based on the thought that you believe your figure to be rubbish.

Sexual gear

Tight skirts, killer heels, T-shirts that show off the pecs, shorts that show off the thigh ... if they make you feel like a sexual siren then go ahead, but only in your own time unless you work as a pole-dancer. Sexy clothes tend to make us move in a sexier way which can make us feel more confident and flirtatious.

One last tip of confident clothing: always prepare your outfit the night before. Decide what you will wear and get it out of your wardrobe to check it is clean, ironed and suitable for the day ahead. Never ever rummage first thing in the morning. Unless you're a very-early-morning person the best time to make styling decisions is not straight after crawling out of your bed. (I once turned up to an image seminar wearing odd shoes, which meant I was forced to lecture from behind a table all day!) Getting your outfit ready and waiting will also make you love yourself as you have taken on the role of your own personal butler rather than your own little slattern who is busy pulling something crumpled back out of the linen basket because you couldn't be bothered to think ahead.

IN A NUTSHELL

- Use assertive behaviour to achieve an aura of confidence. This means being congruent, using confident words and tone of voice and dressing with confidence as well as using confident body-language signals.

- Sell your messages to yourself first.

- Be strategic. Plan your behaviours to achieve your long-term goals.

- Suppress your more instinctive responses, as they can be destructive to your core aims. Recognise your passive-aggressive feelings then learn how to deal with them, especially in business.

- Look at how you communicate verbally and troubleshoot any problems. Practise speaking out loud by reading from a book.

- Check your non-verbal body language and make sure that it conveys what you mean to say.

- Dress to impress – both the people you are going to meet and yourself. Knowing that you look confident helps you to feel confident.

8

SPECIFIC CONFIDENCE FOR SPECIFIC OCCASIONS

SOCIALISING/NETWORKING

Preparation

- If you're at school, get a Saturday job in a shop. If you're at college get one during your holidays. If you're unemployed or in a job that has little in the way of social transactions, try voluntary work. Whether it's poorly paid and mind-numbingly boring or devastatingly fascinating you'll be forced to meet people, talk to strangers in a safe environment, get to know all about service skills and customer care and you'll lose any shyness because you'll be forced to talk. Your confidence levels will rise over a very short space of time and you'll be getting paid for the therapy – what's not to like?
- Join acting classes or an amateur dramatics troupe. Acting is the perfect antidote to a lack of confidence because it trains you to suppress your fears by taking on someone else's persona. Even if it leads to you switching your shyness on and off at least you've found the switch itself. A brilliant way of taming that inner wimp.
- Read out loud. And really, really go for it. Shake the rafters. A beautiful way of losing your inhibitions.
- Karaoke is as good if not better for losing inhibitions.
- Do some voluntary work. Helping other people makes you less self-obsessed and heightens feelings of self-worth. Hopefully it

will be helpful to the people you're supposed to be helping, too. It's not all about 'me me me', you know.

- Learn a party trick or party piece. If yours is a really great, memorable trick you can repeat it whenever you like, in fact you'll become so popular people will be begging you to come to their parties.
- Don't know any? Well, I am letting out a long sigh here because letting you in on my party tricks means I dilute the effectiveness of them but as we're unlikely to be on the same circuit, here's a couple to get you launched.

Levitation

This, I have to say, is top of the shop, a really great trick that involves lots of action and you taking charge so that even if you've been standing like a dumb mute for the start of the event you know you'll end up as the star turn.

- Get a chair without arms and find a victim. This trick should work whatever their weight but try picking someone not medically obese, just in case. Lighter is better.
- Sit them on the chair and tell them you're going to levitate them. Ask for four volunteers and get them to stand beside the chair, one person at each shoulder, one at each knee.
- Get the volunteers to clasp their own hands together with the index fingers out straight, tips joined into a point.
- They then place their index fingers under the bent knees and the armpits of the victim.
- They then try to lift them up.
- They can't, of course.
- Now you tell them they're going to try again but this time they need to do the special, mind-focusing preparation technique.
- Each of the volunteers has to place one hand above the victim's head, then the other, held out flat, palm down above the victim's head, not touching the head. They form an upward pile of hands, again not touching but alternated until all four have both hands in the pile. You hold the pose for a dramatic couple of seconds (if the hands happen to touch you have to rebuild the pile from scratch again), then you shout out 'go' and

they do the same as before, placing their index fingers in the same place and lifting although this time the victim rises easily into the air. Cue wondrous applause and back patting for you.

• They will ask you how this works but you must never tell them. In fact, I can't even tell you because I have no idea; I just know it is very impressive.

The bread-roll levitation

This is great for dull dinner parties that are pretentious enough to supply you with large fabric napkins and round bread rolls (restaurants usually provide both).

• During your meal you need to smuggle a dinner fork on to your lap where you hide it beneath the napkin. If you're shy this should be easy because nobody will be taking any notice of you anyway.

• During a moment of silence ask if anyone has seen you levitate a roll. Place the roll on the empty plate in front of you and raise your napkin with the fork hidden behind it which you have pinched between your index finger and thumb. Bring the napkin down over the roll, cleverly spearing the roll with the fork but without anyone being able to see. Lift the napkin again, with the roll speared on the fork and hidden behind it.

• If you are feeling confident and your audience look suitably impressed you can then twist the fork so the roll emerges as a bulge in the napkin and with practice you should be able to make it move around a bit, possibly then covering the plate with the napkin again to make the roll reappear.

• While the more outgoing guests are probably limited to 'have you seen this new app on my iPhone?' your genuine tricks should leave everyone speechless with awe.

How to do small talk

Does anyone in their right mind enjoy small talk? I'd guess not, but as a process it has huge value in our lives and so learning the skills involved are vital. Don't be put off by fear or boredom. Small talk is just a trick or technique. That person you watch who seems to adore it is just airing a skill they have mastered and you can master it too.

Here are the steps:

1. **Understand why.** Why do we use small talk? We use it as the first stages of networking and rapport building. Social networking means we get to discover new friends rather than marinating in the small pond that is our life-long friends. It also means we have a larger pond to swim in when it comes to finding a partner. You might feel more comfortable with your long-term friends but think what happens if you fail to expand and cross-pollinate. Friends have a habit of moving away, living abroad, going off to study, marrying, breeding and falling off the radar, falling out with you or getting too busy with their all-consuming careers. It's risky to refuse to mix.

2. **Why in business?** Because networking is the best way to get business or jobs. We live in an era where traditional methods of selling have been devalued to the point that everyone's on a hard sell. We have call centres pushing products, charity muggers pouncing on us in the street, spam on email, add-on selling in banks and thanks to the Internet the whole world is beating a path to your door, trying to flog something. Which is why people like to do business with people they know. As we become less trusting we turn more and more to personal recommendation. If I want to get my house painted I will ring a friend to ask who she used, even though I could look in the phone book. We read books that we have heard are good and we buy music that someone has said is great. Your chat with that client at a networking event will be worth far more than picking up the phone and cold calling. If you speak at a conference or get quoted in the newspaper or magazines you build more interest and trust than if you send introductory emails. You might not realise how effective your networking has been because it's a slow-drip experience. But what you build is a reputation based on face-to-face meetings.

3. **Plan your subjects for small talk or chat,** although make sure they sound fresh, rather than scripted, when you deliver them.

   Imagine that you're the host even when you're not as it will keep you mobile, helping you to do the room and mingle with as many people as possible, rather than just standing alone or only talking to one person all evening.

If you go with your partner or a friend, aim to split up to mingle. You can always meet up again after an hour or so.

If you do mingle with your partner make sure you get into the conversation and don't keep looking at him or her for approval after every statement you make.

Plan your introductions to make further conversation as easy as possible.

'Hi, I'm Lola,' is flat, whereas

'Hi, I'm Lola, named after the Manilow song and not Madonna's daughter ...'

'Hi, I'm Lola, I'm the sister the host normally keeps locked up in the attic during parties ...'

'Hi, I'm Lola. I went to school with the host. How do you know one another?' are sparkly.

4. **When you plan to network in business keep your goals in mind,** even if you hide them from the people you're meeting. Hard-selling as you're networking tends to fly in the face of UK business ethics, so keep your business cards in your pocket until the end of your chat (patting your pockets to pretend you're not sure if you have any on you is a good wheeze in UK business-networking events. In the US it would be seen as pretty stupid).

5. **Plan to do the room.** Suppress all your hatred and fear of mingling; this is what you're there for. At a business-networking event you are there to do the room and to speak to a wide range of other people. If you set yourself goals (Eight people per hour? Ten minutes per person?) you will remember to keep on the move. Your physical approach and your speech patterns will be naturally structured around this pace and movement, meaning you have less chance to 'nest' i.e. hunker in for a longer chat, and the people you're speaking to will intrinsically understand the fact you're there for a brief chat rather than a blossoming friendship. Aim to make your business networking a bit like speed-dating in terms of the constant sense of movement and energy, although without making the people you're talking to feel

like victims that you're chewing up and spitting out if they appear to be useless to you as a business contact. The whole point of networking is that you never know how, why and in what capacity you will meet people again. Being polite to everyone is a must. They could turn out to be a client of the future.

6. **Plan your small talk before you go.** Don't worry if this feels contrived. Making small talk is a ritual aimed at getting to know strangers by peeling back layers, like the layers of an onion. You start with general comments then try to find things you have in common. When you find those things you begin to build proper rapport. Years ago businessmen used to play golf because it gave them a method of fast-track rapport. Even guys who were total strangers could be deep in conversation a few minutes after meeting. Although golf is still a popular game it no longer dominates the business scene, mainly because most people are putting in too many hours to spend time hanging around the golf course. So we need to find other ways of getting chatting.

Types of small talk

The smallest small talk consists of the type of comments you make when you first meet a visitor or a client, and it often takes place in a lift or walking to the meeting. This is the easiest in terms of subjects because there really are only two: the journey or the weather.

As both travel and the weather are usually worth commenting on in the UK, confine yourself to them and don't worry about sounding corny. I was in a shop recently and the assistant asked: 'How has your day been so far?' when I put my purchase on the counter. Now this might work in the US retail environment, but in the UK it was plain creepy. I felt obliged to join in the charade, when a swift 'nice day' or 'horrible weather' would have made me feel much more comfortable, because a nod would have done in reply. And there's the rub: visitors are suffering from an overdose of stimulated senses. They're looking at reception, the atrium, your co-workers, the inside of the lift, where to go and how to get there. They're not looking for in-depth conversation. Shakespeare had it right when he started his plays with a bit of non-essential introduction. His audiences were gaping at the scenery and peeling their oranges. It was only later that they'd truly tune in to his prose.

Open questions. When you're making the smallest small talk then, try an easy open question. (Open questions are the type you can't answer yes or no to, you pretty much have to say a little more. They start with words like How, Where, Why and Are? Closed questions make conversation harder as the other person can just say yes or no in response, which means you'll have to think of another question to keep the chat going. These would start with words like Did, Is it, Can, Have, etc.) So 'How was your journey?' is a good first line as it's easy to answer but also easy to talk about if they want. They can provide you with a brief 'Okay, thanks' but they can also tell you all about their traffic jam on the A4 and a pit-stop at the Harvester.

Listen. If they talk a bit, make sure you're listening as your next statement or question should relate to what they've just said. Otherwise you'll sound exactly like you're working off a script, which you are to a certain extent, but no need to let them know that. Your comments should always be made to sound fresh and off the cuff. Try to ask more about them rather than hijacking the conversation by telling them all about your own journey.

Good listening

Good conversation entails active listening with active listening signals, plus your undivided attention. You need to use open questions and you need to feed off the answers.

- Use eye contact while you listen.
- Nod your head to show you are listening, that you understand and that you are keen to hear more.
- Pace your nodding to fit the pace or mood of their speech. If it's a serious story your pace will be slower. If it's upbeat, feel free to pick the beat up a bit but always avoid fast nodding as it's called a non-verbal interruption, i.e. you'll look like you want to butt in.
- Turn to face the speaker.

- Stop what you're doing.
- Don't fiddle, it will look as though your head is full of different thoughts.
- Use subtle mirroring, i.e. copying their pace, energy and type of body movements. Again, I'll emphasise the word 'subtle'. No copying every movement, it will look stupid.
- React to their story, but do listen to what they're saying. People often mask their feelings, meaning they might smile or even laugh when they're telling you how something tragic has happened to them. Mirroring their smiles will look unfeeling.

Avoid

- Queuing – thinking so hard about what you want to say next that you barely focus on what they are saying.
- Interrupting – either verbally or by nodding quickly.
- Faking it – going overboard in your responses: 'That sounds really interesting! No! How fascinating!'
- Hijacking – instead of focusing on their points you're too busy trying to make yourself the subject of the conversation: 'You think you had a bad journey? It took me three hours to get in this morning!'
- Finishing their sentences.
- Assuming that you know what they'll say next.

The next layer of the small-talk onion

Once you've peeled back that first layer via the journey or weather introductions you'll be on to the kind of discussion that will lead to rapport. This is the investigation phase of small talk, a bit like verbal flirting. You will be asking them more about themselves and their interests and possibly telling them a few things about yourself in a bid to find links.

In order to excel at this type of small talk you will need to do a little pre-event homework. This is easy and you should find it enjoyable as long as you keep an open mind. It entails immersing, or just dipping your toe into, the current subjects of the day. What are people using for their chat? What are the 'water-cooler' topics? Try some of the news or gossip websites if you're still stuck for inspiration.

Never ever allow your own dislike for a particular subject to block your ability to display some interest. This is not you pursuing your own hobbies; it's you discovering things that matter to other people. Imagine if the Queen went on her tours only willing to talk about life at the Palace and horse racing? You chat and you listen because it breaks the ice. Embrace the big icebreakers because they will help you out of any networking hole.

As I write, the World Cup is the subject of the month, with Wimbledon a close second. A few years ago you could bond instantly with huge groups of strangers when you spoke about *Big Brother*. It doesn't matter if the subjects make your nose turn up, this is networking chat, not you chatting with your mates. Nobody wins a prize for joining a new group, listening to their chat and then announcing 'I hate that programme/sport' in a superior tone. This is rude and you'd deserve to be ostracised. You've cut their conversation stone dead and they were happily scratching a path through the networking gloom that occurs when nobody can think of anything to say.

Instead of standing silently or trashing the subject when it's one you either know nothing about or you want to know nothing about, register novice interest instead. 'How many games are there left to go?' 'Who do you think will be in the final?' 'How does this compare to other years?' or 'I've never really watched golf. Which would be a good tournament to start with?' This would stimulate the conversation rather than close it down.

There's no need for you to spend your networking time grovelling and agreeing with everything you hear but you should not be a toxic presence, either. Toxic behaviours include the following:

- **Hijacking conversations** by walking in and changing the subject or tone.
- **Trashing the subject** by letting them know you have no interest in it.
- **Dismissing the subject** 'I can't stand that programme'.
- **Getting serious** when they're having a laugh.
- **Moaning**. Although it's good to talk about the weather or football, gripes should only ever be presented with humour and a more positive tone used when possible.

- Being **overly opinionated**.
- **Picking people off** when they have been talking in a larger group.
- **Interrupting** or butting in.
- **Talking to people about other people or events some of the group will know nothing about.** If you do mention someone or something others won't know, add an explanation upfront i.e. 'Did you see what Martin did at work yesterday?' Then, as an aside, tell any guest not aware who Martin is: 'Martin is the firm's HR manager. He organised a paint-ball event and came back still covered in gunk.' It is always very rude to discuss anything that not everyone in the group will know of when you refer to it. If you all work for the same company but have one visitor in your networking group you should either stay off internal subjects and references or explain any fleeting ones. In-chat is extremely rude. Include everyone.
- **Whispering.** Gah! How rude is this? There is also a form of visual whispering which involves the use of body-language tie-signs, small non-verbal signals that we use to flick quick messages across to other people. Eye-rolling, eye-widening, lip-pursing are some of these.
- **Berry-peeking.** Even ruder! Taking your BlackBerry or iPhone out and looking at it or even texting while you're in the middle of a conversation. Or even referring to the fact it's vibrating away in your pocket. Why do you need to have two conversations at once or even allow a trickle of messages to pollute the one you're currently having? I even saw backbenchers busily fiddling with their phones during the debate about the budget. So what if they were being fed facts and info? It's not the pub quiz! Your job is not so important that you need to be on call all the time. You're not a heart-transplant surgeon. Stay in the moment instead of insulting the people you're with.

Asking for help

When you're doing a room you can always get help. If you're stuck trying to mingle, get hold of the host or anyone you do know at your event and ask them who you should meet and whether they would introduce you. (They should be doing this anyway, but hey ho!)

As they walk you across, ask them who you'll be meeting, what they do for a living and anything else that might help create good small talk. Beginning your conversation with the words 'I hear you're a mean guitar-player' or 'I hear you and Sam had a great holiday in Crete last year' is a better warm-up than just 'Hi'.

Announcing yourself

Too many people get smirky and mysterious when introducing themselves. The more simple information you can give someone the easier the conversation will be. 'I'm Karen, I'm not sure if we've met before but I work on the fifth floor in accounts. I'm sure we went to the same all-staff last year. I'm the one who signs off all the expenses but please don't hold that against me!' will oil the wheels better than mumbling 'Karen' when asked your name.

Work alone

Too many people go to business-networking events and take a colleague, who they then spend the entire time talking to. This colleague is your comfort blanket but networking is networking and I can only recommend throwing yourself into the deep end and going alone. If the thought fills you with dread you have my total sympathy as I dread solo-mingling as well, but this book's not about sympathy and jelly-belly, it's about pushing yourself and being brave. Flying solo really is the best way to go. You already know your colleague. Talking to him or her is a waste of time.

Make a good entrance

The way you walk into a room will announce your levels of confidence and approachability more than anything you say when you start talking. Remember, entrances are our prime time in terms of self-marketing and pack acceptance or rejection. Next time you're at a 'do' notice how often you glance up to see who has just walked in. Then analyse whether you thought they looked upbeat, approachable, confident and sociable or whether you thought they might be hard work, either because they looked shy and miserable or because they looked stuck-up and arrogant. Never go into a room thinking you'll warm up a bit later on. People walk in wearing the journey, the weather outside or the trials of their day on their faces when they should be smiling and looking relaxed. How many times did you arrive at a party announcing you'd got lost or had a terrible journey? What do you think that moan did to your face and overall appeal? I know we're talking networking rather than dating but the same rules apply.

Before you walk into an event, take a moment. Remember your Power Pose and entrance-making from the previous chapter (see page 175). Pull yourself up to full height, drop your shoulders back and down, breathe out, shake your hands a little to relax them, keep bags tucked away, keep your right hands free for any handshakes, relax your facial expression and apply a natural-looking smile. (If you struggle with the latter, imagine you've just seen your best friend.) Then walk in.

Keep moving

It's easy to walk into a room when you're networking and then stop for a breather. The problem is it's also easy to find yourself glued to the same spot for hours. Momentum is a funny thing. Keep it going and you'll be okay. Stop and it's much harder to start up again. Walk across and get a drink (drink alcohol sparingly or better still not at all if you're business networking), glance around quickly and then start to 'do the room'.

Breaking into groups

Tempting though it is, try to avoid picking off lone guests who look shy like yourself (unless you're the host, in which case it's your job). Why? Because you want to meet people who are easy to talk to. I can't count the amount of times I've shuffled across to a like-minded shy type, only to find we've ended up having a tricky, monosyllabic conversation. Stuff them. Give them a wet wipe and a copy of this book and move on to the ones you'll enjoy talking to. Avoid duos as they'll probably be well bonded already and go for odd numbers, like trios or groups of five. If you approach a bigger group try to find one where they look slightly mismatched as it probably means they're a tribe of mongrels like yourself, rather than a close-knit group. Walk up with energy, don't dither. Look for the largest gap and walk up to stand in it. Glance quickly to the people on either side of you to smile and nod to register 'hello' then focus on the group alpha, who is the one leading the conversation. Never interrupt the speaker with your arrival. Nobody likes to be cut short in the middle of their best story. Small glances around will be enough to make first introductions. Listen to them talk and use mirroring techniques to build subliminal rapport before you've been introduced. Match the group's pace and style of speaking. When the speaker pauses or finishes, compliment or refer to their story and then introduce yourself, e.g. 'That sounds as though you were talking about Chiswick? I used to work there, is that where your company is? By the way, I'm Nigel ...'

What if they don't let me in?

It happens. People are rude or thoughtless or both. Sometimes I think people who have been or are shy themselves are so damn smug they're in with the in crowd at an event that they feel good rejecting other runts of the litter. Whatever. Plan your exit so you don't lose face by standing lurking wearing a sickly smile as you stare at their backs. And this is what you do: stand hoping they will let you in (I once listened to an American mingling expert and she said you should walk up quickly with your arm stuck out in front which would make them part or risk being impaled on your French Manicure. I'm not sure this is right for the UK though, as I believe we'd part to let someone so attacking to get into our circle then out the other side, so you'd end up standing with your arm still out and your back to the group). Only stand for a few seconds, though. The longer you wait the lower your perceived status in pack terms and the more you risk looking like the drinks waiter or some sad, Billy-no-mates lurker. But don't slink away muttering curses on their first-born. Either look at your watch in a theatrical way or pretend to wave to someone on the other side of the room before you walk off. That way it looks as though you have been hailed or called away to another appointment.

Matching and pacing

Remember to subtly mimic the pace and energy of the people or person you are talking to. Avoid creating body barriers by folding your arms or clutching your bag close or your drink high on your chest. Use your active listening signals. And the key thing about small talk is that you ask a question and then look genuinely interested in the answer. I once saw Prince Philip do a room and that's exactly what he did. He asked everyone what they did but then looked completely engrossed in the answers. It was such a simple technique but the impact was massive. How many times do we ask a question but then look bored, distracted or as though we're set to hijack the conversation when the other person answers.

Here's a quick way to test your listening/questioning skills

Team up with a friend or colleague. Ask them to say 'Corfu' when you ask them a question. Then begin your small talk role-play. You go first:

'Where did you go on holiday this year?'

'Corfu.'

It is now up to you to continue the conversation. It's your job to get it flowing and sounding natural rather than forced. What will you say? Will it be:

'Corfu?' (Reflecting technique, good if you say it in a way that eggs them to tell you more.)

'Oh. Nice.' (Dead end.)

'What part?' (Only good if you have a spankingly wonderful follow-up comment.)

'I thought about going there because my mate went last year but I opted for Greece in the end ...' (Hijack.)

You might have thought this was easy. You don't know. If the conversation never took off or if it died with some silence punctuated by nervous giggling, you know you need some more practice.

How to get away from someone

Hopefully not because they've bored you into a snore, but because you know you need to be off re-mingling. Warn them of your intentions towards the end of your chat by making your body-language signals a little more room-sociable again. You will have been giving your companion your undivided attention up until this point, but you begin to glance away slightly as you talk (not as they do, it's rude), and begin to look to people nearby as though checking they're not looking to join you. Don't tell lies to get away, so no 'I'm just getting a refill' (You should ask if they want one too) or 'I'm just off to the loo'. Make your exit mutual by saying something like: 'I suppose we ought to be off doing the room. Is there anyone you've met so far that you think I ought to be talking to?' This makes it less like a rejection, which some people do think, even at a business event.

How not to let yourself down!

The kind of business/social events like Christmas office parties or even client-hosted parties can easily be misleading. Every year many people blot an entirely clean workplace copybook because they believe anything that involves alcohol and chatter means that you can behave how you like, let your hair down a little and go in with the attitude that whatever happens at the bash stays at the bash. Not true. When you're at a networking event or at any function that is related to your job please keep in mind that the device has yet to be invented that will delete the memory of your dad-dancing, singing 'Delilah', telling that non-PC joke or flirting with the boss's wife from people's minds. You did it. Think how you will feel once the party is over. If you want to let your hair down, do it with friends, not business acquaintances, either that or only let it down a bristle-length or two.

Confident greetings

Greeting rituals are a hotbed of animal survival techniques plus social etiquette rules. Your greeting skills are vital in terms of your projected status and confidence, yet so many of us leave the thought of how to greet right up until the last minute, when our guest or client is approaching with an expression of expectation.

For the animal inside you your greetings are all about survival. When an ape greets another ape he will be expected to offer a selection of submission signals unless he wants to get into a fight. These signals might include head-ducking and body-lowering, which humans have turned into a bow, offering a paw, held out to be bitten off if the other ape chooses, which we have turned into the mutually submissive palm-against-palm handshake, and the teeth-bare, a sign of fear in the ape world, which humans display as the smile of greeting.

Although getting these signals right could mean life or death to an ape, in human terms it's more likely to mean rapport or lack of it. Your first impressions take only a split second in some circumstances, so dithering over a handshake instead of offering a calm, confident, dry palm, or sticking out the classic dead fish or bone-cruncher should not be an option as a weak handshake suggests a spine made of marshmallow, while a cruncher suggests a cruelly competitive twerp.

Wiping your hand right before you offer it might appear polite if you're hosting a small puddle of sweat but it is much more thoughtful and impressive in terms of projected confidence if you wipe the sweat off first, ideally out of sight.

Greetings etiquette

Business handshakes are a good idea as they provide a formal form of rapport building.

- When you're shaking in business it's the host that should extend their hand first.
- If you're the host, use an announcement signal by holding your arm out while you are still a couple of paces away from them. Last-minute offers can lead to awkwardness.
- Give a firm, dry handshake, palm against palm, with your hands going up and down twice.
- Use eye contact and a natural-looking smile as you shake.
- Avoid adding to the touch. Although it's common to see high-ranking people like heads of state add the arm-pat to their shakes the traditional UK handshake involves no other touch than the two hands themselves.
- Never offer a hand-sandwich. This is where you hold the other person's hands in both of yours. Way too dramatic for the UK market.
- Decide to shake and don't dither. Once your hand has started to go out, see the gesture through or you'll appear clumsy and awkward.

- Rehearse your handshakes at home first, until they feel more natural.
- Kissing has become the norm at social events, but also at certain business meetings. In business it's unusual to cheek-kiss someone you have had no quasi-social conversations with, so it would normally be reserved for people you've had chats with about your family and home life. To cheek-kiss you need to place your hands lightly on the other person's shoulders for steering, place your right cheek alongside theirs but without touching, then go to the other side and then part. In the UK one kiss on each cheek tends to be the norm but you will always find some people who are either coming back for more or ducking away after the first peck. If this does happen it's kindest to be firm. If they're pulling away, grab them lightly by the shoulders and even say 'One more' as you go for your quota. If they're in for a third you just need to display pleasure rather than distaste at the added snog-ette. Smile and say 'Oh a third!' and fall in towards them with a high level of social enthusiasm.

IN A NUTSHELL

- Make a powerful entrance.

- Keep the momentum going.

- Work your small talk. Seek out topics to achieve fast-track rapport.

HOW TO EAT OUT/STAY IN HOTELS WITH CONFIDENCE

I have always been fascinated by the fast-food phenomenon. On the odd occasion I've used a fast-food outlet I have seen genuinely unappetising-looking food that people are sitting eating glumly. The price is clearly an attraction, as is the advertising, but I believe the uniformity of the experience must add a lot to the seduction process. Most restaurants are a minefield for anyone lacking confidence. They involve waiting to be seated, menu ordering, confusing drinks menus, cutlery and condiment mastery and things like tips and card payments. Walking up to a till and asking for a brunch burger that is clearly photographed and hung above the counter with its price must seem like a dream by comparison. 'Do you want chips with that?' seems to be the only question asked, compared to the litany of choices that are flung your way in the average restaurant.

Hotels can be as bad, if not worse; being asked if you want a table for dinner and an early morning call/newspaper just as you're trying to focus on writing down your car registration details can cause cerebral overload.

Then there's the added problem that the way you consume food says a lot about your approach to sex. (Hence the teen-appeal of places that offer instant cheap, no-frills food with its instant-gratification solution to filling your face as opposed to establishments catering for older people where delayed gratification and reassuring quality is the order of the day and appetites have to be tickled via intriguing blends of flavours rather than sated ASAP.)

- When you're checking into your hotel make sure you queue at reception, not concierge. It's easily done, especially in the posh places.
- Keep a note of your booking reservation number. I've lost count of the amount of hotels that seem to 'lose' bookings.
- If you get bombarded with requests about early morning calls, etc., tell them you'll pop back down to confirm later.
- In a modern hotel the room key will probably be a plastic swipe card. These never work first time. Look for the strip and the arrow to help you swipe the right way.
- That card often needs to be inserted into a wall-mounted light switch once you get into your room. Most people ring down to say the lights aren't working and get told about the cardholder by a very narky-sounding receptionist.
- If you're trying to impress your partner don't take all the bathroom bits like soap and a sewing kit; it looks mean.

- And don't start tutting about the price list for the mini-bar.
- The electric kettle will work three times slower than your own at home and the hairdryer probably has a heat control switch that makes it cut off after a few minutes of use.
- You will need a degree to be able to use the shower. The ones with the handlebar-style controls are the worst. Always make sure you don't try to run a bath while you are fully clothed. Inevitably the unit will be switched to 'shower' and you will get soaked.
- Untuck your bedding before you retire. Hotel staff have a habit of tucking sheets and duvets as tight as possible, making sex impossible as you'll find you're lying like a tax bill in a sturdy brown envelope.
- Hotel phones cost a huge fortune. Use your mobile.
- Always check the fire exits. Most hotels have regular evacuations, mostly in the middle of the night.
- When you're eating out, check other people's dietary requirements are catered for. I was once taken to a restaurant where the only veggie option was a goat's cheese stew.
- Allow your guest to sit with their back to the wall. It's the way an animal would prefer to eat.
- If you don't understand something on the menu ask the waiter when he or she comes round to take the order. If you don't speak French and the menu is written in it, ask for an English version.
- It's okay to ask for tap water if you don't want to pay top dollar for bottled.
- Bread usually comes up before the meal. Never cut your roll in half and butter it. Break the bread off into pieces to eat it. Don't scoff it all before the meal, it looks cheap.
- The simplest rule with an array of cutlery is to start from the outside and work your way inward.
- The chef gets upset if you salt and pepper your meal before you taste it but – frankly my dear – I don't give a damn.
- The hardest time to catch the waiter's eye is when you want to pay and leave. If possible, go up and pay at the till.
- If you think someone else is paying it always looks nice to make some move towards offering, like patting your pockets or rooting in your bag for your card.

- If they insist, say thank you and add 'My turn next time'.
- Look to see if service has been included. If not, go for about 10 per cent or more if it was exceptional.
- If you're at a business meeting and sandwiches are served it looks deeply unpleasant to prise them open while making your selection.
- In business make it a rule never to be the first one at the coffee pots. They are a nightmare to get working with dials that turn, spouts that miss, plungers that need to be activated and unlabelled pots that pour coffee all over your tea bag. Let some other poor sucker go first while you watch and learn.
- Don't ferret away biscuits at a business gathering. One is okay but a handful looks cheap, as does any food that you take from the food area 'for later'.
- Never take sweets from a business meeting. And however altruistic-looking it is, never stack a pile of curling sandwiches into a napkin 'for the guys back in the office'. What are they? Too poor to eat?
- Never take your breakfast into a business meeting. It's wrong on so many counts but one is that it makes you look poorly time-organised.

IN A NUTSHELL

- Expect to be confused. Most hotels are confusing.

- Remember how the key works, including the lights.

- Never rob your own hotel soap before you've used it.

- Hang back when it comes to the coffee pots.

9

PERFORMING WELL IN BUSINESS, ONSTAGE AND IN LIFE

HOW TO BE CONFIDENT AT INTERVIEWS

The words 'confident' and 'interview' are not exactly the happiest of bedfellows. It's strange for anyone to attend a formal meeting with what could well be total strangers in a bid to prove they are suitable for paid employment, so take it as a given that your lack of confidence is entirely normal.

Your confidence goal, then, is to keep your nerves sufficiently in check to enable you to present yourself and your skills and abilities well. An interview is a form of performance, not because you will be lying your way to the job or promotion, but because you will be placed in unnatural circumstances, meaning preparation is vital, not just on your CV but on the way you intend to meet, greet and communicate with your interviewer/s.

Preparation
- **Prep your TFB (Think – Feel – Behave)**
- **Use your 'sell to yourself first' strategy**
  Pitching up at a recruitment or promotion interview in the hope they'll see something amazing about you is screwball. Be your own marketing manager. What is it about you that makes you right for this job? Create as close a fit as possible between your skills and strengths and the job requirements and where there is a gap see if you can bridge it by adding other competencies

or creating a plan to take training on the job. Remember your Shield Exercise from page 63? Study it. Not all the positives you have listed on your shield will be right for the job but by looking at it you will be boosting your confidence, self-belief and inner resolve.

- **Talk yourself up, both in terms of motivation and ego**
Use your Leader Voice to get your bravery levels rising, and to help muffle any negative inner dialogues to a point where they are virtually silent. Get your mantras out and dust them down, and block your ears to all the bad news about high unemployment levels and the amount of people applying for jobs. To succeed in the job market you need blinkers and a thick skin.

- **Use filleting to plan your dialogue**
This is like pulling the bones out of a fish. The backbone is your main objective, which is to get the job. All the other bones need to attach to this one objective, meaning you plan six or more key reasons why you would be the ideal candidate, keeping in mind their interests rather than your own. 'I would see it as a challenge' is less tempting a reason for the company than 'I have experience in this field and would intend to put all my energy and enthusiasm into being successful at it'. When you plan your main persuaders, always hear them through the ears of your listeners. Then offer proof of your main persuaders. Telling an interviewer you're good at leading a team is offering an opinion. Giving them examples of times when you have been a team leader and achieved the team task is actual evidence.

- **An acceptable degree of nerves**
Cut yourself some slack. Sometimes nervousness can power us up to a better performance. Remember one key tip I learnt from Olympic Sporting coaches:
  'When you feel the butterflies build up in your stomach, don't try to get rid of them, get them flying in formation.'
I have lost count of the times I have managed to control my own butterflies and get them flying in formation to help create a better performance.

- **Remember they're on your side**
It's easy to have your confidence sapped by the notion that the interviewers are somehow the enemy. They're not. They're on

your side. They want you to be the right one for the job. The recruitment process is an expensive and time-consuming one. They're gagging for you to be the ideal candidate. If they do appear dour (not a given, many are friendly) it's because they're trying to excavate for the talent in you, not butter you up so much they miss the real you.

- **Do your homework**
Always find out as much as you can about the company and the job they're offering.

The interview

- **Make a good entrance**
Remember the impact of the first impression. This is called the Attribution Effect, where we make some of our most important judgements of someone within the first few seconds of meeting them. The good news is that many of those judgements are based on visual signals, from how smart you look to your body language. Pause before you walk into the room and adopt your Power Pose, which is done by pulling up to full height, breathing out gently, pushing your shoulders back and down, raising your chin so that it is at about 45 degrees to your neck (no higher, it will look arrogant), relax your hands by shaking them gently, keep your bag (if you have one) out of the way, rather than clutching it, and relax your facial expression so that your eye muscles give a softened expression and your eyes and mouth wear a confident-looking (not fixed or over-performed) smile. See page 175 for more tips.
- **Keep your right hand free for a possible handshake**
- **Wait to be offered a seat**
And when you do sit down adopt a confident pose. Sit into the back of your seat, cross your legs (if you are short and your feet miss the floor then sit further forward), or sit with them slightly apart if you're a guy, and rest your elbows on the arms of the chair (if there are none, rest your hands lightly in your lap).
- **Use active listening signals**
And feel free to pause to consider your answer before you speak. Fast nodding and speedy replies won't gain you any points. There's a lot at stake and it's not a race. If you don't completely

understand the question feel free to ask for clarification.

- **Try not to bluff**

  If there's a question you don't know the answer to and you try to bluff your way out, it's likely they will spot the fact you're bluffing and worry you might be unreliable in terms of trust if you do get the job. Many employers and managers I speak to say they would always prefer to employ someone who will hold their hands up if they have made a mistake, rather than covering it up.

- **Signs of nerves are not always a problem**

  It shows the interviewer you take the process seriously. Blushing or even a neck rash are common sights (try green-tinted moisturiser as it negates the pink, or a higher neckline if a chest/neck rash is the problem). Shaking hands can be warded off by flexing them before you walk in.

- **Gesticulate**

  To look confident as you answer questions, use open, emphatic gestures. Avoid fiddling gestures (if you tend to fiddle with jewellery, leave it off and if you twiddle with your hair, tie it back) or hand wringing, which can make you look desperate.

- **Keep your hand gestures below shoulder-height**

  Any higher can look ditsy or hysterical.

- **Lean forward**

  When you make an important point or when they do, it's good to lean forward a little bit.

- **Use eye contact**

  But with a softened eye expression, not a stare. Look at the person asking the question as they ask it, then look around at the rest of the panel as you give your answer.

- **Mirror**

  Their general body language and mood. If they're formal you remain formal, if they're relaxed and chatty do the same. Never be more relaxed than they are though, it shows a lack of respect.

- **Make a good exit**

  Smile, thank them and expect to shake hands again.

CLIMBING OUT FROM BEHIND THE VIRTUAL CONVERSATIONS

Email, texts and all the myriad types of social networking form a method of communication that seem invented for the shy, hesitant, social-phobic people with low confidence and low self-esteem. As a way of keeping in touch without all the pain of having to deliver your messages in person it's akin to discovering online food that looks, smells and even tastes like the real thing when you lick the screen. But ultimately you'd starve, which is what will happen if you resign yourself to the seductive charms of virtual communication.

It's easy. Which is exactly why you should treat it with caution, not because I subscribe to the 'no pain, no gain' school of self-improvement but because the use of these methods will create the feeling that you're socialising when in fact you're not.

Communications and relationships should be based on face-to-face talks. Email is great as a way of sending factual messages, a little like telegrams would have done years ago, but we began using them for emotional messages as well, which is undoubtedly risky. Because they come with no vocal tone or visual signals it's up to the reader to apply their own version of both. Take any one message that you have written in words and then see how many different connotations you can apply to that message by changing your tone as you read it. I even spoke to one employee who had been sent an email from his boss saying 'Well done, everyone' and who thought it must be sarcastic.

By hiding behind social networking, emails and texts you erode your own social skills. Although they're good for keeping in touch with other people they should never be seen as your core method of communication. If you need to speak, do so face-to-face or at least by phone. Charisma doesn't present via email, irritation does.

Never confuse an exclamation mark or a smiley face for having a personality

Push on with your 'real' communications, even if it hurts. You don't become less shy or more confident by using virtual communication techniques any more than you get fit watching a workout DVD. The only way to make your socialising or networking work is to keep doing it. By popping to chat to a colleague rather than popping an email, by picking up the phone rather than texting, by socialising with your friends rather than just sending one-liners on a screen, by going on a date rather than flirting via your keyboard you keep exercising your communication muscle. Every time you weigh up the options of your method of communication and decide email is easier you erode your own confidence for the real thing.

No great leaders, speakers, motivators or charismatics have ever used email as their method of getting their core messages across. If you are a manager or leader in business, shame on you if you use email in any way to inspire or motivate your teams. You are a coward and don't deserve your post.

Deliver your messages, don't send them, especially the difficult ones.

Why face-to-face?

Because all-important communications should be two-way. No matter how shy or lacking in confidence you are, you should be able to see the person you are talking to so that you can judge the effect of your words, preferably as you say them.

Proper communication is all about sending and accepting messages all at the same time. We speak, we look, we listen.

We then evaluate and we change what's not working.

Your conversations need to involve both eye- and ear-listening to be effective. When we are able to watch someone's non-verbal signals we are able to read between the lines and understand more of their message. In this way we are all experts in body language. You've been reading it all your life and you are already adept at spotting clues that someone's unhappy, happy, anxious or even lying to you.

INTERVIEW AND FACE-TO-FACE CONTACT IN A NUTSHELL
- Do use email and text but hone the skills of face-to-face contact to make 'real' conversations, like interviews, less of a challenge.
- Harness your nerves, get them flying in formation.
- Make a good entrance.
- Sit well.
- Get the handshake right.
- Do your Shield Exercise (see page 63) to remind yourself of your strengths.
- Then be more specific, answering the questions 'Why would I give myself this job/promotion? What can I offer this post/company?'

CONFIDENT BUSINESS MEETINGS

Business meetings tend to rate the top spot in any lists of the biggest business time-wasters. Why? As they rarely achieve anything tangible for many companies they have become a ritual rather than a practicality, plus they can be distressingly boring, meaning people tune out for much of the time, plus (and here's the confidence factor), they can tend to be dominated by the more extrovert characters who enjoy hearing the sound of their own voice while shy or less-confident attendees sit like bumps on a log, too disabled by their own insecurities to contribute in any way that is of value.

Preparation

Think of your meetings like a game of football. Either you're out there on the pitch playing the game, despite any risks that might entail, or you're up in the stands cheering or moaning but ultimately ineffectual. Ask yourself:

- How often do I come away from meetings frustrated because I have not been able to make my points?
- How often do I sit in silence during meetings, only to let rip with my own thoughts, ideas and criticisms once I'm outside the meeting room?
- How often do I sit on an idea during a meeting because I don't have the courage to raise it?

- Only to hear someone else suggest it and then take all the praise that should have been mine?
- How often have you heard yourself say: 'That was my idea ...'
- Or 'I just said that!'
- How often do you speak up only to find no one seems to take any notice?
- How often do you find it impossible to break in because everyone talks over you?
- How often do you find yourself starting your point with phrases like: 'I know this might sound stupid but ...'?

The whole point of a meeting is to join in. If you have already made a name for yourself as a bit of a dummy who sits through them rather than participating in them, you'll need to break those bad habits as soon as possible. This will require discipline. The good news is, nobody died. This is not a life-threatening experience, it just feels like it.

Challenge your thinking
Phrases like:
- It's not worth saying anything
- Anything for a quiet life
- Nothing ever changes anyway
- It's better to just go along with the group
- I'd rather not stand out
- This meeting is not really aimed at me anyway

need to be deleted from your thought repertoire when you have a meeting coming up.

In the meeting
- Ask for a schedule or minutes beforehand including the main points up for discussion so that you can prep your thinking.
- Always turn up on time.
- Again, one key tip in this book, make a good entrance, by which I mean no creeping in trying to get a seat at the back or walking in looking unsure or unhappy. Take a moment before you make your entrance, reboot your body using tips listed in the

book already and walk in briskly, looking positive and upbeat.

- If the meeting is a large one and held in the format of an audience, pick a seat in the front row.

FRONT-ROW THINKING

When you rush to take a seat that is hidden from view, take a moment to realise what you're saying to your group as well as to yourself. You are announcing that your presence is unnecessary and that your contribution will be insignificant. You lower your own status and you diminish your power to zero. Never wonder why nobody took your comments seriously or even heard what you said. You have already informed them that is the appropriate reaction.

- If you're at a meeting around a board table, pick the seat that will create the best profile for you in terms of status and impact. Check out the highest-status person at the meeting. (I'm assuming it's the manager, boss, or chief exec.) The 'boss' seat used to be at either end of the table, recreating the kind of pecking order you'd get around a dinner table at home. These days, though, most bosses prefer to sit in the middle of a long side, more like a Jesus at the last supper-effect. Sitting directly opposite the boss is a bad move as it looks confrontational. Sitting right next to the boss is a bad move as it implies sucker-up, henchman or assistant. But you don't want to be tucked too far out of sight. So a diagonal is the best bet, visible, but not confrontational.
- Take a good pen. Small details count. A good pen looks confident and competent in a way that a shabby old ballpoint with hotel logo down the side never will.
- And good stationery.
- Create your space by laying both out on the table in front of you, but without spreading out over the space of the person sitting next to you.
- If it's a formal meeting, shake hands with everybody first.
- If it's colleagues you know, greet every one of them with eye contact and a nod. Ignore nobody.
- Where possible be the greeter rather than the greeted. Sitting

waiting for other people to see you and say hello will make you look and feel less confident.

- Use names where possible, it sounds confident.
- Don't sit with your arms folded.
- Don't bring your mobile or BlackBerry in and sit fiddling with it.
- Speak within the first three minutes, even if it's just during the small talk period before the presentations or more formal points start. This is a golden rule. Any longer the harder it gets to join in. Speaking at the start means your voice is up there in the air.
- Plan your key points beforehand. What do you want to say, why do you want to say it and why should they want to hear it?
- Never plan to wait until the end of the meeting to speak. That's when most people are mentally getting back to their desks and workload. You'll sound like a time-wasting interruption of that process.
- Be concise and use high-impact speech, like: 'I think this could be a solution ...' 'I've been looking at this idea ...' 'This is a really good alternative ...' 'Has anyone thought about this ...'
- Never speak from the position you've been sitting in. That was your silent listening pose. Move into speaking mode.
- Always join in visually, even when you're listening. Match the pace and style of movement of the others and nod to show you're contributing.
- Announce the fact you want to speak by leaning forward, placing your hands on the table, raising your pen or hand, raising your eyebrows, raising both hands if they still don't shut up. (This is a list of options, don't try them all at once or you'll look like you're having a turn.)
- Or use the speaker's name to attract attention if they still ignore you.
- Remember that being ignored is rarely a personal attack or put-down, they're probably just too lost in their own moment onstage.
- When you have their attention never ramble, dither, moan or 'Yes ... but...' the idea on the table, as in 'That might sound like a good idea, but ...'
- Never use the old passive-aggressive ploy of pulling a face at something that's been said or sitting back and folding your arms but refusing to offer your opinion when your visual dissent has

been noticed. 'No, I'm fine, thanks,' is a nasty ploy when you're quite obviously letting them know you're not.

• Or the ploy of saving all your gripes up for one big go. I recently had a guy at a conference who sat in silence for the first part then right near the end (despite feedback being invited throughout) suddenly rumbled to life to disagree with two points, one use of a word and one key theory. Then said 'No, fine' when offered a longer chat during the break. Behaviour like that just looks like willy-waving.

• When you get to speak, use eye contact on the entire group when possible. When you're presenting an idea it always looks more confident if you appear to be reading reactions and feedback. Looking down or looking away will give the impression you have no confidence in your point and therefore can't bear to see how it's going down with your audience.

• Use all the verbal techniques in the section of the book on words.

• Never start looking at your watch or stacking your papers before the meeting is over. It looks rude and implies you're keen to make a speedy, nervous exit.

• If someone made a good point during the meeting go across and tell them so on the way out. (No need to be too loud doing this in case it gets read as sucking up.)

IN A NUTSHELL

• Go to meetings with your goals in mind.

• Arrive on time and make a good entrance.

• Speak within the first three minutes.

• Use announcement gestures to get people to listen to you.

• Choose a seat that projects good levels of status and confidence.

ASKING FOR A PAY RISE

Preparation

- Timing will be everything. Study your manager/boss. When is he or she the most open to a persuasive communication? Never barge in or catch them on the hop, i.e. in the lift, always book an appointment at a time you know you'll have their full attention.
- Plan your pitch with military precision. Bumbling nervously about wanting more money won't work. Answer the questions: 'Why am I worth more?' and 'Why will they think I'm worth more?' If you can't then now is not the time to be asking.
- See the conversation through their eyes.

The pitch

- Avoid confrontation or ultimatums.
- Include their key objectives in your own dialogue, i.e. 'I know we have pay bands but I do feel I have a special case because ...'
- Don't moan or gripe.
- Know how much extra you want. They could easily ask you. Be realistic but add a top-up so you have room for negotiation.
- Make sure your speech is clear, concise and to the point. Use the techniques listed in the section of the book on communication and words to ensure you don't stammer, waffle or use diluting words or phrases.
- Don't backtrack. Some people get so nervous they end up turning themselves down, e.g. 'I'd like a pay rise, I know it's not going to happen and I know it's a bad time to ask, with the recession and everything but I do need some extra for my holiday although I could get a loan I suppose ...' etc.
- Be polite but sound firm.
- Be friendly but not a pushover.
- Plan your main points before you speak. Never go into the negotiation thinking you'll play it by ear.
- Don't boast but do give facts if you've achieved well over the last year.
- Boost your confidence by studying your Shield (see page 63), repeating your motivational mantras and visualising your

negotiation from start to end.
- Listen well. Remember it's not just you who's going to talk during the negotiation. Listen to their points without interruption to show you're being reasonable.
- If they turn you down, ask what your next steps should be to ensure you're more successful next time. Would they suggest further training or qualifications? When would be a good time to reapply?
- Get your body language as right as your words. Sit back in the chair, hands crossed lightly in your lap, don't fiddle or face-touch, keep a confident, relaxed facial expression and remember to push your shoulders back and down to relax your posture.

IN A NUTSHELL

- Know your objective.

- Know your key persuaders: why do you deserve to earn more money?

- Pick your time and your place.

- Be concise and don't talk yourself down.

HOW TO GIVE A CONFIDENT BUSINESS PRESENTATION

The words 'business' and 'presentation' tend to have the same effect on your confidence as a vampire would have on your blood-stream but there are some simple steps you can take to ensure a lack of confidence doesn't damage your performance.

Preparation
- Understand that the skill of delivering a professional pre-sentation is no longer an add-on for success in the workplace,

it's an essential. People sell, train, motivate and influence via the medium of presentations. Ducking out of doing them or refusing to learn the skill is like refusing to learn how to work a computer. Once you see it as non-negotiable you can move on and become successful. When you make excuses and create sick notes to duck out, you can't.

- Rev yourself up with some motivational mantras. 'I love giving presentations', 'I know this is going to be good'.

- If you're wilting with nerves tell yourself to get over it. Get a grip. Nobody died. You just have to talk. How long have you been talking? From the age of two years. Shame on you if you never worked out how to talk properly. That's all you'll be doing, talking to other people. Only do speak to yourself beforehand. Deliver a bit of a roasting. Get angry with yourself. Egg yourself out of your fear.

- Visualise success, it's the best way to grow your confidence. Instead of sitting imagining everything that can go wrong, close your eyes and make yourself see You walking, standing and talking with supreme confidence. Once you have tuned in to this image, study it and feel it. How does this confident You look? How are You standing? What is Your facial expression like? What kind of hand gestures are You using? See your audience enjoying the talk, too. What we imagine is like a dress rehearsal for the real thing. See yourself doing well and your body will adopt that look. See yourself being rubbish and you can create that, too. Pick success.

- Begin by writing down your objective. A presentation is a communication and all effective communication has a point. What is yours?

- Now sell that point to yourself. Convince yourself it is a message that needs communicating. Know what you want to achieve by doing so.

- Now sell You to yourself. No wobbling or ducking out thanks to nerves. Fear under these circumstances is only destructive if you pander to it. It's not a lion; it's just a talk you are going to give. Your fear is an irrelevant by-product of the process. Feel it, identify it then control it, don't let it control you. Work out why it should be you giving this talk and why you will give this talk well.

- Plan your structure by writing your ideas under the following headings:
  * Subject under discussion
  * Aims and objectives
  * Limits: e.g. time, existing knowledge of your audience, jargon, etc.
  * Objections: what objections might they have to any of your points? Getting inside your audience's minds is vital. Once you know any key objections it will be far more powerful for you to bring them up than waiting for them to voice them.
  * Discussion – your key points, persuaders and proof.
  * Summary – how you will finish your talk, i.e. repeating your key points to add to the emphasis.
- Belt and braces – what could go wrong? Instead of worrying about problems, which will make you lose sleep and drain your confidence, plan what you can do to prevent them happening or how you can deal with them if they do. Over-reliance on electronic equipment or concern about difficult questions will sap your inner confidence. Instead of worrying, plan.
- Questions. It's good to get questions because it means the audience are engaged. But not everyone knows everything. Work out beforehand which questions you are likely to get, and plan your answers. I'm constantly amazed at the amount of politicians of the highest levels that haven't prepared their responses to some of the trickier questions they should have been expecting.
- You also need to plan your responses to any killer questions. If you're presenting in business you need to know why your product is dearer than a rival's, or if there are any skeletons rattling in your corporate closet.
- And plan what you will do if you don't know the answer to a question. It helps avoid the freeze when you stall over your own lack of knowledge. Never look or sound flustered and always avoid bluffing because it breaks down trust. Tell them you don't know the answer, but that you will find out and get back to them.
- Work naked first. What do I mean by that? Essentially, I mean ditch the props. A lack of confidence leads to over-dependence on visual aids, like complicated slide shows that are full of written

facts that speakers tend to use as a script. The only way to gain confidence as a presenter, though, is to prep, plan and rehearse your talk without aids first then only bring them in to add to any of your points. Slides are boring unless they are diagrams or photos. Using them as your own script stops your ideal thought process, which is where you think about what you're going to say and which points you want to make before and while you speak. True presentation confidence comes from a flow of thoughts to the mouth. You'll need notes with bullet points to keep those thoughts structured but reading off a screen will shut down your brain rather than opening it. Remember when you wore a rubber ring in the swimming pool? It kept you afloat but it was cumbersome and prevented you from swimming. To learn to swim you had to take it off and then take the plunge. The same is true of your presentation skills. Switch the slides off, apart from the genuinely illustrative ones, and take the plunge.

The presentation

- Use all your breathing and calming techniques listed in previous sections of the book, including breathing out gently to relax your body, and tensing then flexing your muscles.
- Take a moment before you start. Never rush to speak. Get to your spot, move chairs or other equipment first if necessary to take control of your area, then pause, look at your audience (with a degree of fondness, not fear or hostility) and start with a friendly greeting to break the ice.
- Never assume your audience are judging you negatively. There is a body-language phenomenon called dog-facing that describes the way people in an audience will often employ a deadpan facial expression when they're watching a talk or performance. It's a blank mask that tends to hide true feelings, which can be hugely positive, so don't be put off. To break down the chances of dog-facing, get a response or movement from your audience as quickly as possible. This will help relax them and you.
- Stand well. Use your Power Pose, i.e. stand as tall as possible, head at a 45-degree angle to your neck, shoulders rolled back and down, feet about shoulder width apart (less wide for women), and weight evenly balanced on your feet. Keep your

hands lightly touched together in front of your body but don't clasp them or clutch any other object like notes, pens or pointers. (These are a stand-in for a teddy bear, something you'll find yourself clutching for comfort.)

- Start with some empathy. Use eye contact on your audience (keeping your eye expression friendly and relaxed), and if you can, begin with a thought that's in their head, rather than voicing your own self-concerns. Never begin by telling your audience you're nervous as it's just plain irritating, but do thank them for turning up at a time when you know they must be busy. If your subject sounds dry or complicated you can tell them you know that's how it sounds, but that you'll be aiming to engage them by making it interesting or keeping it as simple as possible by steering them towards the key points.
- Keep a glass of room-temperature water nearby.
- Be funny if you feel that's your forte but don't tell jokes. Jokes require a well-delivered punchline and a laugh from the audience, otherwise they fall flat. If you're feeling nervous you'll risk botching it and if there is a silence great enough for the old tumbleweed to come rolling across the room you'll struggle to overcome the dip. The other risk with jokes is that there is always someone in any audience who will be offended, no matter how PC you try to be. Trust me, I know.
- Choose your clothes with care. Not only do you want to project the right image, you want to tell yourself good things about You too. Never dress like a loser. How does that look? Scruffy, low-status, ill-fitting, busy, dull, complicated, cheap-looking, creased, mumsy looks like long skirts and cardis, pockets stuffed with rubbish, hankies shoved up sleeves, bad ties, shirts that don't do up, ties that aren't done up, scuffed shoes, chipped nails, etc. I recently watched a leading politician who stood up to speak in parliament with a jacket that was too tight to button but which had sleeves so long you could barely see any hands poking out, a shirt that was so low cut you could see cleavage but so ill-fitting that the buttons were gaping. Bad, bad, bad!
- Empty your pockets in case you start fiddling with the contents.
- And if you fiddle with jewellery, take it off. If you fiddle with your hair, tie it back.

- When you speak, use congruent gestures. This means matching your gestures to your words. If you are incongruent, i.e. your non-verbal signals appear to be at odds with your points, you dilute the impact and power of your message. This is known as self-heckling, where you appear to be in disagreement with your own points. An example would be a football manager saying he was sorry for his team's dire performance but shrugging dismissively as he speaks. Or a woman telling her boyfriend she loved him but glancing away or looking at her watch as she said it.

- When you rehearse your speech, rehearse your gestures too, looking in a mirror as you do so. I'm not advising you to create an entirely scripted performance that includes choreographed hand gestures but it would be senseless to focus entirely on your words while allowing your non-verbal signals to do their own thing. By rehearsing them beforehand you'll get used to the feel of congruent, emphatic gesticulation, rather than suddenly waving your hands about for the first time when you stand up to project your message.

- Walk if you feel it suits you. Nobody said you have to stay rooted to the spot when you're presenting.

- If you're using visual aids (and I consider most of them to be the spawn of the devil) avoid looking back at the screen as you speak. Why? Three key reasons:
  1. Because your eyes tend to roll upwards or down to one side when you're genuinely recalling a point. When we look back behind us it will often create brain cut-off.
  2. Reading off the screen is vile. It insults the audience and makes your talk terminally boring.
  3. If you're staring back at a blank screen or flipchart (as many presenters do, in desperation) you'll look as though you're expecting some form of divine inspiration.

- There is a school of thought that suggests you should calm your nerves by imagining your audience with no clothes on, or imagine them sitting on the toilet. The idea is to remind yourself that they're all just people, the same as you and me. If you feel this would work please go ahead and do it but I worry presenters who do could end up either distracted or staring in horror at the audience's crotch area!

IN A NUTSHELL

• Know your point. What is your presentation for? What do you want to achieve by speaking?

• Work naked first. Begin by planning your talk and only bring in slides or visual aids where you think they might help emphasise points for your audience.

• Keep it in your own words.

• Pause before you start and take control of your body language.

HOW TO BE A CONFIDENT PERFORMER

Or 'How to be confident enough to perform' which is a much more valuable goal.

Performers have always suffered from anxiety, and they are known for huge fluctuations between arrogant and diva-like behaviour and an ego that will bruise as easily as an overripe peach. The words 'highly strung' apply to many leading performers who can require copious amounts of praise (and possibly drugs and booze) to get out there treading the boards and giving their best. This is not a requisite and there are many performers who seem to have their nerves nailed down more securely but many do survive on esteem made of gossamer and sticky-tape.

The point with being a good performer though is the ability to harness all this inner drama and turn it into a professional, competent show. It's the contradictory nature of show business that means many of the top performers we watch on a regular basis are depressives, shy, hideously low on self-esteem and even self-hating. The performing arts can be like a flame to these moths, with the puzzle being why anyone so full of insecurities would want to put themselves through such public and critical scrutiny.

I believe performers all share one trait and that is an inner core that is like a steel hawser. They tend to feel they have a right to a larger audience than the one life usually deals out and they will compromise all manner of feelings of comfort to place themselves in front of that audience.

Many performers epitomise the word 'resilience'. They work against the odds, touting their skills in the face of multiple knock-backs and rejections, sure in their soul that what the public really wants to do is love them. This is a form of self-belief that is awe-inspiring to witness. I watched one wannabe children's entertainer who used every trick in the book to get on TV, even masquerading as a birthday balloon-gram to get them in front of a TV exec in a bid to audition. When everything failed they took up TV production on a shopping channel and got their face in front of the screen that way. Yet in real life they were shy and self-effacing. Imagine a fine steel rod surrounded by tissue paper and you'd get the idea of how a performer thinks and feels when it comes to confidence.

A performer will usually spend much of their week attending auditions. This means pulling enough confidence out of your boots to perform well quickly and under scrutiny despite the odds being stacked against you and despite the fact you may have been turned down many times already that week. This type of confidence requires you to turn things like odds and reality off like a tap and it is the epitome of resilient thinking.

The audition

- Even in a flock of other auditioning performers, many of whom will appear to have more talent in their little finger than you have in your entire body, you need to see yourself as the star of your own show. Tell yourself this really is all about you. You are the hero/heroine of this event and the others are bit-players. Heroes/heroines always come out on top because they just do. If you find yourself losing faith, go back and reread all those books you grew up with like the one where the ugly duckling always somehow manages to become the star. They're what prepped you for the person you are today.
- Although Freud's ego-protection techniques can be counter-

productive if they allow you to become deluded and therefore unable to change, learn, improve or even quit, for a performer they're like the breath of life itself when it comes to survival. If you're attending rounds of castings you need to become partially deluded to cope. This means telling yourself you didn't get the role because it required someone more ordinary/older/fatter-looking and the one who did was also sleeping with the producer. Of course if you're the ordinary, old, fat one who's sleeping with the producer and you didn't get the part then it could be time for a rethink.

- You need to acquire the knack of switching on and switching off. Once you step out under the spotlight or in front of the cameras your total focus is on doing well. Anything else is inconceivable. Never go onstage with a head full of any other thoughts. It has to work, you have to perform well, you have to remember your lines. You will play that tune well and you will hit the notes when you're singing. Allowing any other thoughts or worries or 'what ifs …' to intrude at this point is inconceivable. Allow your fears and anxieties to transform into the survival mode they were intended for and then surf all that survival focus, intensity, and clarity of purpose and instinctive sense of what to do next.
- Sell the concept to yourself that this is how to tap into your talent. Focusing on your performance rather than the fear of failure is the only way to go when you're out there under the spotlight.
- If you need further proof of your ability to do this, ask yourself what happens when you have to perform when you're ill. Once you're onstage your illness vanishes. I have gone onstage with no voice or sneezing my socks off with hay fever but the minute I'm out there my voice has come back and I've stopped sneezing. It's an adrenalin thing. Whatever it is, the same can apply to your confidence. Believe it and tap into it. As long as you have the basic talent in place the only thing stopping you is yourself.
- Never drag other turn-downs into the next audition. If you do your sense of failure will be all over you like marsh gas. Imagine you got that last job and your diary is so full you'd struggle to get in this one. (You're a performer, acting should come easily.)
- Talk yourself up to yourself. That positive inner dialogue is essential.

- Tell yourself you're magical and special. For some indefinable reason you are better than everyone else at the audition. There is specialness about you and the people auditioning you will spot it.

- But that means allowing your confidence to flow like a river. Sit quietly before you perform and imagine your inner Confidence Core bursting and gushing throughout your body, like a dam.

- Remember – don't try to get rid of the butterflies but do get them flying in formation. Never be frightened of your nerves and fear. Both produce adrenalin that can be vital for an exceptional performance. Don't rush from them quaking in terror, enjoy them. Harness them and use them.

- If they start to go out of control just prior to or during your performance imagine yourself squishing them up and sitting down hard on them, like a cushion.

- If you do make a mistake remember the key phrase 'Cancel and Continue'. Cut off your thinking at the trip, and then start again as though nothing had happened. Never dwell or speculate. This is not real life, it's the stage.

- If you still struggle, stop being you. One smart trick that people use onstage is reminiscent of the *Stars in Their Eyes* show: 'Tonight, Matthew, I am going to be Ziggy Stardust!' What this means in terms of your performance is you quell your nerves by imagining you are someone else, someone who would easily stride out onstage and give the performance of a lifetime.

- Think this is hard? It's not. You used this technique all the time when you were growing up, pretending to be other people and your heroes in a bid to learn behaviours via mimicry. If you believe in it you will be able to tap into it. When I was modelling I used to walk down catwalks as Jerry Hall, not Judi James. I know Judi James was shy but I saw Jerry Hall as the epitome of cool confidence. Pick your personal icon or role model and borrow them for a bit.

- Visualise confidence. This is by far the very best dress rehearsal you can do. Sit down. Close your eyes. Visualise yourself performing well and your audience adoring your performance. Watch the whole thing in real time, imagining you're seeing yourself up there on a cinema screen.

• Separate your thoughts between Angel and Demon thoughts. Angel thoughts are the ones you'll need to perform well: confident, encouraging and full of positive, useful messages. Your Demon thoughts are the 'What if ...' and the 'Oh my god ...' thoughts, demotivating, anxiety-producing, defeatist.

IN A NUTSHELL

• Use the phrase Cancel and Continue.

• If you dry, think of nothing.

• Separate your Angel thoughts from your Demon thoughts.

• Go onstage as someone else in your mind if it helps.

• Treat your audience as a large group of individuals.

HOW TO CHAT SOMEONE UP WITH CONFIDENCE

Confident chat-ups require a medium level of self-esteem, mixed with an ability to laugh at yourself, surrounded by a skin thick enough to re-cover a Land of Leather sofa. Unlike other confidence skills, doing it a lot isn't always the best way to improve your technique as scorched-earth rubbish chat-ups could lead to a bumper crop of knock-backs causing your ego to be bruised, and you could begin to look sleazy or become too contrived and insincere.

Nobody wants to date someone who is approaching potential mates in a wholesale manner. Some nervousness or anxiety about asking someone out is usually preferable to a smooth-git-approach or an overall image of rabid desperation. Everyone likes someone who is genuine and in the world of genuine people it's natural to feel some anxiety about approaching and chatting to a possible mate.

To overcome this worry, society has created what are called

chat-up lines, which are conversations rituals like social small talk, aimed at over coming that sticky first few moments of conversation.

Unfortunately, most chat-up lines are completely rancid, especially on paper but also when spoken out loud. Some of the most common are:

- What's a nice girl like you doing in a place like this?
- If I could rearrange the alphabet I'd put U and I together.
- What's your star sign?
- You must be tired, you've been running through my mind all day.
- Do you believe in love at first sight? No? Then I'll have to walk by again.

Now, it would be stating the obvious to say that lines like this are ghastly bordering on repellent. Yet it would also be true to say that some of them work. Why? Well if the visual attraction is strong enough then it's likely a man or woman can say almost anything and still gain approval from his or her potential mate. If a guy looks like Robert Pattinson the chances are he could approach with the very worst chat-up line in the universe and still get a 100 per cent hit rate. However, most of us are not in the movie-star league, meaning your opening line will need to have a bit of a twang to it.

Preparation

To be confident chatting someone up, you need to start way before the chat-up line. Although body language is not a precise science, using it to signal interest and then see if there are signs of acceptance will help your confidence levels enormously because it will minimise your risks of a knock-back.

Confident chat-uppers usually have a very attuned sense of visual signalling, meaning they are adept at reading and transmitting messages that allow them to know whether to proceed or not. This is something you can learn to do and although it's not a foolproof technique it should help eliminate the kind of serial turn-downs that can rot your confidence.

Approaching a potential date

Most of the early stage dating/mating signals are visual and the genuine ones tend to be subtle. The major part of your chatting up will have been concluded way before you walk across and check out her star sign or what he likes for breakfast (both those lines are ironic, please don't use either).

- The phrase 'look into my eyes' applies when you're flirting with someone for the first time. The ritual is all about eye-gaze and acceptance signals.
- When your eyes literally do connect 'across a crowded room' or bar or office or wherever, you will hold that gaze for around twice as long as normal. Normal eye-gaze would only take a part of a second, so longer in this case will mean two to three seconds max, but less is still okay.
- It's that extended eye-gaze that will register interest. The eyes should light up a little, or the eye expression should soften. If the eyes remain dull and expressionless you can assume there's no interest there.
- When we see someone we fancy for the first time (and often for the second and third times too!) our impulse is to stare and allow our eyes to soak up their marvellousness. But this thought alone creates embarrassment, meaning we over-compensate by looking quickly away. But the impulse to eye-read is too strong to deny, meaning we'll glance back quite quickly and often keep glancing across as frequently as possible, at which point your friends will be able to see someone is interested in you, even if you can't. It's called checking one another out and if it's mutual you should be able to make your verbal approach with a degree of confidence.
- The other non-verbal flirt/interest signals include:
  * Dipping the head, using eye-gaze and smiling
  * Mirroring your body language. Like-bodied tends to imply like-minded
  * Smiling and face-checking while you're speaking
  * Frequent glances to your mouth
  * Torso-correction rituals. The girl will often arch her back slightly and change her leg position so that her weight is on

one leg and the other is bent at the knee. The guy will begin to splay his legs more and puff out his chest (subtly).

* There can be some self-touch rituals, like small touches to the hair, mouth, shoulders or knees for a woman and for a guy it's subtle touches to the nose, hair, chest and ear.

* When a guy is interested he'll often try to suppress the more open signals, like grinning like the village idiot. But the smile will be hard to mask, so expect some softening of the facial muscles when he looks at you, plus a barely disguised grin that keeps popping up.

* The eye-interest signals should increase so that you have their undivided attention when you speak, rather than the other person constantly gazing around the room.

• Being aware of some of the non-verbal signals at this stage, and then during all the stages of your relationship, should create an environment for sexual confidence as it means you will be tuned into the other person's thoughts and therefore able to respond in a more successful way. Pushing yourself forward when the early signs are negative will mean asking to get your self-esteem battered when you find the turn-down needs to be much more explicit. Most successful flirts are very well tuned to all the signals of acceptable or non-acceptable responses. They can see exactly when someone is interested and when they're not and when to flirt or make a more openly sexual approach and when to back off. When you lack inner confidence it's easy to become self-obsessed to the point where you are too busy thinking about your own signals to read the other person's. This will lead to either backing away too soon because you've missed their signs that should show they're attracted to you, or flipping to extrovert behaviour and pushing yourself too far or too quickly.

• When someone tries to overcome shyness or low self-esteem by being over-loud and/or over-pushy their response to any knock-backs can be extreme, meaning they either become angry with the other person (and then maybe their whole sex in general) or they get angry with themselves and give up trying. Although it's good to be resilient, over-resilience can be deeply unattractive, especially when it comes with some passive-aggressive responses.

IN A NUTSHELL

- Use eye contact to make contact before you approach him or her.

- Avoid corny chat-ups.

- Create a back pocket. What will you do if you get a knock-back?

- Use mirroring to create rapport.

HOW TO GO ON A DATE

Thanks to the rise in the divorce rate, the world is full of daters of all ages, and whatever your experience or lack of it in relationships, it's always easy to feel like a first-timer if you've got a date to go on.

Dating is the culmination of a self-marketing campaign, meaning there's a lot riding on it in terms of future happiness or lack of it. It's like taking your self-esteem out to do ten rounds with Amir Khan. To date well you do need to lay yourself wide open, even though you know some of the blows might hurt, because going into a new relationship wearing the scars from the previous ones will only cut your chances of finding a soulmate in half.

But this book is all about confidence, so how do you fly in the face of the undoubted risks and emerge with your ego intact?

Easy.

The good thing about dating is that – unlike job interviews – there's very little about the selection process that is logical. I wrote a book called *Sex Signals* to divine the aspects in us and about us that will appeal to another human being. What is it that will make them like us, want us, and want to spend the rest of their lives with us? The answer is complex enough to be exhausting. Many of your attraction factors are things that you are either unaware of, or which you may even see as faults or negatives. Your appeal to your date will depend on many subliminal factors from his or her childhood, like comfort factors or the sense of the familiar. When you get ready for your big date you can make yourself as attractive as possible in a universal manner, following the guidelines prescribed by the beauty magazines and the fashion houses but you will have little if any way of knowing whether you resemble his mother or her father, whether your facial expressions are revealing qualities that he or she has learnt to seek out in terms of good breeding stock or to make a complimentary behaviour match, or even whether your smell (even if you're using the top of the range designer scents) will entrance or repel him or her.

In other words, there are so many factors that will create or destroy attraction that you should never take it personally. The only time warning bells should ring is if the lack of interest seems to be happening across the board, and if you have specific clues as to why you might be impossible to like. Here's a swift guide to factors that can make you impossible to love:

- Do you talk about yourself all the time?
- Do you look in the mirror rather than look at the person who is talking?
- Do you expect a date to share your fascination for horoscopes / angels / soaps / football / *Star Trek*?
- Do you enjoy a good laugh, even if your mouth is full of food?
- Do you believe in sharing details and stories of all your previous relationships, especially the ones that have failed?
- Do you like to play it cool by turning up late and letting your date know you're high maintenance?
- Do you talk about your mum all the time?
- Do you like to take a friend on the first date even though you're older than 14?

Booting or re-booting your dating confidence

Before you go on your date you need some Shield work to enable you to focus on your best assets in terms of attraction, sexuality and rapport. This is clearly going to be different from your career Shield, which was linked to achievements and qualifications as well as personality, but feel free to focus on any cross-over traits that you can use to define yourself as dateable and mateable.

Your Relationship Shield needs to consist of four new quadrants:

1. Your physicality/sexuality
2. Your personality
3. Your interests
4. Your life goals

Don't think of this like an Internet dating form, you're filling in the truth, not trying to impress anyone apart from yourself. Like your other Shield, though, do stick to positives rather than more modest comments or even criticisms. When you come to your personality points, try to bolster them up in your own eyes by adding proof and examples. This will prevent them from being mere opinion. Although there's nothing wrong about thinking you're generous or kind it will add considerable value to that thought in terms of genuine confidence if you can give yourself examples of your own kindnesses.

• When you're about to go on a date and feeling your confidence ebb away it's vital to do what's called 'finish the thought'. This means defining your fears by taking them through to the end of the inner dialogue. Write them down, if possible.
• By defining your fears or anxieties you can begin to take control over them rather than allowing them to control you. Everyone has anxious thoughts but there are some people who allow the anxieties to fester and ruin their experiences and some who plan to deal with any problems that break out. You're going to be one of this last group. Instead of worrying about a disastrous date, write down your anxieties before placing them under one of three different headings:
  * Solve it.
  * Create a back pocket (i.e. plan what you will do if the worst does happen).
  * Bin it.
• Here are some examples of finished thoughts that you could learn to deal with, following the Solve it–Create a back pocket–Bin it technique:
  * 'What if he or she doesn't turn up?'
    Back pocket: plan how long you'll wait. Plan how to get back if you're meeting away from your home or workplace. Plan a

reasonable evening that doesn't include eating cookie-dough ice cream until it's oozing out of your ears and sitting telling your cat how nobody will ever love you because you're deformed in body and warped in mind. A trip to the gym would be ideal. You'll turn up looking a million dollars and get all that pent-up resentment out in a far more esteem-boosting way than pigging out and navel-gazing.

* 'What if I'm so nervous I look stupid?'

Unlike with workplace skills you could break the ice and gain points in terms of attractiveness if you tell your date that you're feeling slightly nervous. Why? Because – although confident people tend to dominate the first-pick dating scene, a degree of nervousness can be seen as adorable. Or at the very least the admission of it will get your date off the hook in terms of their own paranoia and struggles with self-esteem. It's one thing going out with someone you know is only quiet because they're nervous and another to feel your date is sitting in silence because they think you're as dull as ditchwater and about as attractive as the same.

* But if you do admit you're feeling nervous, don't keep banging on about it. Just because the first hit works doesn't mean you then have carte blanche to rabbit on about the how and the why of your timidity, i.e. that previous affair with the serial insulter or the way your parents would subject you to ritual humiliations by forcing you to enter for the egg and spoon race on school sports day. It's truly, genuinely dull and your date will be searching for the butter knife to slit his or her own wrists by the end of the first five minutes of your litany of wrongs.

Dating is networking

Okay, so that does make it sound rather clinical but unless you're the sort of person who can easily shine on a date, it will help increase your confidence levels if you put in a little pre-date planning when it comes to behaviour and conversations. Of course it's important to 'be yourself' too, but it's vital to remember that there are many different facets of You and that displaying them in freefall when you're under pressure to impress someone new is asking a lot of yourself.

- Be relatively casual about your dress and styling. Both should be clean, fresh and well groomed but over-thinking is always a disaster. You could end up wearing a new outfit that is too styled, and might as well have the words 'Dog's Dinner' written all over it.
- Pick an outfit in a colour that flatters your skin tone and in a style that flatters your shape, but which is low maintenance, i.e. you can move in it easily, forgetting about it while you're wearing it.
- If there's an outfit that makes you feel confident, wear that. Your clothes should enhance you, not upstage you.
- Avoid loud colours (red is a special cliché that blokes only pretend to be keen on) and anything wholesale sexy, like a short skirt with a low-cut top. Guys should take the boy-next-door option over the groomed-to-within-an-inch-of-his-life look.
- I've warned against talking about exes, and don't wear trophies from them either, i.e. rings, lockets, ankle bracelets, etc. It's like a guy rolling up his sleeve and displaying a line of tattoos of women's names.
- Avoid anything too quirky too soon. Quirkiness is fine but so is introducing it gradually rather than all at once. For safety's sake restrict yourself to anything that says 'normal', like good jeans and a white shirt/T-shirt or top, or something simple but more formal if the date's somewhere posh. 'Normal' is an important word on first dates. You understand your quirky side but dressing like Helena Bonham Carter then taking him back to your flat to meet your ten cats and your cuddly toy collection might not have the same instant appeal for him.

On the date: confident verbal bonding

- Suppress any lurking (and potentially alarming) obsessive side until your feet are well and truly under the table. Of course there's nothing wrong with (most) obsessions and of course you should feel free to be yourself but it might be less off-putting if you decide to leak your obsession slowly over a period of time rather than welcoming your date into your bedroom that has been decorated as an homage to the flight deck of the Starship Enterprise and then expecting a night of first-date passion in your Captain Jean-Luc Picard all-in-one pyjamas. Unless you actually met at a Star Trek convention, of course. We all have our hobbies but referring to them more than once per date can only cause concern, even if you do start each conversation with the words: 'Of course, I'm not an obsessive ...'

- It's only in movies that the kooky eccentric gets the girl or guy, especially on first meeting.
- Ask questions and use your active listening signals to register your interest. Good listening is good flirting, especially if you have tapped into one of their favourite subjects. But be careful about allowing the questions to sound too much like a grilling.
- Remember Janice from *Friends*? That awful laugh and the 'Oh-My-God!' catchphrase? We all have our verbal foibles but these can become magnified when we're under pressure, i.e. on a date. Bite the bullet. Ask a close but also honest friend what verbal habits you have that could turn off a date. Then spend some time learning how not to do them. This entails the 'Learn what to do, not what not to do' philosophy, meaning instead of priming yourself to *not* laugh in that way or say that thing, you plan what you should say or laugh like instead.
- Never tell someone what you are like, e.g. 'I'm mad, me!' or 'I'm a people person', etc. It sounds too much like the hard sell. Let them find out. People love finding other people's depths out for themselves. 'Oh he's really shy deep down', 'She's very kind when you get to know her', 'He comes across like an intellectual but he's got a really wicked sense of humour', etc.
- Go with some thoughts in mind. There's no need to fill the date with jokes and stories, in fact doing so can make for a boring few hours for the other person, but do think of a few interesting topics that you'd both enjoy talking about, even if they're no more creative than favourite films or music.
- If you're back on the dating scene after a long gap, avoid sounding too out of touch, judgemental or set in your ways. Here's some phrases divorcees on the dating scene again have told me crop up regularly:
  * 'I'm looking for a woman/man who ...'
  * 'I never watch TV. Won't have it in the house.'
  * 'I'm afraid I like the old-fashioned type of woman, one who is feminine.'

⋆'I suppose you're mad on football. I never understand what it is you blokes like about it so much.'

⋆'My kids never answer me back.'

⋆'I thought about a dating agency but it was much too expensive.'

⋆'Me and my mates go off to Thailand for a month every summer.'

⋆'I can't stand men/women who let themselves go.'

⋆'My last wife was gorgeous, a real stunner. I learnt my lesson there though, never again.'

⋆'I don't mind a dog as long as it doesn't bark or make a mess.'

Confident visual rapport

- Use mirroring to create fast-track rapport. This means subtly copying their pace and style of movement.
- Try touch-tennis, where one of you touches the other during the date (start with a small touch on the arm or hand as you're talking or link arms or hands as you're walking) then wait to get some form of reciprocal touch before you touch them again.
- If you're happy with the touches you do get, confirm that with an eye-gaze and a gentle smile.
- If you're choosing the venue, try to pick somewhere that has a relaxed, unpretentious atmosphere. A meal for two is the ideal first date in terms of psychology as it allows you to sit opposite your date to speak with and watch them, and the food keeps your hands occupied as you do. This means you begin to get a much better reading of them and their personality than you would at a club, theatre or cinema. However, a restaurant can feel like a minefield if you're lacking in confidence so it's a good idea to try it out first. If you're nervous, skip the type that uses what I call 'lap waiters', by which I mean the waiter holds the chair out for you and places the napkin on your lap. In terms of choreography and 'doing the right thing' these can be a nightmare. Stick to the type of eating place where the menu is understandable, you place your own napkin and they don't rush across to fill your wine glass every time you take a sip.
- Always pick food that is easy to eat. Avoid anything that requires the kind of skill levels that you'd only have under the most calm of circumstances, like lobster, unshelled prawns, spaghetti, etc.

- Do avoid glugging back the alcohol. When we're nervous or lacking in confidence, a couple of glasses of wine can feel like the perfect way to loosen up and relax. However, nerves can also make us very bad regulators of the amount we're guzzling and the speed at which we're necking it. It's never a good move to get tipsy on the first few dates as it makes you look like a lush. Again, it's only in the movies where the guy finds the drunken woman adorable or visa versa. In reality they're more likely to think you can't be bothered to stay sober and soak up their company instead. To say it's unflattering to your poor date would be an understatement.

- Don't be picky. There are always foods we don't like but the actual act of turning your nose up is rude. I have met many people who try to cover a lack of confidence by over-compensatory behaviour like turning food down, pointing out when the wine is one degree below what they consider the ideal or announcing the food their date has ordered is making them shudder. Phrases like 'I don't know how you can eat/drink that' aren't funny or clever. It's always important to remember your date might be as lacking in confidence as you are and feel humiliated by comments like these.

- When you're nervous always check your date is going to be joining you in every course you order. Sitting eating alone while your date watches you is a challenge for anyone save for dyed-in-the-wool extroverts. I once went on a date and was asked if I'd like some champagne. My arm got twisted until I agreed but when it turned up there was only one glass with the bottle and my date announced he never touched alcohol.

- Be careful about jumping the gun. If it's a first date and you're already using the term 'We' – as in 'Next time we can go to that club round the corner', 'We could get a cheap deal flight to the Canary Islands for the holiday this year' or 'We could get a puppy' – or if you so much as mention marriage, babies or your mum and dad, then you'll come across as too much of a bunny-boiler.

- Pre-plan the ending of your date. Know how you will get home and whose home you will be going to. I don't say this for moral reasons but leaving it open-ended can put pressure on you if you're dithering throughout the evening, and that pressure can mean your confidence is at risk. Knowing you're not going to have sex is one good solid decision that probably also means you can order the dessert without worrying about a bulging stomach. Deciding you probably will have sex (with certain provisos, of course) means you're prepped up and oven-ready, rather than sitting worrying about your Spanx or the fact your back-wax needs redoing.

IN A NUTSHELL

- Do your Shield Exercise (see page 63) to reboot your self-esteem.

- Plan your venue carefully.

- Don't over-dress.

- Plan some conversation points but don't sound too rehearsed.

- Be a good listener.

MEETING HIS OR HER PARENTS

When you met your partner you were able to charm them into loving you. (I assume this is true if they've invited you to meet their parents.) So far so good. Your partner's parents, however, are a totally different ball game. Their objectives are different. Whereas your partner was probably hoping to be swept off his or her feet, their parents' role will be to use an eye that is unaffected by rose-tinted lenses in order to unmask the charlatan and ne'er-do-well. Their role is one of protector and therefore, however warm their greeting rituals and however many types of cake they have slaughtered in your honour, it is always wise to treat them like an overly suspicious pair of nightclub doormen.

You might hold the trump in terms of your partner's heart and loins but their Ace card is time. They have plenty of it and they know which buttons to press to manipulate their offspring.

A confidence disaster then? Not really. Your overall confidence should be boosted by the fact that you're meeting them at all. The rest is all down to simple psychological trickery.

Preparation

- Never ask your partner if his or her parents will like you. Always ask if you'll like them. When you ask if they'll like you you'll probably get a false affirmative but you will also learn very little about them as your partner will be unwilling to define your personality to you, as in 'Oh yes, they love gobby girls who can down a pint in 30 seconds'. If you ask if you'll like them you'll be far more likely to hear some telling details about them that you can use to your advantage as in 'My mum can be a bit prudish but my dad's got a great sense of humour'.
- If you do ask about their opinion of you take no notice of his or her answer. He or she loves you and probably also love their parents, which to him or her adds up to an all-round love-in. You, of course, will know better. Be shrewd and be strategic. Think competitive rather than instantly accepting.
- Discover your role in your partner's life. You might be the 'one to take home to mum', i.e. a decent, house-trained type who will impress the parents by being a safe bet. Or you might be the mummy-punisher, i.e. the one who is symbolic of your partner's rebellion against his or her parents, meaning they're supposed to be shocked by you and hate you, that's all part of the plan.
- Don't know which one you are? Ask to see a photo of the mum if you're a girl and the dad if you're a boy. Do you resemble them in any way? If so you're the 'one to take home to mum'. If you dress like a Goth or curse a lot or enjoy hard-core PDAs (public displays of affection) and the parent looks top-to-toe Marks and Sparks then you're the living embodiment of your partner's two fingers up to his or her parents. You could rock the psychological boat by scrubbing up well and not dropping an aitch all through dinner but then you'll be letting your partner down, a classic no-win scenario.

The meeting

- When you meet the parents (assuming you're not the mummy-shocker), any tendency towards shyness should be seen as a USP (unique selling point). Parents love shy partners for their offspring as it boosts their status (you're scared of them), as well as implying you're not a sleaze who is into his or her fifth marriage.

- Feel perfectly free to act shy, but do ensure you skip any of the shyness signals that can get misinterpreted for being aloof or sulky, like sitting quietly without joining in at all.

- Your greeting rituals are important. Hugging is good, but only if they haven't got in first with the offer of a handshake. Put everything you have into your hug as it will store up points that you might lose as the afternoon wears on. A good hug is disarming and suggests affection tinged with relief. Don't cling like a limpet but do get some torso contact in.

- Avoid throwing looks to your partner. These tie-signs are fine at a crowded venue when you're with your peers but will be very excluding when you're with his or her parents, like whispering in front of them.

- Avoid noticeable displays of close affection, especially any pseudo-sexual ones. It will look as though you're spraying your territory.

- But don't knock or mock your partner. Siding with his or her parents over their smelly feet will show a lack of loyalty.

- Never reveal anything dodgy in your past. And by dodgy I mean the fact you even had a steady relationship with anyone before.

- No matter how old you are, never refer to the fact that you have sex with their offspring. To them, he or she will always be a child.

- Be polite. It's a power thing. Dress smartly, sit well, listen, smile, and don't be cheeky. The real you can emerge later down the path.

- Don't become so nervous that you end up flirting with one of his or her parents. It happens a lot. It's ghastly and it will mean only one of three people will end up liking you and it won't be your partner or the other parent.

IN A NUTSHELL

• Get to see a photo of them first.

• Get some ground knowledge about them and what they do.

• Shyness will work to your advantage.

• But not if you are too quiet, in which case it could look like arrogance or rudeness.

• Be polite and look polite.

HOW TO HAVE CONFIDENT SEX

Never is the difference between men and women made so obvious as in the types of confidence we require to have average, good or outstanding sex.

Women might be brought up to be more sexually wary and even diffident but when push comes to shove we can afford to be passive in our input and we can lie about our enjoyment, lying back and thinking of England before we fake a triple orgasm.

For a girl a lack of confidence will – at worst – only lead to some fear and some difficulty. For a man it's the end of the performance. Negative Inner Dialogues might lead a girl to worry about her body shape or technique but once it kicks in for a bloke it's stage fright transferred to the bedroom. Why am I telling you this when it's only making matters worse instead of better? Because I'm glad I'm a girl, that's why. Now let's get down to the sexual confidence-boosting.

Preparation

• Sex is really just a thing animals do to have offspring. It shouldn't be a big deal. It's humans who turned it into an Olympic sport. We watch too many films and read too many books. Two actors simulating sex with their underpants still on should never really be seen as the yardstick by which you judge your own performance. They're worrying about their cellulite showing on camera. You're worrying about keeping things going for long enough.

- Celebrities who perform all the massively sexual red carpet PDAs are rarely at it in real life. Often the relationship's been set up by their PRs, meaning the couple barely know each other, or if they do they're usually masking the fact they're about to split up.

- Nobody has the perfect sex life because everybody's different.

- Even when sex is good it's rarely good all the time. And good tends to fade after a couple of years, when nature assumes we've bred a couple of kids. After that the lust often dies away and you find yourself reading magazines containing articles called: 'How To Keep Sex Alive in your Long-Term Relationship' that contains heaps of goodies like 'Dress up in bondage gear' or 'Go on holiday to a hotel'. Most people are suffering from sex-envy. Don't be one of them.

- Sex really is all in the mind. If you're a guy and you worry about being able to perform you'll probably fall victim to a self-fulfilling prophecy. Some guys tell women they're rubbish at sex, just in case.

- It's not only those with perfect bodies that are able to have sex. People are attracted to and turned on by a whole myriad of different shapes and forms. There's a saying in nature that there's no such thing as an ugly monkey when it comes to sex appeal. You might not like to compare yourself to an ugly monkey but the point is we're less picky than we like to pretend.

- Never complain to your partner about what you see as your less-attractive body parts. They might have been hugely turned on by that bit but now you've given your view they'll feel like a bit of a pervert for admiring it. I once watched a girl who was curvy to the point where less-confident girls could well have had a hang-up lie back on the sun bed in front of one a hunky guy, only for him to point out she had a few armpit hairs she'd missed. She just started picking at them happily and told him she'd got some more stubble on her legs. He smiled happily and admiringly, not put off her one jot.

- Get used to your naked body before you bare it during sex. If you have the space and privacy at home, pull the curtains and walk around in the nip for a bit as often as possible. Your naked body is your proper body so getting in touch with the feeling of air on skin can be liberating and confidence boosting.

- Try to read books that write about sex in a realistic and entirely natural way. If the heroine is primly historical or if she's screaming for more after her tenth orgasm in as many minutes, skip them for something more morale boosting.

- And beware women's magazines. They are often preoccupied with sex and orgasms in a way that is guaranteed to produce sex-envy. If you're actually doing it you rarely have the spare time to read up about it.

- If you're a guy, stop believing you should be like some sexual robot, ready; keen and able to have sex anytime, anywhere and anyhow. When you're discussing sex with your mates, remember everyone lies. A bit. A lot. It's a power and status thing, the alpha males get the first pick of the females as part of their power display. Blokes boast. Don't be diminished by their boasting.

- Enjoy the fun and the humour in sex. It only looks spiffing in movies where – if you remember – they not really doing it, just pretending. I've lost count of the amount of films I've seen where the sex scenes would be physically impossible, nothing's in the right place or the right angle for lock-down, but the heroine's bouncing up and down fit to bust.

- Knowledge is always power. Find out how everything works and where to put it. I'm not saying that the secret of confident sex is to do a thesis but it will help if you know what you're doing. Many people don't, they just muddle along on facts they found out at school. You'd be amazed how many people don't know how their bodies work. Arm yourself with a couple of good sex manuals but keep it basic. '100 Orgasms in One Hour' might be a bit too advanced, as will anything with the words 'Tantric' written on the cover.

Doing it

- Use music. It's a cliché but true, a lot of music is written to get you in the mood for and relaxed enough for sex. Find what works for you. As a confidence trigger it will work well, especially hand-in-hand with a glass of wine.

- Confident kissing is important because it's a bit of an hors d'oeuvre for the real thing. It's the pause before the kiss that counts, when you look into his or her eyes and then lock lips. Analysing some celebrity kisses the other day I realised how rubbish most of them were, even with their long-term partners. Lips were missing lips, heads were straight rather than tilted, most had left their shades on, many had their eyes open and quite a few were looking away into the far distance as they snogged, as though scouring the horizon for something or someone more interesting. Perhaps the best kiss was Paris Hilton kissing her dog.

- Get your heads close, employing some body touch, like a hand on his or her shoulder. Lock eyes and cup one hand on his or her face (maybe both hands if you can) to ensure you appear romantic while controlling the action. Tilt your head and start with the gentle, exploratory kiss, i.e. half-parted lips pressed lightly against theirs, pull back a bit and then go for the proper, open-mouth, saliva-exchanging kiss. Regular kissers are usually happy doing their own thing but novice kissers might need to do a little rehearsal with a balloon or anything head-shaped first, and ditto for returning kissers, i.e. people coming out of a long-term relationship where kissing either dropped away or was less passionate.

- Remember that sexual confidence, like any other form of confidence, comes from a solid sense of self-esteem, but not from arrogance. You do need to fancy yourself (throw yourself some admiring glances next time you're prancing naked in front of the mirror) but not in a way that is narcissistic (boring and excluding for your lover).

- Part of your duties as a lover is to stroke the ego of your partner. Their confidence will be your gain because it will help them to relax and lose their inhibitions. Compliments, groans of delight and gasps of wonder and surprise work well, so do remember that a little acting can be hugely beneficial. Most people have hang-ups about their bodies. If you can quietly tune into any body parts that your partner might feel less than secure about and compliment it while you're doing foreplay you could find the favour is returned, boosting your own confidence. A groan of desire will do better than scripted words, as saying 'I thought you said you had cellulite' or 'Your bum doesn't look that big lying down' will not form part of an effective seduction process.

IN A NUTSHELL

- It's no big deal, it's just sex.

- It doesn't have to be an Olympic sport. You can thank writers of third-rate novels for all the focus on gymnastics and staying power.

- Just do it. If it's bad, do it again only differently this time.

- Never draw attention to your bad points by trying to hide them.

- Compliment your partner, it makes them sexier.

- Remember that humour is an important part of sex; if it weren't we'd do it some other way.

DEALING WITH DIFFICULT PEOPLE

Other people come in all shapes and sizes and most of them come with the capacity to be difficult. I'm aware that word sounds like a bit of a euphemism. Okay, they can be horrible, hateful, rude, angry, backstabbing, crafty, selfish, unreasonable, competitive, thoughtless, charmless, etc.

The key point to remember though is that they think what they are doing is right. This is the key to confident and effective handling of them. Work out what their 'right' looks like first. Then take action.

When you lack confidence your responses to difficult people will probably only come in two varieties. Either you:

1. Do what they want, i.e. act passive in a bid to avoid confrontation

or

2. Act passive for a certain amount of time, then get fed up and turn passive-aggressive.

The problem with these options is that neither of them work. Go back to the section of the book on Assertiveness and you'll see you need to be strategic and set goals.

Preparation

- Ask yourself what behaviour they are using that you see as 'difficult'. Write it down, sticking strictly to the facts. No 'I think' or 'I feel', just a list of what it is they do, that would stand up in court. (Hopefully it's not going that far but it's a good discipline to apply to any people problems.)

- Then ask yourself why you think they do it. What would their reason be if they were asked? Where possible try to apply some positive reasons. It always helps to have a balanced view.

- How does this behaviour make you feel? Write your feelings down. (While remembering that part of your confidence plan is to disallow thoughts that give other people control over your responses.)

- Remember that – unlike on TV – people are rarely either 'goodies' or 'baddies'. The difficult person you're dealing with will probably have some very good traits, too. I've met bullies that can be the kindest people at times and love-rats that are loyal and adorable when they're not cheating. The problem with these switches in behaviour is that it creates cognitive confusion in you. But don't be confused. People are multi-faceted. Just because your boss can be as sweet as a nut at times doesn't mean you have to put up with the bullying behaviour at other times.

- Does their behaviour constitute bullying or harassment? If so your response will be affected by the fact that these behaviours are not allowed in the workplace. If you feel threatened you will need to keep a log of incidents and you will need to report the behaviours as a company needs to prevent it from occurring again.

- Create your own set of values. This will be intrinsic to your own confidence levels as it will ensure that basic inner steel Core of You isn't compromised. Remind yourself who you are and what you stand for, e.g.: civility, reasonableness, intelligence, maturity, honesty, etc.
- Deal with any problems as quickly as possible. The longer you put up with bad behaviour the more you appear to condone it.
- Be honest to yourself about any reason why you haven't taken action. Pretending something doesn't worry you, when it's the fact that you don't think you have the power or status to make change, you fear their reaction if you do point out the problem or you enjoy their liking or approval and are scared of losing it, etc., is deluding yourself. Even if you still decide to do nothing at least you have a realistic view of what's occurring.
- Think about your current patterns of behaviour. We all have life and transactional patterns, meaning they do X and you do Y as a result. Your response could be providing this difficult behaviour with the reward it's seeking. Or to put it another way, if you always do what you've always done you'll always get what you've always got. By changing your own behaviour or response it makes it very hard for the other person to continue doing the same things.
- Never fall for the line: 'I can't help it, it's what I do. It's just the kind of person I am,' either from the other person or from yourself. We are all able to change our own behaviour. If we can't we are suffering from severe mental problems.

Confronting the difficult person

- When you're looking for behavioural change from your difficult person you will need to be specific about your feedback. For instance, 'You're not pulling your weight' or 'I don't like your attitude' will just lead to disagreement or confusion, whereas 'You have been late the last three mornings. I need you here at 9am' offers a signpost for change and improvement.
- Try appealing to their values. I have always used a four-box system to help me define other people's communication and behaviour values. As long as you don't over-stereotype, the boxes help you see that other people are just different rather

than awkward and it helps you to deal with them in a more effective way.

* **Drivers** are people who speak in an abrupt, concise, non-chatty style and who like to get to the point without any waffle. They are competitive and focused and often suffering from stress. They can also create the biggest problems for anyone suffering from a lack of confidence as they can appear impatient, bossy and controlling. When you're dealing with a Driver remember to speak clearly and concisely and stick to your points. Don't over-speak but don't challenge them front-on, either. Appeal to their sense of achievement and personal glory. If you're their manager, get them to suggest some solutions to the problems they're causing. They are the behavioural type most likely to put the blame back on you, telling you you're wrong in your assessment and it's not what they're doing but the way you're perceiving it. Always be armed with facts and evidence when you're dealing with a Driver.

* **Actors** are entertaining, energetic and outgoing. They use humour as both an attack and a defence, have a short attention span but loads of enthusiasm, although that enthusiasm will die quickly along with their interest. Their dislike of planning and detail will make them hard to pin down to any planned work and they are the group most likely to agree to change but 'forget' to do so. An Actor will use charm and humour to get their own way. To deal with an Actor, keep coming back to your point until they are forced to listen and give specific steps that you will be checking in future. They're used to problems just going away so you need to exhibit tenacity.

* **Empathists** will usually cause the least difficulties, unless they have a tendency to be passive-aggressive, i.e. storing up gripes and grievances or doing you so many favours and good turns that they have grown bitter. Always notice an Empathist, as the fact they're the last to complain can make them easy to overlook. I work with a lot of people who leave Empathists last on the list of getting things done as there are others who shout louder and complain more. However, an Empathist tends to believe that their good nature will be rewarded and can suddenly turn if they find they're being walked over instead.

* **Analysts** have a love of detail and planning that can make them difficult if they feel they're being rushed or if you're not taking a job seriously or not looking at the small print. They always have facts to back up their argument, making them difficult to manage if you don't. You need to do your homework if you're going to deal with an Analyst because they are the most stubborn of all the groups and set high value on a concern for detail. Have a grasp of your facts and respect their values in terms of dotting all the 'i's and crossing all the 't's.

• When your difficult person is a customer, make sure you have a system for dealing with complaints. A system needs to be flexible though, as scripted responses and overly diagnostic problem solving will make them feel they're being dealt with by someone who doesn't care.

• Maintaining your confidence in the face of a difficult or even angry customer takes resolve, so make sure you plan your techniques before you face the problem, rather than playing it by ear once it has occurred. Your main challenge will be persuading yourself to not take the behaviour personally. Once you do you risk two consequences:

  1. You take a dip in your self-esteem.
  2. Your animal responses kick in and you start to get into a state of aggressive arousal or you start to get upset.

• Remember when you last complained about something. There were probably two aspects of your complaint: The Physical, i.e. the product that didn't work or the delivery that didn't turn up, and The Emotional, i.e. the upset, irritation, anger or inconvenience that was caused as a result. When you're handling a complaint always remember these two are equally important and ignoring one of them will make the complainer more difficult.

• Begin by pausing. There's no need to do what's called solution-eering when someone has a complaint. This means rushing to resolve it without first listening to the whole story. Sometimes it's too late to resolve the problem and the complainer just wants to do an emotional dump. Your pause should be used to remind yourself not to take it personally, to breathe out gently and quietly to allow your body tension to dissolve, and to use active listening, meaning you not only focus on their story and their problems, you also show you are listening by making all the right noises if you're on the phone or using eye contact, nodding, etc. if you're face-to-face.

- Your next step is to imagine things from their point of view. Letting them know the delivery is on its way doesn't really make up for the fact they've just spent three hours peering through their curtains waiting for it to be there on time. Take care of the emotions and the inconvenience first.

- Then you clarify their main points. This will show you have both listened and understood what they've told you. When someone is resolving a complaint we like to think they have got a good grasp of the total problem. By repeating their main points back to them you'll also be most likely to gain your first agreement from them. ('So you were promised a call back at four?' 'Yes.')

- Then you tell them what you're going to do to resolve the problem. Never over-promise because it means you'll under-deliver, so swearing to get the product back to them before the weekend is risky unless you can repair it yourself. If there's anyone else in the line of command, like a supplier of certain parts or another department in your firm, it's hugely risky to make guarantees on their behalf. Avoid explaining your problems to the customer though, especially in detail or with a hope they'll feel sorry for you. There's a phrase in customer care that says: 'Don't tell me about the labour pains, just show me the baby.' Keep that phrase in mind.

- Ask your customer if your solution is okay. This gives them a small feeling of choice and control that could reduce their levels of anger, irritation or stress.

- Know what you will do if you need to switch the problem off. By this I mean dropping the problem if their behaviour goes beyond that which you should be reasonably expected to be subjected to. By which I mean shouting, swearing and possible physical threat. Your company should give you guidelines in terms of what is and isn't appropriate and you should plan your dialogue for if and when that happens. Most companies use a line like: 'I do understand that you are angry but if you continue to shout/ use that type of language I will have to terminate the phone call/

conversation.' This should be said calmly and assertively.

- Telling someone to calm down or insisting they'll have to calm down is like pouring petrol on to a fire in a bid to put it out.

- You will probably be given the advice to stay calm when dealing with a problem person but this can be counter-productive if you are too calm, which will look like indifference. Use some subtle mirroring to display concern for their problem. This can include a concerned facial expression, leaning forward slightly if you're at a desk or moving more quickly if the problem seems to be urgent.

- See your complaint/problem handling as part of your job and something to use solid skills on, like those listed above. Too many companies employ people who are expected to handle difficult clients/customers and complaints without having any idea how to do so. Our only experience of handling a complaint is often family/friend-based, but skills like sulking, crying, shouting or insulting back aren't the type you'd be looking at in a business situation.

IN A NUTSHELL

- See it from their point of view. They don't think they're being difficult.

- Be honest with yourself about your own behaviour.

- Be adult, not aggressive or passive.

- Know your goals.

- Plan your strategy to fit those goals.

10

YOUR TROUBLE-SHOOTER GUIDE FOR INSTANT QUICK-FIX TIPS

This section of the book is for those panic moments when you need simple, instant solutions on the hoof. If you feel like browsing through it during times of calm in a bid to make your reactions pro-active please feel free to do so. Otherwise leave the book within easy reach for those moments when you find yourself in the middle of an emergency and about to go into your famous impersonation of a headless chicken.

I have an exam coming up and I'm too nervous to sit down and study

Solutions:
- Do some instant exercise, like running on the spot, dancing or a quick workout to burn off some of that extra energy and manage your stress levels.
- Repeat your mantra: I feel calm, confident and in control.
- Turn off all external distractions including your phone, PC (unless you're using it to study) and radio.
- If you need background noise, play light classical music. It calms you down and helps you learn.
- Use the magic ten-minute rule: start your revision for ten minutes. It's the best way to get going.
- As you read keep repeating the command 'soak it up, soak it up' to help you memorise.
- Stop telling everyone and anyone about how nervous you are.

Chatting about that will cost you precious time. Just sit down. Turn on. And get going. Soak it up, soak it up.

• Work towards rewards. A cup of coffee after you've mastered that first section or a couple of biscuits after the next.

I suffer from nerves during my exams

Solutions:

• Breathe slowly before you start, focusing on the out-breath to create calm.

• Try to get a good night's sleep the night before but if that's impossible just lie still with your eyes shut. Your brain will still be active but you won't wear yourself out tossing and turning.

• Always finish your revision an hour before you go to bed. Soak in a warm (not hot) bath.

• Peppermint or lemon oil can help you relax without making you too sleepy during the day of the exam. (Smell it, don't eat it!)

• Choose six key headings or facts you find vital to your exam subjects and focus on them as you go in the room, rather than panicking.

• Use a magic stress touch technique like rubbing the tip of your thumb or earlobe to help you relax during the exam.

• Repeat your mantra in your head: I feel calm, confident and in control.

• If your brain goes blank during the exam, focus on nothing for a few seconds. Close your eyes if you can. This will allow the thought to pop up in your mind.

I hate using the phone, especially at work

Solutions:

• Try to use fewer emails and more phone calls. Frequent use creates confidence.

• Plan your conversation before you pick up the phone. Imagine you'll be answered by voicemail, which normally makes you think your points out beforehand.

• Don't say 'sorry' or 'it's only me' when they answer.

• Ask if they're busy before you launch into a chat.

• Headline your points: 'Hi Jane, about that hotel you asked me to book …'

- Write your key points down on a pad to check you made all of them.
- Keep it concise.
- Repeat the main points at the end of the call.
- Breathe out before you start to speak as it releases tension.
- If you're female, bring your vocal tone down a couple of notes.
- Sit well in your seat rather than slumping or folding your arms.

I have to make a speech at my daughter's wedding

Solutions:

- Write notes rather than a speech.
- Write in lettering big enough to read from the table when you're standing.
- Skip the set jokes. They're embarrassing if you're feeling less than confident.
- Write down your core messages: what do you want to say about your daughter?
- Think those messages through. They should come from the heart, even if the delivery is a little awkward.
- Keep it simple. Long rambling stories bore people who are keen to get on with the party.
- Don't drink until after you've spoken.
- When you stand up, push your chair back and move into the extra space.
- Pause a moment to collect yourself and look round at the guests.
- Empty your pockets before you speak. Fiddling in pockets looks awful.
- Remember a sincere message is better than a polished one.
- Speak in your own words, don't get too formal or long-winded.
- Do your vocal warm-ups in the loo beforehand.
- Rehearse by talking out loud, glancing at your notes if necessary. Do the whole-body mime too, using your hands and going through all your facial expressions.
- Don't tell guests you're nervous at the start of your speech but do try a little self-effacing comment: 'Most of you will be amazed I'm still on my feet by now, let alone making a speech' or 'You all know me as a bit of a windbag but this time I'm going to try to make sense.'

I can never get a word in at meetings

Solutions:
- Plan your points beforehand and sell them to yourself.
- Arrive looking confident (your Power Pose).
- Meet and greet your colleagues, using a firm handshake.
- When you're chatting beforehand tell them in advance that you have some important points to make.
- Sit in a chair that will ensure you are visible.
- Speak up within three minutes to get your voice in the air.
- Join in physically, nodding and reacting.
- Make some notes as the meeting goes along.
- Use announcement gestures, sit forward, raise a hand to shoulder level, raise both hands, fingers up, palms outward.
- Use the chair's name to interrupt.
- When you have a gap to speak in make sure what you say is positive, concise, but high in impact.
- Never display resentment that you're excluded. It will make you seem sulky.
- Never make your points in general chat after you've left the room. If they want to hear them they will have to listen during the meeting.
- If you're talking over the others keep your tone low. A raised tone will sound borderline hysterical.

I struggle getting information out of other colleagues

Solutions:
- If they see the information is for your benefit alone you're going to have to illustrate how the benefit will be mutual.
- Do this by using phrases like 'I can speed the whole process up if you happen to have those invoice numbers for me' or 'If we can go through it now it will mean you won't have to have me on your back for the next two weeks'.
- Use their objections during your intro: 'I know you're busy and this must feel like an intrusion on your time but it is vital we go through it because ...'
- If they don't want to speak, ask them what would be a good time to sit down and go through it.
- Always write as they speak. If they don't think you're listening

they won't play ball.

- If you're approaching them via email you're letting them off the hook. Emails requesting information are often seen as low priority and they'll hope you'll go away if they ignore it.
- If your hunt for information is going to be regular, always introduce yourself in person. It's easier to ignore a request from someone you don't know.
- If you do send an email and get no reply, follow it up with a visit 'to make it quicker and easier for them'.

I always lack confidence speaking to my boss

Solutions:

- Remember it's you not them. It's not what they're doing, it's how you choose to respond.
- They're just a human being, like you.
- They probably trigger old memories of school teachers or other bossy people.
- Lock a wall around your response.
- Create your own list of values and stick to them, e.g. 'I will be polite and assertive', 'I will speak clearly and concisely', 'I will stay calm and act intelligently'.
- Never attack but don't back down either. Stay your ground, albeit politely.
- Use eye contact, a relaxed facial expression, avoid fiddling or body barriers and no nervous giggles.
- If you don't understand – ask.
- Avoid covering up mistakes. Tell them and fix them.
- Dress up. Certain clothes carry certain levels of status. Smart jackets, primary colours and smart shoes will make you look and feel like less of a pushover.

Other people take credit for my ideas

Solutions:

- Never sound or look bitter after the event. The phrase 'that was my idea' is rarely fruitful.
- Did you flunk talking about your idea in a way that made it sound good? If you made it a throwaway comment don't be surprised if someone else picked it up and ran with it. Next time

tell the right people and use impact.
- Avoid moaning to your boss. They'll think it doesn't matter whose idea it was as long as it was implemented.
- Learn where the leaks were. If it's a colleague who beats you to the block, keep quiet in future until you're at that meeting with the boss.
- Then make sure you put your idea across. Don't flunk it.
- If it's your boss stealing your thunder you have a bigger problem, especially if you don't have access to the next level. You could ensure your idea sounds complicated and ask if you can go along to explain it yourself.
- Or tell your boss you have a good idea and would like to know how you can present it to the next level.
- Keep yourself in the loop. At the very least ask your boss what the reaction was to your idea.

I can never delegate

Solutions:
- Next time someone comes to you with a problem, discuss possible solutions by asking them how they would handle it.
- Stop using phrases like 'No problem' or 'If you want anything doing round here you have to do it yourself'.
- It's possible to delegate in all four directions: upward (your boss), downward (the people you manage), sideways (your colleagues) and outward (getting customers and suppliers to join in) but the techniques for each will be different.
- Before you delegate, work out exactly what the job entails and who will be the best person to do it.
- Never dump on the one who is easiest to delegate to.
- Never use a baby voice: 'Would you just mind doing this ickle thing for me?'
- Be assertive and use assertive dialogues.
- Explain the task and brief them thoroughly.
- Explain why it needs to be done.
- Delegation is not abdication. Be there to offer advice but don't hover.

I can never haggle

Solutions:

- This can be cultural. Some people see it as natural, others would rather chew off their own arm. Decide you're going to haggle. Once you've made that decision the rest is just technique.
- Set your goal. What price do you want to pay (within the bounds of reality and fairness, of course).
- Ask the price. Look at the shopkeeper for a moment. Look back at the product. Then say 'Is that your best price?'
- As you ask, remember not to nod, giggle or move your head from side to side. By doing this you let them know you're caving in before the haggling has begun.
- Silence is the great tool of the haggler. Look at the product, and then look back at them. Say nothing. It's amazing how many sellers cave in when you say nothing. I had one that caved in three times during my silence. I was happy with the first deduction.
- When they tell you the price, say 'Three hundred pounds?' in a slightly incredulous tone. Then look at them in silence. There's no shame, you could be wondering why it's so cheap. Let them crack first.
- If you're selling and have reached a haggling impasse, break the deadlock by offering them something of low value to you: a free manual, a disc, a discount voucher. It will help them back down and buy without losing face.

When I fancy someone I can never look at them without getting embarrassed

Solutions:

- Turn an affliction into a pulling point. Bashful body language looks adorable.
- Get yourself in their proximity. Standing near them shouldn't tax you too much as long as you don't appear weird.
- Keep the dimpled smiles, blushing and body barriers but combine them with your eye contact.
- Princess Diana excelled at this. She would smile shyly and dip her head but fix people with a huge eye-gaze at the same time.
- Practise in the mirror first. Chin down then eyes up to meet your own eyes. Keep rehearsing so that it looks and feels natural.

- Plan your chat-up line. Keep it simple. 'We keep smiling at one another but I thought it was about time we introduced ourselves too. I'm ...'
- Plan your exit strategy just in case. 'No no, I'm just dashing off too, nice to finally meet you though' should do.
- If you're approaching someone during the daytime carry a serious novel in one hand. It always makes people look normal.
- Don't overdo the perfume or aftershave. It will make you look desperate.

When I get nervous I get sweaty

Solutions:
- Wear natural fabrics like cotton rather than anything with nylon in the blend.
- Avoid fitted shirts in dark colours.
- Wear shirts or tops with baggy armpits.
- Avoid cold showers or splashing your hands or face with cold water as your body will over-compensate and reheat quickly.
- Use an antiperspirant deodorant. Ask for one that is super-dry.
- Take a deodorant to work.
- Avoid plastic seats.
- When you get anxious, slow down. More rushing, more movement, more sweat.
- Use a matte cream that will stop your face from getting shiny. Ask in Boots. They do one that you can use on a bald head, too.
- Think cool. It's mind over matter.
- Carry some wet wipes, just in case, and use one before you shake hands.
- Keep a large hankie to mop quickly if your face sweats during a meeting or presentation.

I struggle with saying 'no' to people

Solutions:
- Stop saying 'yes'. That's not a trite comment. It's easier to stop yourself saying yes to everything than it is to start saying 'no'.
- Get used to the 'no' word. Role-play it by saying it at home and with friends first.
- Sell your 'no' to you first.

- Remember you're not rejecting the person, just the request.
- Use assertive body language. Eye contact, open gestures, a relaxed posture with no fiddling.
- Don't waffle. Say your piece and then shut up and listen.
- Never use a bald 'no'.
- Show you understand their request 'I know this job is urgent ...', etc.
- Then say 'no' with your reasons, if you want.
- Then negotiate if possible.
- Make 'no' mean 'no'. When you back down you show weakness.
- Know what is and isn't negotiable.
- Stick to your bottom line.
- Never make a non-negotiable sound possible. Avoid phrases like 'I'll have to see'.

I always judge myself against other people

Solutions:
- Stop treating the whole world as some sort of beauty or talent pageant. Why judge? Just be accepting.
- Assess yourself independently. Know what's good, what's attractive, what's a skill and what's not.
- If you can't stop judging, find a few people who will make you look good.
- Tell yourself to stop being so self-obsessed. This is a form of vanity.
- If you do make comparisons, do so without judgement. Saying 'They have bigger boobs than I do' or 'They are taller than me' are statements of fact. Saying 'They're better, prettier, more attractive than I am' is voicing judgemental opinion.
- Make one key rule: 'I will never, ever voice these thoughts. It's pathetic to think them. Speaking them out loud is boring.'
- When you do you're seeking reassurance, flattery and approval from other people. Never make them join in your own little inadequacy games.

I worry about my partner's exes

Solutions:
- Unless you marry or date a virgin your partner will always have a past. Most men come with terrible baggage called 'the one

that got away', i.e. they are fixated on a love they lost.
- This is normal and it means nothing. What isn't normal is for you to obsess about it, especially to the point where you ruin the relationship.
- Never ask about ex-partners unless you're checking sexual history for a health angle.
- Never be jealous of history.
- If the sex, love, fun was so great, why were they single when they met you? If they're telling you, they're trying to make you jealous, that's all. Your self-esteem should never rest in the manky lap of someone who means nothing to you.
- Read *Rebecca* by Daphne du Maurier. It will teach you a lesson you'll never forget.
- If the ex is fighting to get him or her back and you're encouraged by your partner to watch the fun, try dropping your partner. It's better than getting caught up in their stupid little games. You're better than that. If he or she wants you they'll have to come minus the baggage and game-playing.

I have no body confidence on the beach

Solutions:
- Humans come in all shapes and sizes and most of them are just fine.
- Pick a costume that feels confident rather than one that stretches you.
- Take the plunge straight away. The more you unveil like a timid stripper and sit shielding bits with your hands the more negative attention you draw.
- Wear your swimmies under a wrap or your clothes and just rip the top layer off as soon as you hit the beach.
- Swim or play some kind of beach game straight away. Once you've been stretching or jumping for a beach ball and falling over and laughing the inhibitions will have lifted like a cloud.
- Never moan about your body shape or bits. If you do you might as well attach a neon sign saying 'Look here!'

I lack the confidence to complain

Solutions:

- See your complaint as a negotiation, focused on getting you what you want. Otherwise it's just moaning.
- Only ever complain to the person responsible for your problem or the person who can resolve it. Telling other people means you risk it getting back, meaning you'll look weak.
- Set out your points before you complain.
- Keep to the facts and try not to get emotional.
- If you think you're going to lose it you will. Repeat your mantra: I feel calm, confident and in control.
- Be assertive. Look up the skills in this book.
- Tell them what is wrong and what you would like to happen.
- Use acceleration techniques: polite to start with, firmer if you don't get what you want, very firm if it still doesn't work.
- Know your rights. Never make them up or believe what someone else has told you. There are too many urban legends about consumer rights.
- There should be a difference in your approach when you assert your rights to when you're asking for a favour.
- Speak clearly and be concise.
- If you get no joy, ask them what they would do.
- Be careful about using threats.

I lack confidence with technical things

Solutions:

- There are many different types of intelligence and some people struggle with IT, maths and technical things while others can't tap into their creative side or do well at sports. I'd suggest that – as we're all equipped with the basic tool, i.e. the brain – your lack of ability is down to some form of barrier that is caused by your own lack of confidence.
- De-wrinkle your thinking. When we're trying to learn or understand something new, expectations play a large part in how well we manage. Because you have a script running in your head telling you there's going to be a struggle you're creating wrinkled thinking, which means you can't keep your mind open in a useful way.

- Every time you feel wrinkles appearing in your brain, sit back and repeat 'I feel calm, confident and in control'.

- We also have different preferred learning styles so discover whether your approach to all things technical is failing to penetrate for that reason. You could be Auditory (better listening to messages to learn), Visual (better reading handbooks or maybe watching someone else do it) or Physical (better doing it yourself with instruction or help). Remember when you were last successful learning something and apply the same technique you used then to your current technical study.

- Learning occurs when we see, listen, read, say and do. Doing something creates around 60 per cent of our remembering when we learn but if we listen, read, say and do we get a 90 per cent hit rate.

- Find a good coach or mentor. Not all technical types make good tutors. Sometimes they can be impatient or unable to speak in a way that mimics basic English. Find someone who talks in a way you can understand and learn from.

- Arm yourself with the phone numbers of help lines for the equipment you're using.

- Always focus on what you can do. Computers appear to have unlimited potential but there's nothing wrong with the fact that you can turn yours on and use it for documents and emails. At least you've mastered something.

- Technical learning can drop out of your brain if it's not being used regularly. Write down instructions for any things you're not using regularly.

- Tell yourself you can do it. Your brain is not odd. Visualise doing well and you can do well.

- Avoid the barrier of anger. When we can't get to grips with anything technical we often respond with barely suppressed rage against the machine. Anger makes learning impossible. The PC is not programmed to make your life miserable and to make you look a fool. It's trying to help you; make friends. Shake hands (or your mouse) and get on with it.

I need to give a confident presentation but I don't really know the subject

Solutions:

- Many business people get asked to give presentations that are on a subject they have little knowledge about.
- You need to negotiate for time to acquire that knowledge.
- Being confident when you're bluffing during a presentation would be foolhardy.
- When you present you need to know about three times as much as you are going to say.
- If you don't you are right to lack confidence. Your integrity will be on the line.
- Learning is fine but if you have no time to learn then you need to say no to the presentation if at all possible.
- If you're absorbing someone else's knowledge don't attempt to absorb their presentation as well. We all speak best if we put things into our own words.
- Take the facts, learn the detail then restructure the talk so you know you can exhibit mastery.
- Consider doing the bones of the talk but recruiting a second speaker who does have the knowledge to act as your expert.

I have to give a conference speech. Large audiences terrify me

Solutions:

- Keep your talk in your own words and your own style.
- A large audience is just a bigger group of individuals, so there's no need to formalise or introduce long words that are unfamiliar to you.
- Walk the stage prior to the talk. Most people pore over their notes but you should be rehearsing the technicalities as they can make or break a talk. Where will you be sitting? How will you get on to the stage? Is there a remote for your slides? Where can you put your notes? How will you know when your time is nearly up?
- Avoid using a lectern. They look stuffy and horrible.
- Be in charge of your own slides. I know the IT guys say they'll know when to change them but somehow that system tends to go wrong when you're in full flight.

- Use a lapel mic, if possible. Hand-held feels and looks like you're going to sing.
- Like your subject. The message is the whole point. What is yours? Why do you have to deliver it? What is your key point?
- Like your audience. They want to like you.
- Pause, greet them using eye-gaze. Breathe out. Then start.
- Begin with a planned start although be happy to change your introduction if you notice anything current you can use.
- Start with a high-impact opening. Get their attention. Never warm up as you go along.
- Only use slides to add to their interest. Not as your script.
- Walk about the stage if you want to.
- Speak with energy and allow your passion to show through. If you lack passion, avoid using the word as you'll sound false ('We feel really passionate about this product').
- If you're taking questions and are taking them at the end, plan what to do if you get none. Never allow a tumbleweed moment to go on for too long. Say: 'Does this mean I've covered everything for you? Great.'

CONCLUSION

When you're working on your own confidence you need to be coach, mentor and motivator, as well as the person who will lead yourself to great achievement by pushing you through the pain barrier.

A kind, gentle approach doesn't work. I have proved that being understanding is similarly useless, because understanding why you're afraid does nothing to help you trip that switch you'll need to override your evolutionary processing.

The reason I have defined the causes of your fear is to allow you to fly above them, not to marinate in self-pity. Your lack of confidence makes sense in evolutionary terms, but your task in modern life is to work to overcome all those fears that are now largely redundant, like fear of strangers in a safe environment like the workplace or fear of drawing attention to yourself when you have to appear onstage.

Recognising and identifying your fears helps you to conquer them. Knowing them and wallowing in them does not. You can't touch fear or see fear (although it could be argued you can smell it!) so it won't stop you achieving unless you see it as a tangible barrier. Your fear is the amber traffic light, warning you to take care. It's up to you whether you see your amber light as a red light or as a precursor to a green light.

I want you to see your fears as an amber light that warns you to take more decisions. Is this likely to hurt me, kill me or be dangerous to me? When the answer is 'No', you switch to green and proceed.

The technique is flipping the amber light off at will, and that's what this book has been all about.

Proceeding takes effort but your effort is worth it because you are allowing yourself to grow. By taking control over your responses and behaviours you learn self-respect. By learning self-respect you automatically acquire confidence.

Never again allow yourself to hide in the dank gloom of shyness and low self-esteem. Tap into your Confidence Core and use my simple techniques to keep tapping in. Be resilient and move forwards, never backwards. Don't allow your ego to be the victim of other people's criticisms, insults, rejections and bad behaviours. Remember the cartoon character that gets knocked to the ground? Shake your head madly to clear it (blubber-blubber-blub-blub), get up, dust yourself down and carry on. Take responsibility for You. Cherish it, protect it, promote it and allow it to shine.

INDEX

INDEX